LETS GO!

PUBLISH

Taxation
Without
Representation

Third Edition

Can the U.S. Avoid Another "Boston Tea Party?"

This book relies on the Constitution, the founding documents, Articles of Association, Declaration of Rights and Grievances, Declaration of Independence, and the Bill of Rights.

Taxation without Representation unearths and explores a massive dilemma for U.S. Citizens. The US began without representation. Then, the Colonies fought a war of independence to acquire representation. Now, our beloved representatives have fallen for the candy coated wiles of the new kids on the block--obscenely rich mega-corporations and members of the establishment of both parties.

This book offers a walk-though about how our government once was, how it improved, and how it again eroded and regressed from freedom to a new set of oppressive roots. The book highlights the major issues affecting the American worker, particularly the wholesale exportation of jobs to legal and illegal foreign nationals. The book also discusses how both political parties are preventing independent candidates from appearing on ballots and the problems presented by voting machines surreptitiously designed with technology that enables an interested party's surrogates to manipulate and even override the people's choices.

Our representative democratic republic is definitely in trouble. While pointing out definitively that we pay too much in taxes, this book also offers a number of unique solutions to help get us back on a trach of which the founders would smile. Enjoy!

LETS GO PUBLISH

BRIAN W. KELLY

Copyright © 2010, 2017 Brian W. Kelly

Taxation without Representation Third Edition   Author Brian W. Kelly
Can the U.S. Avoid Another "Boston Tea Party"?

Disclaimer: Though judicious care was taken throughout the writing and the publication of this work that the information contained herein is accurate, there is no expressed or implied warranty that all information in this book is 100% correct. Therefore, neither LETS GO PUBLISH, nor the author accepts liability for any use of this work.

Trademarks: A number of products and names referenced in this book are trade names and trademarks of their respective companies.

Referenced Material: *The information in this book has been obtained through personal and third party observations, interviews, and copious research. Where unique information has been provided or extracted from other sources, those sources are acknowledged within the text of the book itself or at the end of the chapter in the Sources Section. Thus, there are no formal footnotes nor is there a bibliography section. Any picture that does not have a source was taken from various sites on the Internet with no credit attached. If resource owners would like credit in the next printing, please email publisher.*

Published by: LETS GO PUBLISH!
Publisher: Brian P. Kelly   Publisher: Brian P. Kelly
                  P.O Box 621
                  Wilkes-Barre, PA 18703
                  brian@brianpkelly.com
                  www.letsgopublish.com

Library of Congress Copyright Information Pending
Book Cover Design by Michele Thomas, Editing by Brian P. Kelly

ISBN Information: The International Standard Book Number (ISBN) is a unique machine-readable identification number, which marks any book unmistakably. The ISBN is the clear standard in the book industry. 159 countries and territories are officially ISBN members. The Official ISBN For this book is on the outside cover:
978-0-9977667-1-4

The price for this work is :   **$17.95 USD**
10   9   8   7   6   5   4   3   2   1
Release Date: July, 2016

Dedication

I dedicate this book to Angel Kathleen and Joseph McKeown, wonderful people, wonderful first cousins and avid supporters of all of my writing efforts.

Thank You and the Best!

Acknowledgments

I appreciate all the help that I received in putting this book together, along with the 68 other books from the past.

My printed acknowledgments were once so large that book readers needed to navigate too many pages to get to page one of the text. To permit me more flexibility, I put my acknowledgment list online at www.letsgopublish.com. The list of acknowledgments continues to grow. Believe it or not, it once cost about a dollar more to print each book.

Thank you all on the big list in the sky and God bless you all for your help.

Please check out www.letsgopublish.com to read the latest version of my heartfelt acknowledgments updated for this book. Thank you all!

In this book, I received some extra special help from Dennis Grimes, Gerry Rodski, Wily Ky Eyely, Angel Irene McKeown Kelly, Angel Edward Joseph Kelly Sr., Angel Edward Joseph Kelly Jr., Ann Flannery, Angel James Flannery Sr., Mary Daniels, Bill Daniels, Robert Gary Daniels, Angel Sarah Janice Daniels, Angel Punkie Daniels, Joe Kelly, Diane Kelly, Angels Fluff & Puff Kelly, Brian P. Kelly, Mike P. Kelly, Katie P. Kelly, Ben Kelly, and Budmund (Buddy) Arthur Kelly.

Table of Contents

Preface:

Brian W. Kelly wrote this book because our representatives in the House, the Senate, in state legislatures and city councils have forgotten their duties as representatives of the people. Additionally, the president, the governors, the mayors, and other prefects of the people in the executive branches of governments across the land have conveniently forgotten that the primary fundamentals of our representative constitutional democracy (republic) start with representation.

"No taxation without representation" was the catch phrase in the period of 1763-1776 to summarize the major grievance of the American colonists in the Thirteen American Colonies, incipient kernels of what would later become the United States of America. When King George III of England and the English Parliament began to impose new taxes on the colonists (Stamp Act, Intolerable Acts, etc.) without their concurrence, Reverend Jonathan Mayhew of Boston coined this term during one of his sermons in Boston.

Another Bostonian, a politician by *the speak of the day*, James Otis, changed this just a bit and he is well known for the phrase, "taxation without representation is tyranny." Tyranny it was and in this book, you will see that tyranny it surely is again.

In 1773, American Colonists violently opposed the tax on tea imports at the most celebrated Tea Party of all time. The Boston Tea Party is recognized as the first experience in which the colonists acted against the Crown. Of course, the British could not accept this "illegal act" as they saw that it would undermine the authority of the Crown and Parliament. When the British Government began to crack down on these "illegal activities" performed by the colonists, the colonists chose to defend themselves in case the British Government did not hear their pleas to correct the abuses.

Though today the tea still may be in the ships in Boston Harbor, millions have expressed discontent of the government several years ago by holding their own tea parties all over the US in protests against the American government. Bernie Sanders and Donald Trump have awakened the same spirit of "NO" today to a government that thinks it owns the people of this great country.

Beware the lulling idea that your government cannot be taken over by rich members of a *Ruling Class* or de-facto by corporations, or even by a powerful president with disdain for capitalism. The quickest way to assure this can happen in our time is to stop paying attention; stop caring; and stop voting and to let them simply have their way.

Brian W. Kelly wrote this book because he cares and I am publishing this book because I care. Together, BWK and I hope to energize Americans again in the new millennium as in the 1700's. Our mantra is that this magnificent democracy of which much blood was shed, continues to be worth fighting for.

I hope you enjoy reading this book and that you will remain vigilant and take the actions necessary so that this experiment in democracy, this United States of America can persevere and succeed for many hundreds and hundreds of more years. For now, I wish you the best! Yes, we suffer from Taxation without Representation but as we awaken to that reality, we can make it much better by paying attention to our elected representatives.

Sincerely

Brian P. Kelly, Publisher
Lets Go Publish!, PO Box 621 Wilkes-Barre, Pennsylvania

About the Author

Brian Kelly retired as an Assistant Professor in the Business Information Technology (BIT) Program at Marywood University, where he also served as the IBM i and Midrange Systems Technical Advisor to the IT Faculty. Kelly designed, developed, and taught many college and professional courses. He continues as a contributing technical editor to a number of technical industry magazines, including "The Four Hundred" and "Four Hundred Guru," published by IT Jungle. Kelly often writes for blogs such as Conservative Action Alerts.

Kelly is a former IBM Senior Systems Engineer. His specialty was problem solving for customers as well as implementing advanced operating systems and software on his client's machines. Brian is the author of 69 books and hundreds of magazine articles. Over half of his books and articles are about patriotic topics. He has been a frequent speaker at conferences throughout the United States.

Brian was a candidate for the US Congress from Pennsylvania in 2010 and he ran for Mayor in his home town in 2015. He loves America but has no love for corrupt officials.

Chapter 1   We Get the Government We Deserve

America Is a Representative Democracy?

When the following thought marched into my mind only a few short years ago, "America is a representative democracy," I began to ask myself, isn't it time that we actually had some real "representation" from our so-called representative government? The way it now works provides far too much separation between us, the electors, and them, the elected officials coordinating our pooled resources for the alleged benefit of "everyone." But who is everyone? A genuinely compelling concern for our government or Disney-like utopian myth?

I propose the latter. Our government is wholly unaccountable. Our lawmakers have no trouble going with the flow and commit us to years of debt without even taking the time to read the legislation for which they vote. Even worse, its members, allegedly our civil servants, do not even seem to care for our own wellbeing. They care for their leadership and themselves but they just can't get it into their heads that we the people count at all.

While running for office, it seems that incumbent and aspiring prospective officials saturate our consciousness day-in and day-out, wheedling us into their self-perpetuating power games with promises of responsiveness, unity, and even candor. Yet, even then, only one primary concern lurks on their minds, that *sine qua non* of their very daily existence, the next election.

A forthcoming election could be as distant as two years and still your impending loss of job, perhaps due to a plant relocating to China, or one closing in Michigan, is at best a secondary afterthought to the very men and women promising you change, when you want it, and stability, again when they believe you want it.

Unfortunately, their priorities are one dimensional and your job going to China or just no longer existing, isn't the focus. Eventually they get re-elected and go off to Washington for yet another term. The cycle starts again with the eternal candidate alternating between Washington and their well-insulated, gated communities far enough from the common people that they don't have to care what you think.

It's Never Them

When they are about to raise your taxes, they are particularly inconspicuous. Being numbed to the excesses and decadent corruption of everyday politics, you may not expect communication and straight answers and so you are not disappointed. You hear about the tax issues on TV or in the paper, not from your elected because your opinion on the matter really doesn't matter. They would rather converse via cellular or Blackberry or iPhones with some of the only entities who truly can garner their attention, co-Congressmen, the affluent, the corrupt media, and of course, major campaign donors.

Discussing an important issue with you, while seeming like a charming noble way for a representative to spend an afternoon, is discarded as wanton. It's dismissed simply because it would not tangibly benefit anyone's reelection campaign which, as we have all learned, begins the day oaths of office are sworn.

They want us to think that any tax increase is caused by imaginary rival agents or economic forces beyond their control. They will convey this to us with the sole purpose of acquiring our hard earned money. Apparently, they promise, any burdens will fall on some imaginary "other person" and we will remain unscathed.

Horrifically but as expected though, when we get our tax bills from the bureaucracy, we find out that we were that "other" person. Since the bureaucracy sent us the bill, we blame the bureaucracy, and again let our politicians off the hook, just like our "representative" hoped we would. And again, they live to run for another election, their only professional motivation in life.

Talk to the Hand

Most individuals feel that their needs and opinions are not taken very seriously by elected representatives who occupy the hallowed chambers of our government buildings. We would call it a communication break-down but there really is no communication. Despite our inability to get legislators to know our side of important issues, such as taxation, jobs, illegal aliens, etc., and more recently, bailouts, and healthcare, we treat them with too much respect. We intrinsically know that they care only about the desires and opinions of pressure groups, lobbyists, corporate executives and owners, as well as the plain old rich.

Only these voices reach our representatives. Yet, time and time again, we let them off the hook. Politicians cut themselves off from their electorate by choice to be spared from accountability. Yet, whenever necessary, they make a resurfacing experience and always in time for the next election. Why are we so nice to them?

You may not see them in action when they work the halls of congress but you do see them work the wedding halls when it is the height of the election season. In Congress, the typical representative appears to have some sort of godly mandate, on the basis of which, whatever they put forward must be good for everybody. However, whether it is a good idea or not, and they rarely are, you know the idea more than likely came from the whispers of the chosen elite. Politicians do not serve most of their electorate and they get away with it because again, we do not hold them accountable, and we do not break their pattern by showing up on their doorstep with our needs.

It's Time to Fire Them—Every One of them!

What would happen to the placid world of the politician if its constituency took them to task? What might happen to these politicos if the citizens suddenly became extremely active? How would the elected representative handle such a massive increase in constituent contact? Would they become beneficent and magnanimous? Or would they choose the hermitage approach and lock the gates and doors and hope the rabble will go away?

Especially if we think they would never put up with our entreaties, we should deluge them anyway and help power our representative democracy back to working order. In our hearts, we know we would see nothing more than congressional aides coming out of the woodwork to "see if they can help matters." That of course is code for "see if they can shut us up!" And, for their lack of efforts on our behalf, we should do the only humane thing: fire them! Throw the bums out. They've had their day.

Regular People Are Taking Notice

There is a clear and fundamental problem with our government, even when we are on different sides of most of the other issues. In Mitt Romney's campaign, he said that Washington was "broken." With Obama now, it may be just "broke."

Either way, it is almost beyond repair. For the broken government that gave us the infamous Bush Dubai Ports deal, whose ex-Presidents represent foreign nations, and who have passed laws such as the "uniform labeling of products" fiasco, a fellow citizen of mine, Rik Reppe, a regular guy and self-described performer, writer, raconteur, and occasional business geek, ripped the establishment a new item in his blog at the URL below.

http://reppe.blogs.com/reppecom/2006/03/because_we_get_.html

Reppe believes that we the people get exactly what we deserve because we elect these talking heads and empty suits, who owe their allegiance to some corporation someplace. To demonstrate the rage that is out there in cyberspace about what an absolutely abysmal bunch of political louts run our government, I picked two paragraphs from Rik's rants on the labeling topic. Though many things are Obama's fault, even more as days goes by, lack of representation is not a recent phenomenon. These caught Rok's ire, for example, back in March, 2006

> "But why should we believe the House of Representatives is looking out for us and not sucking at the corporate t...t? That's easy. You know the House has got your back...you know they're grandstanding for votes...on any and all issues on which no public hearings are held. Because we all know that politicians who are looking out for the people hate it when those efforts are brought to the attention of the people. Hate it, hate it, hate it. The last thing...the very last thing in the whole wide political universe any politician wants to do in an election year is to trumpet efforts to help the voters thus securing easy camera and soundbite time.
> ...
> And ain't it grand that on the same day the Senate passed a completely impotent and toothless "lobbying reform" bill that contains no actual provision to enforce

the increased disclosure the impotent and toothless product of their collective minds created (passed by a vote of 90-8 proving that as much as I want this to be a Republican issue it f...ing well isn't) it takes up an issue that had been voted down by every Congress since 1994 and is only back to the influence of lobbyists? You may hate what our Senators are doing but you gotta love that kind of brazen chutzpa, don't you?"

They Work for Someone Else

The chasm between electors and the elected is widening as we speak. The John Does and the Jane Q. Publics have lost faith in their representatives. Many have become fully disinterested in the political process, though the healthcare "debate" and the fresh air at the "Town Meetings" may be just the cure for this malaise.

For some time, with good reason, the public has felt disenfranchised from the basic right of a citizen to participate in the democracy. Some may handle this by ignoring politics. Others may find alternative ways to attempt to influence the course of events, sometimes through friends and associates, but not always with very positive results. Sometimes as we have seen in our history, the frustration of humans in our democracy leads to violence as in the civil rights movements and the anti-war rallies of the 1960's and the riots in Los Angeles in the 1990's. Are we there again? Perhaps the main reason that the system even seems to work is that constituents do not make many demands -- at least till now, and like Reppe says,

"We Get The Government We Deserve."

This is the root cause that permits politicians, masquerading as our representatives, to represent other interests. It is an understatement to suggest that representatives are out of touch with the will of the people. Even the newly elected begin to share the wealth of their constituency with others as they begin their "service." They have this need to redistribute income and now they are redistributing healthcare.

This is a common malady of the often elected and the newly elected are quickly infected. For a politician, it's "catchier" than the Swine Flu. Elected "representatives" have no problem taking your money and buying votes with it -- even if there is nothing left in the treasury.

Until they got caught by John Q., how many of the "honorables" voted originally to have the non-working and the illegal aliens receive the tax rebate of 2008? This trick was like buying future votes but the motivation was the same. It wasn't really intended for the downtrodden, hapless, illegal foreign national struggling to make ends meet. Not a chance. It was to puff up the elected to demonstrate their magnanimity and vote-worthiness.

Besides your money, they will also take your means of earning a living if it serves their purposes. To please their corporate sponsors, they have no problem taking your job and giving it to a foreign national, either here in the U.S. or in the worker's home country, in China or India. They have just one mission and it is accomplished if they get elected again. The next term of office, not the current one, is all that matters. We get the government we deserve.

The House of Lords

Senators are above it all. They breathe the rarified air reserved for the Gods. If you see a Senator once in your life, it is a memorable event. Perhaps you are among the lucky. Perhaps not! Senators have so many people to represent that they operate as Lords, clearly of the nobility (though nobility is expressly forbidden by the Constitution), and they have no need to ever mingle with the common folk. They can't anyway. In Pennsylvania, for example, the state in which I live, it is the 6th most populated state in the U.S. with an estimated population of 12,500,000. That means that between the two senators, each gets to work with over six million people. No way no how! The Senators know they do not have to represent the people and so they represent whoever they choose and they still get sent back every six years like it is an entitlement. A sure thing. We get the government we deserve.

The House of Commons

What about our representatives? Why don't we ever see them? Remember that our Constitution clearly specifies the number of senators and representatives. The ratio is fixed at 1 representative for each 30,000 in the electorate. Now, that is still a high ratio but it is workable. Regardless of what is in the constitution, however, in the year 1911, the representatives themselves decided to break this basic tenet of the Constitution by adopting a new law. Now, only 435 maximum seats are allocated regardless of the population. This of course has made them all more important and thus worthy of a large salary and expenses. In 2009, for example without unvouchered expenses, your congressman pocketed $174,000.00. Not bad for a part time job.

With a growing population, the ratio in the House of Representatives right now is about 1 in 700,000. That's an awful lot of hands to shake for one just person. So, they don't. And, you don't miss them. But, you should! We get the government we deserve.

If you are good at math, you'll be able to tell this puzzle isn't over yet. Take the twenty-some mostly permanent staff members for each of the 435 representatives and multiply that (about 22) by 435 and add that to the 435 representatives. The number approaches 10,000. With the approximate U.S. citizen population just over 300,000,000 (technically illegal aliens have no representation), it can be argued that the ratio of 1 to 30,000 has magically been maintained, if you're happy talking to an aide instead of your representative.

Why they need 22 or 23 staff members is an enigma I will let hang for another day. The point is that we actually need about 9500 more Congressional Representatives to comply with the Constitution. That would certainly make our representatives much more accountable and maybe we would actually be able to reach them and maybe they would even live in our communities. And, of course they would not be so "important and honorable," which would be good for the people. It would be a bummer for the Congressman, however, not being quite as important, but so what? Remember, we get the government we deserve.

There are lots of other sound arguments for this notion postured at the Jacksonian party blog at:

http://thejacksonianparty.spaces.live.com/blog/cns!3E751362FDD59519!143.entry

Our Benign Oligarchy Can Use A Dose of Direct Democracy

You may choose to read more about the forms of government in the Civics Lesson included at the back of Chapter 2. In this lesson you will learn why our form of government is known as a representative constitutional democracy. Instead of every person having a say in every decision, we elect representatives and we hold them accountable through the Constitution to make sure they don't hijack the government.

When a government is of the rich, for the rich, and by the rich, we would call that an oligarchy--rule by the few over the many. Substitute special interests for "rich," and it means the same. As long as we get no representation from our elected, we really do not have a functioning representative democracy. In practice it is an oligarchy and this is very dangerous.

As long as the oligarchy is benign, there is not much reason to be concerned other than that long before the year 2000, the government was already hijacked and still nobody is calling anybody on it. The great insights of Dr. Michael Savage, a well-known syndicated Radio Talk Show Host suggest that the time to get really worried about your free speech is when the few start sending out the big black cars and one at a time, the many begin to disappear into the gulags. In 2010, of course, it seems the Obama Czars have all come equipped with questionable integrity and a tailor made government hijacking kit. Watch out. We get the government we deserve.

In a Direct Democracy, the people have the vote, not the representatives, and this type of democracy is based on the principles of Initiation, Referendum, and Recall. Many of the states of the union also have these notions, but our founding fathers believed at the time that the checks and balances they built into the early government would permit the constitutional democracy to last for quite a long time. They originally thought that professionals, such as our Senators, one from each state, would be the proper way to run the country. As the Articles of Confederation were woven into the Constitution, this notion changed to two senators per state, not elected directly by the people but by the state legislatures, and a House of Representatives of the people, elected directly by the people.

Checks and Balances Aren't Working

As they say at realdemocracy.com, "DEMOCRACY WON'T WORK UNLESS YOU FIND THE TRUTH AND KEEP YOURSELF INFORMED." Stay ignorant of how things really are and you will almost certainly reap the government you deserve.

The checks and balances of the Founding Fathers include (1) the Constitution itself, and (2) the three "equal" branches of government. But the big trick they had up their sleeves was that the (3) representatives in the House were elected, not appointed and there was a huge electorate to make sure that bad representatives would not be reelected.

In other words, they believed that the American people would weed out the bad guys so the bad guys could not corrupt the government. These three notions were intended to keep the representatives of the government serving the people and not special interests. If this were the case in practice, however, I would not have been challenged to write this book.

Since the government is beginning to behave as an oligarchy and this was never the intention of the Founding Fathers as they drafted the Constitution, an injection of Direct Democracy might just be what the doctor ordered. It is fully in line with our U.S. Constitution, which vests ultimate sovereignty in the people, to create a mechanism that would permit the people back into our government process.

Through a constitutional amendment, for example, the people could gain the right to initiate national legislation (Initiative), create national referenda (Referendum), or demand the recall of officials (nowadays called scoundrels), who do not represent the people (Recall).

When the amendment passes, these activities could be sponsored by various public groups, or through the local and state governments. These three pillars of a direct democracy are presently reserved for the states whose constitutions specify these rights. It would be a relatively minor addition to our political system to engage the public in having a role in setting the political agenda. With how far our representatives have hijacked our national government, the time to act is now. We get the government we deserve.

Unfortunately, as noted above, not even all states have constitutions which permit the three prongs of a direct democracy. For example, my home state of Pennsylvania, has no statewide initiative or referendum rights, though Philadelphia and Allegheny (Pittsburgh) counties have it at the local level. A group of Pennsylvanians called the "PA Taxpayers for Referendum Organization" are planning legislation to create a state constitutional convention to give PA these important rights. Many notable historical figures have noted that our representative constitutional democracy could be improved with Initiative and Referendum. Their reasons seem to fit the national mood and the national need.

Theodore Roosevelt, for example, in his "Charter of Democracy" speech of 1912 said, "I believe in the initiative and referendum which should be used not to destroy representative government, but to correct it whenever it becomes misrepresentative." Abraham Lincoln is well known for his words, "Government is of the people, for the people and by the people." Referendum is recall of government if the government does not act in a responsible way.

Back in 2005, the League of Women Voters of Pennsylvania took heed and offered that it "believes that citizens should have some means of taking direct action if their elected representatives fail to enact laws that voters support, or if they pass laws that are not wanted by the people." Does any of this hit home?

Whether at the state level or the federal level, any thought of the public as a whole being able to participate in the political agenda, with majority rule and one-vote-one-value, would send shivers down the spine of political operatives. The corporate owned corrupt media would go nuts. It would even appear to be a menace to all minority groups who today exercise disproportionate power through representatives.

But, fear not. As you know the Irish are a minority and I am Irish. The Catholics are a minority, and I am Catholic. As minority groups, this change would affect both of these groups, but maybe that is OK and for the greater good. I don't have a problem with the notion at all. It would actually be a way of controlling the idea often referred to as the tyranny of the minority in which the voice of a few have disproportionate power to their numbers over the many.

Watch Your Words; The Media 'll Get You

Elitists in the media and the bureaucracy who claim the right to know what's best for us every day pour forth a deluge of abuse and character assassination arguments to keep "We the People" in our place. In the presidential election, for example, the media anointed Senator McCain as the winner of the GOP nomination after Super Tuesday, though my state, Pennsylvania, and many other states had yet to express their opinions on the matter. These volleys and even attacks don't come from nowhere. They come from the power-packed corporatocracy that owns the corrupt media. Watch what they say a little more carefully if you please, because they slander anybody who disagrees with them or who can alter their grip on power and propaganda.

Some think that John Edwards' story and how he was summarily removed from the primary elections right from the beginning is actually a case study for the abuse of corporate power. Edwards, though selfishly motivated could be seen as a champion against the established corporate power chieftains. He was a kick-butt trial lawyer who ate corporate chieftains for breakfast and salted away a huge nest egg for himself. He was defamed by the corporation-owned media simply because he was a "nasty" trial-lawyer.

The irony is that the Democratic Party was and is still in bed with the trial lawyers. They wanted nothing to do with Edwards' promises to end the problems of "greedy corporations." Media surrogates instantly plopped the "trial-lawyer" label on Edwards and he was gone even before Super Tuesday. Since the election, we've learned a few more sordid details about John Edwards but perhaps we were the people duped before Super Tuesday by the corrupt media? We get the government we deserve.

As you will note in Chapter 10, corporations are a huge
threat to our democracy and need to be toned down a good
measure so that real little guys do not feel their sting and so
companies such as General Electric do not have undue
influence on our lives through their media holdings. In 2009
Forbes declared GE as the largest corporation in the world.
Having GE control NBC and MSNBC and CNBC may give
the corporate behemoth a little more influence on American
life than is good for the people.

The Brave New World

Note: http://en.wikipedia.org/wiki/Brave_New_World,

Aldous Huxley wrote the Brave New World as a novel
in 1932. The book is about the future and its setting is
London, 2540 A.D. The novel anticipates that all of the
reproductive advancements that today are just notions
in a lab someplace, including biological engineering,
and sleep-learning, will be commonplace in the future
and will be used to change society. The book talks
about drug use as pacifiers to make the people feel
better and loudspeakers used to get across the message.
Later Huxley wrote two other books on the topic, one
thirty years later in which he saw the future coming
much sooner and the other, The Island, which took the
sterile notions of Brave New World and made them
more attractive and more positive. For example,
loudspeakers are replaced by pleasing parrots trained to
offer uplifting slogans.

Is our current day, " the Brave New World revisited," is a
new deal in which the Government hands out pacifiers to
keep the citizenry in a state of euphoria? What does such
euphoria look like? For the politician, it is a no-cost notion

since they get elected by bribing you with your own money. Many citizens want there to be "no problems" so much so that they can't or won't listen to hear that there actually is a big problem that requires them to pay for its solution. Yet, that is the system we have. Politicians who speak the truth are rejected because the voting public would rather be served denial and sugar and some pacifying stimuli.

Very early in the 2008 primaries we saw the media at work with sugar packets for those of us that don't mind being fat and Splenda for the slender among us. The media early on picked John McCain and Hillary Clinton as the only viable candidates. They just as quickly switched to Barack Obama. The media, and the Independents took the Republican primary from the Republicans without a whimper and they brought their man McCain in from sure doom to be the primary victor. Somehow, they found a faux conservative in the lot and that's what the Republicans got by going along to get along.

The utterly corrupt corporate media, the low ratings media I might add, helped voters come to the media way of thinking with a constant barrage of propaganda for their guys and against all the others. The sinister part of the deal is that the propaganda sounds a lot like hard news. Intrinsically we all know that there is no free lunch but "don't ask me to pay!" We get the government we deserve.

Can We Stomach the Change We Need?

Both parties are spending more and more money while in office because they get rewarded for spending our money. They get reelected. Even the Republican Party were big spenders during the Bush years. What was that all about? Republicans and Democrats of course do not want to pay for spending with taxes, which affect their reelection opportunities, so they borrow.

Of course the Democrats can always get a little more from the rich by implicitly invoking the subtle principles of class warfare. Both parties seemed to have no problem borrowing from and bankrupting Social Security, which was supposed to have been in an Al Gore style Lock Box.

Nobody talks about it because it serves no politician well but the biggest tax is the inflation this spending behavior causes. There is no bigger spender in history than Barack Obama and his team of czars. Ironically, inflation is the worst and heaviest tax on the working poor. Each year more Americans fall below the living wage because we pay for government's excessive spending with inflation and not taxes. Taxes are already high enough but somebody has to pay for political pork (porkulus) and you know it won't be the politicians or the Ruling Class.

Each year the shrinking middle class fakes its standard of living by borrowing more, the only sensible thing when you have inflation. Greed of the ruling political class finished the Roman Empire and it is well lined up to finish the American economic empire. "Free healthcare" may be the final nail in the US coffin.

Until the healthcare debate of 2009, I did not have overly high hopes that the electorate would opt to change anything as long as they too are greedy for what benefits them in the notion of "someone else will pay politics." The revolt of the summer of 2009 that has continued tell me that the people now seem more interested in the US as a surviving entity as any other issue I have ever seen.

The free lunch is over folks. Until Barack Obama caricaturized government largesse with free-fall spending like never before, it seemed like many Americans, getting by OK, stubbornly were hanging on, sending back the political hacks for two more years or four more years or six more years even when they chose not to represent us.

The sun seems to be shining on this folly now as more and more people are crying to throw the bums out. This downslide must end. It won't end, however, until we choose to end it at the ballot box and we forever hold the "honorables" accountable or better yet, we just send them home to get real jobs like the rest of us. The question always was, "do we have the stomach to do what is right?" Your friendly neighborhood politicians, all the way to the lords of the national ring are banking that you and I don't have the guts to do it. This time, I think they are wrong. We get the government we deserve.

Shall we cast off what is left of our independence and join the major political parties and ask for more government control and then we can loudly applaud our political leaders at important reelection functions? Maybe we can carry around their nominating petitions, and even hand out how-to-vote cards at elections. Or, should we clamp down on this big problem with our democracy, speak up, demand action, and if we are not satisfied, now really, shouldn't we just throw the bums out?

Democracy is a relatively new phenomenon in its modern forms. It has developed over the last few centuries to a somewhat acceptable level in perhaps 40 of the world's 200-odd nation states. Judging from the U.S., it must further evolve. It cannot remain fixed in the face of accelerating change in all other aspects of society and the outright threat of takeover by corporate power and influence or as John Edwards correctly characterized it, "corporate greed."

The elements of direct democracy such as Initiative, Referendum, and Recall are anathema to politicians and governments at all levels. Yet, all three of these tenets could help enliven the political experience for the people and make government at all levels more accountable. In all western democracies, including the good ole U.S. of A., there are high levels of dissatisfaction.

Thus, there is more and more interest in politics by the yet-to-be-disillusioned young and things that can improve politics such as the Initiative amendment need to be brought forth and adopted. The mood of the country, voiced often by the young in the past presidential election brought forth the current administration and now the American people are getting changes many had never considered possible and every day it seems there is more.

The Bush years brought great division over the war in Iraq and a very unpopular president, from his own doing along with the help of the corrupt, left leaning media. So, now, we have trillions of dollars of debt, give-away programs for the rich (Wall street and the Bankers) that are better than PowerBall, and a big war in Afghanistan that does not seem to be fought well.

We also have a CIA that is being emasculated, and we seem to have no fear at all of terrorism as the name was even stricken from the federal dictionary. It seems that Michele and Barack must now be living with Alice and the Tin Man to not notice America crumbling. On top of the new stuff, there is still the same old deep division in this country about open borders, the full response to terrorism, and the ongoing Iraq and Afghanistan wars. I fear these are just a few symptoms of a much deeper malaise.

Familiarity Breeds Contempt

People everywhere seem to want to push the bounds of democracy further than their governments will allow. Both Prime Minister Blair in the UK and President Bush in the U.S. led incredibly unpopular governments. But, they are of the past and new guys took their places. Gordon Brown got off to a great start as the #1 in the UK and our own Barack Obama was so popular he was almost declared a King and ruler for life. Americans actually loved everything about the Obama's, from the kids to the new dog. Never have I seen such a high level of satisfaction for any President. Brits who were sick of Tony Blaire and the Iraq War were likewise quite pleased with Gordon Brown, though not at the level of the American love affair. Congratulations to both for their fine early showings. Those days too are gone.

In addition to the big new rap of fiscal irresponsibility, the dissatisfaction with the U.S. government at all levels stems from many reasons such as a steady slide in social, economic and environmental conditions in the past 20 years; the increasingly overt nepotism, careerism, cronyism and outright corruption in our political system and in the government itself. Who do you trust? What once was a Johnny Carson game show is now a question that beckons to be answered well but seemingly cannot be. In 2009, more and more blog contributions were asking, "Do you trust your government?"

On top of a major dislike for having unpopular notions rammed down the public collective throat, much of this is fueled by public revulsion at brain-dumbing political campaigns, the blatant disregard for the public in official decision-making, the dominance of big business, big unions, and big government, the flaunting of wealth by the Ruling Class, and increasingly fat salaries for politicians.

Meanwhile the general public (that's us) is chopped liver, theoretically living beyond its means, and they have no recourse but to work harder for less money. With the economic collapse of late 2008, living beyond ones means has actually taken on new meaning and many individuals have been forced to follow this mantra. Not to be outdone, the Federal government finds no need at all to have balanced checkbook, and those trying to balance theirs find it a bit disingenuous of our politicians to take pay raises while they are systematically draining the US treasury for their pet reelection projects. Is Nero fiddling again?

We the people have to tighten our belts to compete with those who would take their jobs while living either legally or illegally in the U.S., as well as those who would be pleased to do their jobs in China, India, or Russia or a host of developing nations. It's not pretty on the streets. " Let them eat cake" seems to be the government's response.

The public in ever increasing numbers, is also recognizing the structural defects of its political system. The centralization of power within the major parties so that there is no longer a two party system nor room for independents is becoming quite obvious. Bush, Clinton, Bush, Clinton was almost not just a bad joke; it was almost a reality. President Barack Obama benefited on that one.

Add to all of this bad stuff the negativism and personal abuse inherent in adversary partisan politics, the domination of public decision-making by small elites, major party collusion depriving the public of choice, an institutionalized "broken promise syndrome," the failure of the government to be able to handle organized minority groups--legal and illegal--and undemocratic electoral systems and machines where only by chance, and sometimes in spite of devious manipulation, does the resulting government reflect the will of the people.

When representatives of the government call citizens at Town Hall meetings Astroturfers, and disingenuous, while at the same time they send their bought and paid for thugs and operatives (yes, the operatives of our legislators vs. the people) to combat and disrupt the "undue influence" of John Q Public on the fair and open legislative process, isn't this really an awful ugly pot calling the kettle names. Did anybody mention the words "healthcare," and "government control?"

In a democracy it is axiomatic that the majority can only govern with the consent of the minority. Yet it helps to have a majority. Our last set of presidential elections show that there is a deep divide in this country. Yet the good old boys in Congress seek bipartisan labels for their "solutions." It makes no sense since the biggest problem may just well be the political parties that breed our representatives.

They can never consider electoral matters except in terms of their partisan advantage. Underlying the alienation and powerlessness people feel is the lack of a true representative democracy, the accelerating rate of change since the 1980s, the information revolution, the forces of corporate globalization and the ongoing tyranny of the minorities. And they were the good ole days.

Today, as we now have a president with about a year under his belt, and as a country we got the change we asked for, the rift is still huge. And though the above underlying principles and all of the symptoms of no representation that once existed still exist, the debate to many has gotten more personal. It has shifted from just plain old poor and often corrupt representation to a new and deep concern that the actions or inaction (lack of reading legislation and voting for it as an example) of the elected may change the nature of the country forever.

Whether it is a fear of full-bore socialism, or a fear of giving up ones whole paycheck or one's own healthcare to get just a piece of it back, the people have been awakened and life for politicians will never be the same. And, that is good. But the politicians will not take this sitting down. Will they actually consider taking over the country to keep the will of the people in check?   We'll talk about this and many other things as we ponder about whether the people will get the government they deserve, if the people work to deserve better!

Elites Are No Longer Elite

In 1774 the English Whig Party member and Political philosopher Edmund Burke offered that representatives should be elected to govern rather than the people directly. Burke saw that such representatives should exercise their superior wisdom and judgment irrespective of the wishes of the electorate. The electorate in Burke's eyes would be easily characterized as "We the People." He saw their governance as being aided by an elitist private service -- not a public service.

For Burke, that was not only OK but highly desirable. He believed that the public would always reject the "necessary hard decisions," and thus would be incapable of meaningful governance. Today we would call him naive but back then, there appears to have been a substantially higher level of integrity in the political class, thereby making his ideas more acceptable for the times.

Many, including the framers of our Constitution were influenced by Burke but the elitists envisioned by Burke in his writings were not greedy politicians and corporate profiteers who also happened to be wealthy. For Burke, the elitists were in fact the elite of society, the cream of the crop by all standards. They were people you would like if you met them. They were not pretentious. They just happened to be better schooled and in many ways more intelligent and more capable of grappling through the tough decisions.

The overall Edmund Burke philosophy is no longer acceptable to a vast number of people, though it is still promulgated by elitist editorialists, bureaucrats and some academicians. The problem with this notion is the tacit acceptance of an indefinable inequality and the fact that the good unquoted elite can very easily become members of the bad "elite," a group who are well characterized by taking substantially more than they give back.

No Secrets!

The more eyes that look at the machinations of government, the safer and more prosperous we all will be. There are many arguments against open government at all levels, but history tells us that secrecy is a formula for corruption and long-term failure. Additionally, secrecy in government all too often provides for the perpetrators to avoid the responsibility and accountability that would be required if their actions were well known.

The fact is that corruption scandals are regular occurrences in governments across the world, and as you examine these failings, secrecy is always a required ingredient. If government is not always open, then what is it? Closed? If it is truly closed then how is it that in this closed scenario, the secret decision-making is always known by a privileged few who profit from the knowledge?

Watch to see if Jeffrey Immelt, CEO of GE, world's largest corporation, formerly director of message for NBC and MSNBC before GE unloaded them, does not get to enrich his company through some secret deals with his new buddy, President Barack Obama. Obama, the champion of the little guy, in his inner chambers has room for people of all backgrounds, including corporate profiteers and plain ole filthy rich people.

Watch closely to see if there are any rewards to Immelt for being in on the secret meetings which do not occur. It is intuitive that in a closed government, only John Doe and Jane Q. Public are kept in the dark. Somehow, speculators would bet that Jeffrey Immelt gets the full lighted treatment. As open as our government is on paper, secret meetings are commonplace. Thus, we must be wary since these closed sessions occur with "our" representatives at all levels. When they are out of sight in secrecy, we can bet that they are representing somebody other than "We the People."

With an educated populace as exists in the 21st century, it is in fact dangerous to merely trust our representatives with our government. We can be assured that they will not do the right thing. We must, as Ronald Reagan would say "trust but verify." It is all too easy for elected representatives and even their minions, the bureaucrats, to assume that a shroud of wisdom comes down on them once they have arrived in their office.

It is so much easier to serve the private rather than the public interest when dressed in the veil of secrecy, steering clear of accountability. Without a doubt, our most recent history furnishes abundant proof. Open the shades and bring in the light of day. Open the windows, please, and let the stink out of the room--for good. We get the government we deserve.

Chapter Summary

The Representative Democracy that our forefathers brought to this country is not functioning properly. Our elected representatives at all levels of government view the notion of representatives in a much more opportunistic way than intended by the Constitution. To solve this problem, we must admit that government is out of control and no longer is of the people, for the people, and by they people, and we must have the guts to correct it, even if it means not getting something for ourselves from the largesse pile. The time to fix it is now, perhaps before those really in charge become aware of their full power and we never have the opportunity again to gain control. The time is now. We get the government we deserve.

I am very happy to announce that Thomas Dawson has contributed four essays to help complete this work. The full text of these essays is included in Part II of this book in four chapters 5- 9. I predict you will enjoy them immensely.

Sources:
http://reppe.blogs.com/reppecom/2006/03/because_we_get_.html
http://www.samuelgriffith.org.au/papers/html/volume5/v5chap8.htm
http://thejacksonianparty.spaces.live.com/blog/cns!3E751362FDD59519!143.en
try

Chapter 2   Too Many Honorables

The Issues of Today

Something happened to representative government from the
time of the Declaration of Independence and Constitution to
the present. Though our representative constitutional
democracy has survived for about 230 years, it is not at its
healthiest right now. Here are just a few of the major
problems that we are facing as a nation:

- The threat of Socialism from the Government
- The war on terrorism (whatever they call it now)
- Wars in Iraq and Afghanistan
- L-1A and L-1B foreign national visas
- H-1B and D-1 foreign national visas
- Illegal immigration
- Excessive legal immigration
- Corporate power and greed
- Labor arbitrage / offshoring
- Jobs
- Election process corruption
- Healthcare availability and affordability
- Institution of marriage
- Respect for life
- Influence of special interests
- Lobbying
- Private property confiscation
- Political and corporate corruption
- Energy and oil
- Homeland security

- Social Security
- Free trade
- Tax reform
- Economy
- Education
- Crime / drugs /gangs

No book can attack all of these issues (listed in no specific order) and be substantive enough to be informative. So, this book concentrates on the elements of taxation and our lack of representation on all fronts. It focuses on the ability to earn a living and the trouble with corporations as non-equal equal citizens, labor issues, foreign nationals, illegal immigration, and labor arbitrage / offshoring.

The book also takes a look at controversial election laws designed to facilitate fraud for the good of the two party system at the expense of We the People. There are more than enough topics in this abbreviated list for us to examine and offer possible solutions. We'll have to leave the rest to our elected representatives.

Our congressional representatives, and presidential representatives (yes, even the president is supposed to administer the will of the people) have to deal with all of the issues in the big list above as well as others. In 2008, while in the midst of the presidential campaigns, through all sorts of media and the Internet, Americans were able to see what the potential presidential representatives thought about these issues and what they would do to "change" things for the better if they could sell us on putting them in office. Change certainly was the theme in 2008's presidential primaries and it continued into the general election. Now, many who sought change in 2008, 2012, are had buyers' remorse in 2016.

Along the way, we even learned from Mitt Romney that not only was Washington broke, it was broken and needed quick, yet lasting repair. Now, with Barack Obama, it is even more broke and there is concern his quick fix may be from Carl Marx's playbook. .

Promises, promises, promises. How can you tell when a politician is lying? The comic answer of course is, "when their lips are moving." That's because there is a big difference in the spoken words of politicians prior to the election and after being elected. Let me tell a short story to make my point. About the man tied for best presidential orator of all time with Bill Clinton, our own Barack Obama, the word is, don't even listen to what he says, watch what he does. If I were a comedian, I might suggest that only his teleprompter knows for sure.

IBM: Don't Confuse Selling with Installing

While I was with IBM, I worked in local sales offices in Utica, New York, and Scranton, PA. I was a technical guy at the time. IBM called me a Senior Systems Engineer at the time I retired. Delivery time for IBM equipment during my career was anywhere from a month to two years. Because large computer sales people got paid something when they sold a machine and something again when the company shipped the machine and the field engineers installed the gear in a customer premise, there were rules of engagement during the sell and the install cycles. The sell cycle was very much like our elections in which politicians promise, promise, and then promise to make more promises. Sales reps made promises in the same fashion. Yes, it can do that. Yes it can do that. Yes it can do that... Until they got the order.

Theoretically a computer could do any business task if programmed properly. So, the yes answers could be true if the programming were available, and the sales rep intended that the machine would be able to do all the things promised--not that it would necessarily do them--but would be able to do them. You see the difference.

Then there was the install or implementation cycle in which the Systems Engineer had to prepare the customer for their new computer so they were ready to use it when it arrived, and most importantly, that they were confident enough that they would pay IBM for it as soon as possible. There were few unfulfilled promises in this scenario since if the machine did not do the job as the customer saw it, they would send it back to IBM and the salesman would forego all the commissions and pay IBM a penalty. However, there was a difference in the frankness of the discussion during the sell cycle and the install cycle. Before the salesman got the order, nobody was supposed to say anything negative, regardless of whether it was true or not. Thus, IBM people always joked that nobody should confuse the sell with the install.

The same goes for our promising politicians. During the election process they sell, sell, sell using the level of promises necessary to get the order. Nobody in the campaign can say anything negative about the candidate or a proposed solution to an issue even if it is true. Much like an IBM salesperson, if you can't get a promise from a politician on the sell side, you will never get one on the install side. Once elected, (install side begins) all bets are off and the truth and facts and real intentions take over.

Unfortunately for the American people, when politicians as legislators choose not to fulfill the essence of their promises, we cannot send the computer back shipped and uninstalled. We cannot assess a penalty for lying to us about their real intentions. We do have initiative, referendum, and recall at the state level but not at the federal level. Moreover, it would take a groundswell and an act of congress (literally) to make that work. So we wind up being stuck with politicians instead of being supported by our elected representatives.

The Honorable Congressman from Blankety Blank

Then what? Then we have to treat them like gold and call them "the honorable so and so from such and such." We always must be wary that they do not hurt us too bad. Somehow in the last fifty years and perhaps longer, the notion of the representative as a noble person as in "nobility" has been creeping into our etiquette. Yet, not only are most politicians often dishonorable, they are plain and simple corrupt and they do not represent the people once elected. We know who they represent - special interests, corporations, and the Ruling Class of elite citizens.

They tax us and tax us and tax us, but they do not represent us. This is clearly taxation without representation but not quite as it was before the Tea Party. The tea is brewing today in a bigger way and it is much hotter than when I wrote the first edition of this book in 2008. Just like before the original tea party, the people on the streets are getting more and more riled about this. Originally it was the young and they elected Barack Obama as the answer. Now it is everybody and Obama has become part of the problem, not the solution. ,

The young have surely become more active in the election process. For example, without using these words, the first meaning of their buzzword "change" is "Throw the Bums Out!" And, for how "the honorables" they have treated us when given the privilege to represent us, they are worse than bums, indeed. Even the young did not expect Obama to be more like Mayor Daly than Abraham Lincoln. And the seniors, they think that the change they asked for was just, "no more Bush," and now many believe that the new guy is going to steal their healthcare to pay for somebody else's healthcare. .

The lack of representation is a big problem for regular Americans, young and old, and it manifests itself in legislation or lack of legislation to protect even our most basic rights. Among their despicable acts, our representatives have tried to give our healthcare to 50,000,000 more potential voters, given our jobs to legal foreign nationals, have permitted greedy American corporations to swindle stockholders and employees and to take American jobs overseas, and they have permitted illegal foreign nationals to settle permanently in the U.S. to take our jobs and take our tax money. Then, to add insult to injury, our representatives in the Presidency as well as in Congress have told us that we don't really want our jobs or our own healthcare and that all of this charade is good for America. Phooey!

A Method to Solve Problems

Problems that can be solved fit nicely in a notion called *The Scientific Method of Problem Solving.* The idea is to know the problem, come up with some solutions, test the solutions, and then draw conclusions from the observations and testing. The problem, which I would like to tackle using the scientific method is that representative government is not working and it needs to be fixed. Unfortunately, that topic is too big for this chapter and it is addressed throughout this book. But, we can attack a more discrete subset of the issue and we can have some fun at the same time.

The problem for today is that we the people honor despicable politicians with large titles though they do not deserve them -- and of course this contributes to the lack of representation. Analyzing and posturing solutions to this problem about our leaders will both enlighten and amuse as we walk through its solving via the Scientific Method.

The Scientific Method deals with problems, not symptoms. A runny nose, for example, is a symptom of a problem. The problem may be a cold, the H1N1 flu, or perhaps an allergy. For argument's sake, let's say a problem is *a real issue that can be solved by the scientific method.* It can be defined as a question to be considered, solved, or answered. It may also be a difficult situation, matter, or person. On the lighter side, a problem may also be a misgiving, an objection, or even a complaint. A symptom, on the other hand is a *characteristic sign or manifestation of some underlying pathology.* That pathology is most often the problem.

The six basic steps in the scientific method are as follows:

1. State the Problem - No problem can be solved if it is not identified. In a nutshell, the problem we are exploring in this iteration is that that representatives at all levels of government, no longer representing the people from which they were elected, are emboldened by the honorable titles given them for merely holding office. This undue tribute affirms the pitiful work of the representative as being even more than acceptable.

The more powerful the representative, the more toxic the effect of this callous disregard. Representatives have created their own class of people, which is a notch to many notches above the common person on the street. A root cause of this in the year is that representatives of the people in all levels of government enjoy the adulation that comes with the office they hold... in fact they enjoy it too much.

They enjoy the separation from the hoi polloi and the sense of nobility they gain by praise and extra respect. The public feeds this notion by granting them such titles as the "Honorable" as is frequently done in Britain and which was part of British politics at the time of the Revolutionary War. Because of the Colonists disdain for the notion of the "Nobility," the Constitution expressly forbids the granting of such titles unless authorized by Congress:

The Congress is expressly forbidden to grant titles of nobility or permit federal officials to accept gifts or titles without Congress's consent

The lawyers have probably all focused on the words, "*without Congress's consent,*" as a viable loophole, whereas the people well recognize the intent of the founding fathers.

When elected to public office, the pomp and circumstance that begins at the inauguration starts a process that sets the newly elected on a path far different from mere mortals. It is clearly irrevocable and for the rest of the politician's life, the "notion of once-elected" clearly sets them apart from those they represent or once represented. If it weren't for the laws keeping them in the territory of their constituencies, surely, they would be able to find their just segregation. Thankfully, there are rich neighborhoods in almost every election district and the rich and well-to-do people in those neighborhoods are also "of the people." Thus, the new politician has the opportunity to find new friends of proper status so as not to have to mingle with the common electorate.

Is This Bad Behavior?

Today's finest psychologists who are always quick to find a "rational" explanation for all bad behavior might suggest that there is nothing wrong with politicians finding elite rather than humble companions worthy of fraternization. Why should a politician for example, once elected, have to break bread with a plumber, an electrician, a computer programmer, a salad tosser, or a hamburger flipper when there are people with fountains of money in their pockets and a taste for powerful friends? Hyperbole and oversimplification aside, there is no doubt that in general, the rich and the powerful have perennially been consenting bedfellows, a symbiosis that leaves nary a crumb for the toiling paeans who bake their very bread.

It is proper and even dutiful to now ask. "Are our representatives in government excessively elevated and exalted?" This singular question expands into many. Do they quickly begin to exhibit a sense of self-importance and arrogance upon accepting their office as in the case of the infamous *pompous* politician? Or by virtue of their office, have they in fact become magnificent, illustrious, of great renown, deserving and entitled to honor? Does the praise and high respect given even the newly elected arise because it testifies to their creditable conduct or their consistent untarnished reputation?

Does it mean that intuitively at the end of the oath, and at the end of the day (a phrase very popular for politicians today) they have become guided by a high sense of honor and duty, characterized by a massive gob of ... well, let's just say it ... integrity? Or is Nero Caesar alive, healthy, and among us? Surely these are all good questions and I think you know on which side of the argument our esteemed psychologists would find themselves.

If there were something wrong with all of these compliments attributing the finest attributes of a person to our political class, surely, the psychologists would have identified it and would already be correcting it. But, why does the proletariat accept all of this pomposity from its representatives as if it is the only way it should be? I would answer the last question by suggesting that Jane Q. Public does not spend a lot of time on the question.

If Jane Q. spent the time required to analyze what this is all about, she would more than likely conclude that it is nothing more than innocuous puffery. She would see that it serves to ingratiate the representative to be more inclined to offer benefits to the represented who offer such tributes. The bottom line for Jane Q. and quite frankly for John Q. also is that they would let it happen because there appears to be no harm done.

Should We Care?

Being a John Q. myself and knowing lots of other John Q's, I must admit that the puffery is getting old to many of us and you the reader are now included in our lot. This book in many ways is about the effects such puffery has on the laws and the enforcement of laws in this country. We are not talking about the emperor and his new clothes since the constituency of ourselves, unless feeling direct pain from the hand of a politician, do not even look to see the emperor unmasked or unclothed as "hizzoner." Basically we do not care about the platitudes given and we give them sometimes ourselves, though with misgivings.

Does this attitude of honoring the "Honorables" because it is what everybody does, hurt John Q.? In a word, "Yes" it does, because this flattery, harmless as it may be given, does inflate the political ego and thus creates more separation of the representatives from the represented. It does not promote the common good. Additionally, it can be argued that it prompts the political class to care more for themselves and other elites than for the man on the street. And, my dear readers, that means that John Q. is really not being represented in our government today.

As you will read in further chapters of this book, our forefathers could not stand the notion of taxation without representation. If the truth be known, they could not stand any notion imposed on the subjects of the Crown, without representation from those imposed upon agreeing to the imposition.

To show their disdain for a non-representative government with the power to enforce taxation, colonial Americans chose to fight a war to gain the right to their most important demand, representative government. Using other terms, the founding fathers called this government of the people, for the people, and by the people. Unfortunately for America, many of our elected were not in history class the day this theory was explained.

This right in many ways is being squandered today by ordinary citizens who think that politicians are more than who they are. The political class in many ways is viewed by the people as if they are the ruling class and the people are their subjects. This is a bit like one would expect from a constitutional monarchy or an oligarchy, not from a democracy. Hopefully this book and the words of others will help the people of this nation remember that we run the country and that the politicians, once elected must become public officials. To the extent we permit them to remain as politicians with some public duties, we remain unrepresented. The next election has nothing to do with the duties of those currently in office, yet an incumbent never is more at work than when involved in getting re-elected.

Those Days vs. These Days

Shortly after the Revolutionary War and after the formation of our representative government, there was a problem for the constituency. Somebody had to send representatives. At the federal level, it was not too easy for a local farmer to give up his farm and head off to Washington by wagon or horseback to represent the folks back home.

Recognizing this difficulty, in appreciation for representing the constituency, the neighbors, who were not of the aristocracy but of the commonplace, tended the representative's farm and protected the household, the mom and the kids and the animals, until the hero representative would come home and resume his life. During this period of American history, the representatives were clearly honorable, but they did not demand the title.

The irony of those days compared to these days is that in those days the representatives performed for their constituency from a sense of duty. In these days, though one cannot strike a broad negative brush on the political class or a good person will never agree to help our cause and run for office, it seems that instead of from a sense of duty, today's "politicians" go for the office from a sense of opportunity. That's about it and that is the big problem.

I can probably end the book right here but there is lots more I have to say. When one is motivated by the sense of opportunity, one's interests lie mainly in oneself. So, I could rest my case right now but I will continue since we not only need to change the notion that the governors are elite and the governed are subjects, we must convince the best and the brightest of our country to take up the yoke as in days past and do for America from a raging sense of duty, not opportunity... and not for a lifetime.

A Country of Honor

The State of Pennsylvania is not unlike the other 49 states. So, as I speak about PA, think about the similarities with the political business in your own state. Surely some who come to office come from a sense of duty and they are fine people, while others come from the draw of opportunity. Hence, with the dismal track record of politicos from all states and the federal government, It is better for the constituency to not trust any in elected public office until given proof that such trust is well deserved. Just like your state, the state of Pennsylvania in which I have lived all but two of my years in this life, is a state with a mix of the duty class and the opportunity class.

A number of the names in the next section are people who I know from my own area of the state. As I mention names and titles, please do not draw any conclusions on the specific individuals that I mention (at least in this chapter) A number of office-holders, such as former magistrate Martin R. Kane, and William H. Amesbury from my City of Wilkes-Barre, I know are very good men.

However, I admit that I do not know all about even these two. I met Kane as he was serving as a Justice of the Peace at a wedding of a young man who was like a son to me. The Honorable Martin Kane could have easily dismissed this family's request to travel to the far corners of the county on a sunny holiday to marry them but instead, he welcomed it. Amesbury and I met in a Little League game when we both were 11 years old, and in all the years that have passed, I still haven't heard a bad word about hizzoner. I am also friends with our Mayor, Tony George and thankfully for Wilkes-Barre, he is about as good a guy as it gets.

As many states in this wonderful nation, the state of Pennsylvania has many politicians bearing the title "The Honorable." Are they honorable? That is for their constituencies to examine and decide. It is absolutely amazing how many yeronners and heronners and hizzoners there are in all states, so I have chosen PA, my state, as my example state.

To put some names next to some of those honorable representatives, executives, and justices, permit me to use those with whom I am most familiar from a local standpoint and then pick them at random the further from my home town they get. For example, the list of honorables includes the Honorable Senator from Pennsylvania, Robert P. Casey, the Honorable Matt cartwright (U.S. House of Representatives), The Honorable Thomas Wolfe (Governor, Commonwealth of Pennsylvania), the Honorable Elisabeth J. Baker (PA State Senator), the Honorable Eddie Day Pashinski (PA State House of Representatives), the Honorable Anthony George, Mayor of Wilkes-Barre City, The Honorable Seamus McCaffrey (Pennsylvania Supreme Court Justice), The Honorable Christine Donohue (Pennsylvania Superior Court Justice), The Honorable Richard M. Hughes III, (President Judge, Luzerne County Courts -- , The Honorable Ray Cronauer (District Justice, Luzerne County), The Honorable William T. Amesbury -- Judge of the Common Pleas in Luzerne County). .

With no disrespect intended to any of the above, that is an awful lot of "Honorables" and it doesn't touch the number of hizzoners, heronners, and yeronners in just the state of Pennsylvania. If you begin a calculation based on current appointees and elected offices, the national total of the "Honorables," would be in the hundreds of thousands.

That's an awful lot of honor that is implicitly taken by this branch of the political class. Think of your own list in your own state and you are probably not surprised that this list is large and in almost all cases, except for Amesbury, I chose just one of many in the chamber who hold the same office.

So, as a major preamble to a problem statement using the scientific method, I have described the situation (problem) in adequate detail. The big problem is that there is taxation and there is not representation. Yet, somehow the "representatives" are all honorable.

The situation is quite similar to when King George III and Parliament in the 18th century directly levied taxes on the colonists and the colonists rebelled. Though outright rebellion is not necessarily right around the corner, the current set of "Honorables" need to pay attention to the mood of the people on this topic because the public mood is not very good. Those representatives who enjoy the game need to come to the realization again that the people come first.

Unlike the 18th century, however, there are living representatives. There just isn't real representation. The litmus test is whether that representation is of the people, for the people, and by the people. Take a look at the Honorable So and So's in your home state and in your locale, and ask if you're gifting them with the title of hizzoner has minimized the representation you receive. I say yes it has in most cases and thus the problem statement for this problem using the scientific method, with due poetic license, can be written as follow:.

Completed Problem Statement - Scientific Method

The use of platitudes and pufferies to describe elected representatives diminishes their desire to represent the people and increases their desire to represent themselves, the elite and the special interests classes of the elite. It also decreases the expectation level of the constituency as they, by their own words, place their governors in a higher socio-political class and they submit as subjects to "what comes down the pike."

The next phase of the scientific method of problem solving is as follows:

2. **Form a Hypothesis** - Using the Scientific Method of problem solving, this represents a possible solution to the problem formed after gathering information about the problem. The term "research" must be properly applied here.

Can this hypothesis be as simple as an admonition to stop doing what we are doing? Stop giving puffery and stop accepting puffery. Is it that simple? Yes it is but there are some other issues that we need to discuss and these follow:

From henceforth, let the representatives serve as unsung and humble heroes about whom songs of distinction will rarely be raised unless the distinction is truly earned. Let them represent the people and nobody else. Let their inner selves guide their votes and let their inner selves give them praise for jobs well done. Let the pomposity and the arrogance end and end quickly.

Puffery Leads to Improper Allegiances

Let no special interests be permitted anywhere close to the hallowed chambers of our government and the buildings in which the business of the people is conducted. Keep the lobbyists and those backed by the money of the unknown, including that of the enemies of these United States, from the legislators (our representatives) as they are making laws for the common good of the states.

Lobbyists and those whose income depends on influencing America's lawmakers should be permitted no contact with the

representatives of the states, or any local constituency. Such
activity in proximity of lawmakers is not for the common
good and the lobbyist crowd should not be permitted to
intimidate or influence any representative. The notion of
important lobbyists trying to influence legislators can have a
negative effect on the clear thinking of the people's elected
representatives. Let the lobbyists identify themselves and
lobby the governed, not the instruments of their government.

The notion of lobbyists, however, is just an aside. If our
representatives, paid well of course, ($174,000 per year as of
2009 not including expenses --- for each house seat knew that
they could not receive additional compensation from
lobbyists, bribers, or whatever you want to call them, ever, no
how, no matter how they voted, they would not be as
inclined to favor those for private interests against those for
public interests.

Pay Them Well

Politicians live in elite neighborhoods. This is not good but it
would not be right to dictate the neighborhood in which your
representative lives as long as it is within your district. Our
representatives must be paid well for their service and they
should believe that they are being paid well. Otherwise, their
honesty may be compromised as they turn to the elite in
order to receive more compensation.

They must be paid well during their terms and their terms
must be short so that they do not become untouchable by
mere mortals. The temptation of being for oneself while in
office clearly must be minimized. This is as we say, a
representative democracy and our representatives cannot do
well by the people if they represent themselves or those who
are not of the people. It really is that simple. The primary
point of this discussion is that we the people must reengage
our government within the honorable laws (and we need to
get rid of the laws not so honorable) that benefit all of the
people.

Minimize the Opportunity for Corruption

Sending our newly elected into a quagmire of corruption and deceit and seeing who survives is not a good recipe for the future. Let's figure out how to get rid of the corruption and all the bad that comes with that. Calling the newly elected "the Honorable" and paying homage to her or him as a new governor of subjects is clearly not the right approach. It is unfortunately today's modus operandi, an operandi that has long failed the people.

Thank-you's are most appropriate for good service. The notion of a required "hizzoner" that starts a period of aristocratic living from the first waltz of the Inaugural Ball breeds just more separation from the people. In a democracy, the rich and the plebeians have the right to a voice in their government. So, what do we do? Well, first of all we must realize that nothing is going to change for the better unless the people are very insistent. Corruption begins as the corrupt begin to believe in themselves and not the mission of helping their whole constituency. Rule # 1 for the people is to pay attention.

Unfortunately as innocuous as it may seem, this notion of "The Honorable" and all that means is ingrained deeply into the fabric of American political culture and etiquette. Until recently, however, one could also rely on the ethics and morals of the representatives as an additional inhibitor to corruption, and thus assuring proper action. It seems that in the latter part of the 20th century the culture of "anything goes" has permeated American society and its morals and its ethics. Not all politicians are corrupt but it is easy for our representatives to get sucked in to something that is much bigger than they themselves.

Therefore, one can no longer count on one's own ethics and one's own morals if elected to serve as a countervailing force against bad representation. Consequently, it is up to the people to create an environment, which is more personally rewarding for our representatives to do their jobs, than it would be to accept praise for merely being elected.

Political corruption is actually what we hope to prevent. When it was once safe to speak of religious values in this country without fear of reprisal or a lawsuit, there was an apparent social conscience with which to gauge all actions. Much of the writing of the founding fathers reflects a Christian bias for example. The underlying Christian faith, which is based on love and honesty and goodness is not really a bad model upon which to form a government. I know of no Christian or Hindu or Jew who by ideology alone wants to kill me.

Ethics and Morals

As our representatives get further removed from their original neighborhoods and become rich in one way or another because of their public service, this may help the representative but it does not help the people. One teaching of the Christian church is the "eye of needle" analogy. Christianity holds that this is bad news for the rich, because it is easier for a camel to go through the eye of a needle than for a rich man to enter the kingdom of Heaven.

So, according to Christian teaching (the faith of the founding fathers), the tendency of a politician to work with the well-to-do and live in their neighborhoods while becoming rich makes them less likely to be worthy of Heaven. Less likely for Heaven means more likely for corruption and so, if honor is given in any form, perhaps it should be from the people to its representatives -- those representatives who stay in the regular neighborhoods and live humble lives. The representative would be honoring the people by doing so and would have more of an opportunity to avoid the needle test.

What might be the curing hypotheses using the scientific method that we pass to the next phase in the process (testing)? As my wife would say, "'What's the point?" Well, since you asked, this is exactly the point:

Representatives of the people at all levels of government are of the people and must therefore be for the people so that their laws can be recognized clearly as being by the people. When situations occur that exalt the representative regardless of their service or lack of service to the people, merely by their elected office, this is reprehensible and the laws put forth under these circumstances should be viewed accordingly and scorned. How can a pack of nothing but "Honorables," who have distanced and disconnected themselves from the ordinary people that elected them, represent us fairly in our government? The fact is that as a whole, today's representatives are not doing the people's business. They are doing their own business and the business of their elite sponsors. This problem is the very essence and the rationale of this book.

Thomas Jefferson had great disdain and mistrust for the propensity of man, once given the power to rule, to use that power for the good of the people rather than himself. He warned of what could happen when such people create issues for society that require more and more debt and ultimately more taxation, with the implication of poor representation. With historically high deficits and mounting national debt, we seemingly have not learned this lesson well:

> "We must not let our rulers load us with perpetual debt. We must make our election between economy and liberty or profusion and servitude. If we run into such debt, as that we must be taxed in our meat and in our drink, in our necessaries and our comforts, in our labors and our amusements, for our calling and our creeds...we [will] have no time to think, no means of calling our miss-managers to account but be glad to obtain subsistence by hiring ourselves to rivet their chains on the necks of our fellow-sufferers. And this is

the tendency of all human governments. A departure from principle in one instance becomes a precedent till the bulk of society is reduced to be mere automatons of misery. And the foreshores of this frightful team is public debt. Taxation follows that, and in its train wretchedness and oppression."

Does it not seem in these words that Thomas Jefferson is looking at us from the grave, knowing his words have been unheeded and working for God now to make sure we get his message and we act accordingly?

Completed Hypotheses - Scientific Method

The solution to the "Honorables" is quite simple. Our elected representatives, while in Washington or in the state assemblies and even in the courtrooms and the lower legislatures, executive branch chambers, and councils should be treated with respect and should have amenities to compensate them well for their time away from home. However, they are not entitled to the title, "honorable" merely by taking the oath of office one time. The title "honorable" no longer can be an expected gift from the public to the representatives without them having earned the title. It is the legislators, executives, and justices themselves who should strip themselves of the title immediately and be done with it. It is nonsense and should be ceased immediately.

Additional Thoughts

Those once in office but no longer in office who still get a kick out of being called the "honorable" can receive a replacement title if it is that important to them, from the body from which they retired. Ex-presidents and ex-Governors and Ex-Mayors can request the title from an ad-hoc committee respectively made up of ex-Presidents, ex-Governors, and ex-Mayors. A suitable respectable title that does not imply honor can be created, such as "the public servant" or the "friend of the people," and this can be used in etiquette from henceforth rather than force a vote about honor for each public official above a certain level of office.

A different term for judges than "Your Honor " should be instituted and while in session, judges would thus be greeted as "Your Judgeship" while presiding officially in a courtroom. Since "judgeship accurately reflects the high respect needed for the position of judge, not the person behind the robes, it is a responsible compromise from the "honor" system.

In all other social events other than those purely political in nature and sponsored by politicians or friends of politicians, all of our duly elected servants should not be greeted as "the Honorable" or by their official title. In a democracy, if these people are of the people, and they are or should be, they should be addressed as all of the people are addressed. As an example, I do not want to be known as His Authorship.

If we think about it, we are all pretending about the elected being honorable anyway and that is just silly. It's actually pretty stupid besides. It's pure puffery at its best and in this day and age in which the constituency is questioning the loyalty of its representatives, considering ones-self as "the honorable," is not the side of the puff on which a representative should want to find himself.

The next phase of the scientific method of problem solving is as follows:

3. **Test the Hypothesis** - In this third phase of the scientific method, an experiment is performed to determine if the hypothesis solves the problem or not. Experiments are done to gather data. It is very important that good observations and records are made during an experiment.

Mary K. Mewborn, writing in the November 19, 1999 edition of *Washington Life Magazine*, in an article aptly titled "Too Many Honorables?" has done most of my work for me in testing the hypothesis. The solution as noted above is to not haphazardly bestow the title of "Honorable" - period. Ms. Mewborn notes the asininity involved in granting such a title in her first examples. Here are three priceless misuses of the title from Ms. Mewborn:

"A socialite in Wesley Heights thinks it adds personal distinction to her many listings on fundraising invitations."

"A former ambassador living at the Watergate uses it to remind others of his long-ago diplomatic posting to a small Caribbean nation."

"Appointees to even the most minor Presidential commissions are apt to believe it bestows instant social cachet- with invitations to A-list parties sure to follow."

She points out in this article that it is illegal to take the title "honorable," although she acknowledges that which cannot be gained legally can be gained by political process. In other words, the politicians can do what they want once they run the country -- and they do -- and they have -- and quite frankly that's why she and we are upset!

Test the reasonableness of no longer conferring the title honorable on our representatives by reading the following several paragraphs, again taken from Mary K. Mewborn's timeless article about "Too Many Honorables." Before the paragraphs, here is the URL of the article, available online for the surfing. It's a fun read.

http://www.washingtonlife.com/backissues/archives/99nov/honorables.htm

Whether it is the roster of the Board of Governors of the Smithsonian Institution or the benefit committee of a typical Washington charity gala, there are always a number of names preceded by "Honorable," instead of the usual Mr., Mrs., Miss or Ms. How this came about in a country whose Constitution expressly forbids the granting of titles amuses some and irritates others. At the very least its widespread usage raises some eyebrows.

Traditionally the British use the "Hon." (originally abbreviated from "The Right Honorable Magnificence of Nobles"), to identify certain family members of hereditary barons and earls, i.e., their daughters, younger sons and the younger sons' wives. In America, however, such inherited titles were rare among the early colonists, and after independence there was no king to grant new ones.

That did not mean this country developed along totally egalitarian lines. Even in a democracy it was only natural that ways had to be found to distinguish the elite from the hoi polloi, the rulers from the ruled. The conferment of titles, although prevented by the Constitution, was effectively achieved by political success.

Political primacy is now well-established in matters of protocol and etiquette and is, according to the U.S. Government, a matter of procedure and form. Consequently, it would be very improper indeed to refer to the "Hon. Bill Gates," even though he may have billions in the bank and pay his taxes, or to the "Hon. Cindy Crawford," although what man wouldn't hope to flatter her? Nobel Prizes and great humanitarian deeds won't make you Honorable either, though getting elected Mayor of Bladensburg, Md. definitely will.

By the rules of etiquette, you can become Honorable by getting elected to the White House or Congress, or by having the President nominate and the Senate confirm you to an ambassadorship or other political post (judge, commissioner, etc.). Once you are made an Honorable, you stay that way for life, regardless of what an independent counsel or district attorney may subsequently uncover about any untoward activities. "In Washington, as Betty Beale, longtime social columnist and observer of the Washington social scene, bluntly puts it, "The title 'Honorable' has nothing to do either with honor or character."

The next phase of the scientific method of problem solving is as follows:

4. Collect the Data - Using the Scientific Method, this is the place in the process in which you record your observations, measurements, or information from experiment.

The collection of data in the scientific method can be represented by the copious research work that permitted Ms. Mewborn to uncover the fact that the title "honorable" is not and cannot be a conferred title and therefore it is a title that is improperly used to refer to the people's representatives merely because of their representation. The raw data from her research is not here for us to examine but there is enough in her article to suffice as data well collected.

Moreover, you and I have observed the notion of the "Honorables" in our daily lives and we have also seen the impact of such pomposity in the behavior of our elected officials. If you have looked at the same news accounts as I throughout 2009 and 2010 and long before, it is clear that our representatives have become so honorable that there is now so much honor, there is no longer any room for shame. There is a lot of collected data in our observations and those of the media.

In the Federal Government, it is clear that Senators are further away from the people than members of the House of Representatives. They behave as Lords from old England and have a major disconnect with the people. Even when they commit a crime, they believe they are better than the represented.

Among just about every highlight reel from the last five years is the story of a US senator who said he would resign in the midst of scandal surrounding his arrest in a police sting targeting lewd behavior in a men's public restroom but then flip flopped believing his own admission of guilt was not enough to prove he was guilty. Remember Senator Larry Craig, 62 at the time, who had been arrested in June, 2007 and then pleaded guilty in August to a lesser charge - disorderly conduct. He apparently paid the $500 fine, and was given a 10-day suspended sentences and a year's probation. But, he was only kidding...

Another class act is Democratic Congressman William "the Freezer" Jefferson of Louisiana. Jefferson has been dubbed the "Freezer" though he has no major football skills but until recently he has been able to avoid the rush. In the first edition of this book, I was able to say that he had not been sacked yet but his sack was found in his freezer with $90,000 of cold, in fact, frozen cash. He's in jail now. His constituents more than likely gave him the cash from a number of lemonade sales they undertook to help him with his future defense if he were ever to need cash. OK, I lie but the story is pretty close.

The Congressman faced 16 charges of being a thief more than 2 years after the FBI found the cash in his freezer. He was convicted on 11 of the counts. That does not mean he was not guilty on the others. He was guilty of taking a bribe from a foreign official and the $90,000 was left from the marked $100,000 that he received (from an FBI Informant). After all, $100,000 is a lot to spend. Fearing he would take off to a remote island, Jefferson was remanded before sentencing. How's that for honor?

As a result of these two and others of recent vintage such as Republican Duke Cunningham, Republican Bob Ney and Democrat Jim Traficant and probably hundreds more like them, it has become easy to presume guilt. As noted previously, "How can you tell if a politician is lying? He's moving his lips" That says it all and it helps to repeat it to remember it.

Dr. Gerhard Falk, writing an article in blog form on http://jbuff.com/c012705.htm performed his research and collected data in order to shed some light on the subject of respect for politicians. Whether you agree with all of what he says or not, Falk certainly catches the spirit of the great disdain with which our leaders were held in 2008 and not much has changed since. Mewborn and Falk and many others with whom we would probably agree, note that the "Honorables" have created an ironically dishonorable circumstance, some by their conduct outside of office and some by their poor representation. The moniker of "honorable" being used to describe those looked upon as of questionable repute does not help matters. Dr. Falk adds his own few words about the Honorables to the mix as he discusses the vile of politicians in his blog:

> Politicians of all parties are evidently convinced that the whole world revolves only around them. They do not want to meet the voters, i.e. the ordinary taxpayers, for fear that they may be asked what they do all day and what happed to our money. They call themselves "the honorable" this and that...
> ...
>
> Politicians love to aggrandize themselves. Bill Clinton spent $42 million on his second inauguration and George W. Bush spent $40 million more. These expensive theatrics are obscene and have no place in our democracy. Read the life of George Washington. He was sworn in for a second time as President of the United States on March 4, 1793. His speech was only 134 words and he then walked home alone. No parade. No speeches. No dances. No gross exhibition of ego.

Falk had not met Barack Obama, the first combination
Sultan. King, and President of the US. Because of the triple
duty, Obama was forced to spend upwards of $170 million
for his inauguration. Was it inflation or excessive love? For
the pure scientist who is reading this, please forgive my poetic
license regarding the scientific method and the idea of data
collection to back up the hypotheses. Once all the data for
this phase would be collected, there would be plenty to affirm
the validity of the hypothesis and the analysis.

The next phase of the scientific method of problem solving is
as follows:

5. **Analyze the Data** - This part of the Scientific Method
asks the question: "Just what does all that data indicate about
answering the problem you are solving?"

The problem of self-aggrandizement and the notion of self-
importance are well documented and well observed even
without deploying the scientific method. Will the inability to
use the title "honorable" actually solve the problem of (1)
inappropriate claiming of title and (2) the resultant lack of
true representation of the people for the people by the
representatives of the people?

The scientific method helps us here even though we cannot
observe the results of the blocking of the use of the title since
there is no real data and no true table upon which to
experiment. However, since this problem limited itself to
part 1 of 2 above, the answer is logically clear that if the title
"honorable" can no longer be used in a whimsical manner by
any politician at any time, then the problem statement is
solved by the hypothesis. Thus, we can stage the analysis to
draw such conclusions in Step 6.

However, there is no real set of data that can be collected
(Step 4) that would tell us that our representatives would
actually change their behavior and be more prone to
represent the people rather than themselves or special

interests. We would hope so but there are no assurances. Most reasonable, prudent people would believe that it would contribute to a better situation but it probably would not be enough.

The next phase of the scientific method of problem solving is as follows:

6. **Draw Conclusions** - After examining the data from the experiment, at this point in the six point Scientific Method process, conclusions can be drawn. In its simplest form, the conclusion will be "yes" the hypothesis is correct, or "no" the hypothesis is not correct.

The solution as noted previously is simple to the problem of the "Honorables." If they no longer are bestowed the title merely by gaining an office or an appointment, the problem of "too many Honorables" and not enough honor is on its way to a successful ending. Once politicians can no longer use the title, "honorable," their egos will no longer be instantly stroked and the people will have eliminated one major source of puffery for our duly elected representatives.

Let honor be reserved for honorable deeds and not because politicians may be offended if there is not an aura of puff surrounding their entrance on the scene. So we can say **Yes** to this conclusion and I would suggest that we should say it loudly.

-- End of Scientific Method ---

But Is Puffery Really the Problem?

Heavens no! But, puffery is a big problem since it is the arrogant, puffed-up politician who is more likely to choose to disrespect the will of the people and go on his way to legislate for the good of special interests. Politicians go out of their way to bring wonderful legislative gifts to the privileged class and the special interests. The current "Honorables" have a hard time saying "No" to friends in high places.

I received a number of emails this year from cohorts who, like you are interested in this U.S. government succeeding. Most, like you and I find major fault with such a representation process that puts so many buffoons in office. We all know intuitively that the notion of humor is the quality that appeals to a sense of the ludicrous or absurdly incongruous. For those schooled in high school geometry, it's like when CPCT is not equal.

When things do not add up and nobody is hurt, at least at the time of the adding, it sure can be funny and it can induce a big belly laugh. The puffery that comes with political office and the buffoonery of many of the "Honorables," is what I will attribute to this email that I received from one of my associates. I have no idea of the original source of this email but it sure captures what I have been trying to say about the perception of character of our elected officials.

Subject: Haircut

One day a florist goes to a barber for a haircut. After the cut he asked about his bill and the barber replies, "I cannot accept money from you. I'm doing community service this week." The florist was pleased and left the shop. When the barber goes to open his shop the next morning there is a 'thank you' card and a dozen roses waiting for him at his door.

Later, a cop comes in for a haircut, and when he tries to pay his bill, the barber again replies, "I cannot accept money from you. I'm doing community service this week." The cop is happy and leaves the shop. The next morning when the barber goes to open up there is a 'thank you' card and a dozen donuts waiting for him at his door.

Later that day, a college professor comes in for a haircut, and when he tries to pay his bill, the barber again replies, "I cannot accept money from you. I'm doing community service this week." The professor is very happy and leaves the shop. The next morning when the barber opens his shop, there is a 'thank you' card and a dozen different books, such as "How to Improve Your Business" and Becoming More Successful."

"Then, a Congressman comes in for a haircut, and when he goes to pay his bill the barber again replies, "I cannot accept money from you. I'm doing community service this week." The Congressman is very happy and leaves the shop. The next morning when the barber goes to open up, there are a dozen Congressmen lined up waiting for a free haircut.

And that, my friends, illustrates the fundamental difference between the citizens of our country and the members of our Congress.

This little email joke may not say it all but it sure says a lot about the breakdown in real respect that the people have for the representatives of the people. As you will see in the other chapters of this book, there are lots of real reasons for this feeling and it is not just a matter of puff.

Chapter Summary

In this chapter we used the scientific method to determine whether there was a real problem with all of the fluff and puff that is associated with our political class. The use of the word "honorable" was the point that was debated in this chapter. Should our elected representatives be entitled to the title "honorable" merely by being elected. Using the Scientific Method, we concluded that the answer is no and that it hurts our democratic system of representative egalitarian government to suggest that all men are not equal.

Chapter 3   Civics Lesson: Constitutional Democracy

This chapter introduces the notion of the importance of representative government to the citizens of the United States and it also introduces the notion of taxation without representation as our elected leaders fail to accomplish their duties. In this Civics Lesson, we examine the form of our representative democracy and we explore other forms and variations that make the US form of government about as good as it can get.

This brief civics lesson is presented in this book to give the reader the opportunity to understand the basic tenets of the US representative constitutional democracy. For a deeper appreciation of the notion of the US government and its underlying political principles, there is an excellent free course available on the Internet and I encourage you to visit the Cyberland University of North America at the following URL:

http://www.proconservative.net/CUNAPolSci201HOutline.shtml

Dr. Almon Leroy Way, Jr. University President & Professor of Political Science in his free Internet course titled Political Science 201H - The American Political System: Politics & Government in the USA captures the details of politics and government in America. It is an excellent reference for just about any facet of American Government and Politics that you would like to examine. My hat is off to Dr. Way for a wonderful work and a thank you for sharing it with us all. Below, you will find the course description taken from the Web Site:

COURSE DESCRIPTION:
A free, self-study, non-credit course in American Government and Politics designed to benefit (1) the

general reader interested in politics, government, law, and public affairs, (2) the advanced high-school student enrolled in an American Government, Advanced Civics, Modern Problems, Problems of Democracy, or Political Science course, and (3) the university or college student enrolled in or planning to enroll in a Political Science or International Relations course or in a History, Geography, Sociology, Economics, or Business course with substantial political content.

Constitutional Democracy and Other Political Regimes

The United States of America has been formed as a *"constitutional democracy."* Democracy can be defined as government by the people or by their elected representatives. A "direct democracy" or as it is sometimes called, a "pure democracy" is a system in which all the people of a country or entity who choose to participate do so directly without elected or appointed representatives. The latter is referred to as a representative democracy.

Attributes of a direct democracy are included in the notions of Initiation (opportunity to propose legislation) , Referendum (opportunity to offer ballot resolutions in elections) on a ballot, and Recall (the ability to vote to have representatives come back home so that another can be chosen. These are not included in the federal government of the United States, but are included in a number of state constitutions.

The specific makeup of a direct democracy may take on different capabilities depending on the will of the people. Depending on how the system is structured, the members of this assembly might pass executive orders, create laws, elect and dismiss leaders and conduct trials. When elected officials conduct the people's business in a direct democracy, they are considered executive agents or direct representatives and thus are bound to the will of the people. Considering that many citizens of the US are upset with our leaders because of little accountability or so it seems, the notion of leaders being tied to the will of the people at first seems to have substantial merit.

With over 300,000,000 and counting as the population of the US, one can also see how it may be unwieldy for such a system to be fully direct in practice regardless of how attractive it is in theory. Thus, for a direct democracy to work, intermediary public groups are needed. Theoretically, this group can be the state legislators but, this too has issues in that the notion of "Honorables" and poor representation of the people's interests is also an ailment of state governments.

The vehicles that are used in a direct democracy - namely, Initiative, Referendum, and Recall all have merit and need to be included soon as amendments to our constitution for our Federal Government. When the representatives choose not to do the will of the people, a form of government that inhibits actions directly by the people gets in the way of being able to handle the situation. There is always the wonderful idea that when they are not doing their jobs, we can throw the bums out, and we should. But with the entanglements that our elected find themselves with the Ruling Class, waiting two to six years to throw them out can be "taxing" and it makes the system less effective and less responsive than employing some direct democracy notions within our constitutional democracy.

You see, it is a constitutional democracy that governs the US using the representative democracy form of government. And thus the term *constitutional* democracy implies a number of structural points as follows:

- The basic principles upon which the society of the United States of America operates
- The institutional forms and processes of the U.S. government

- The distribution of political authority among the major offices and institutions of the government
- The resulting power relationships among these government offices and institutions.

The notion of constitutionalism strengthens democracy as it defines the underlying principles in which the democratic structure is to operate. It clearly differs from other forms of government not chosen by our founding fathers such as dictatorships and oligarchies -- though many scholars today suggest that the US in practice, with the tacit acceptance of the political class and the governed, is becoming more of an oligarchy in which the few rule the many. This was clearly not the intention of the founding fathers in developing the outline for constitutional democracy that has worked so well for so long.

Now that we have defined the notion of a democracy, what then makes a constitutional democracy that much different? A constitutional democracy can be described accurately as a system of government in which the power of government is defined and thus limited, and it is distributed in a body of fundamental written law called "the Constitution." Additionally, the electorate (that's us - the people -- a.k.a. the general voting populace within our political society) is given the effective means of controlling the elected representatives in the government and holding them accountable for their decisions and actions while in public office.

A constitutional democracy thus has two essential ingredients, (1) a *constitutional* ingredient and (2) a *democratic* ingredient. Let's examine these ingredients:

The *constitutional* ingredient of a constitutional democracy is the "*constitutional government*." As noted above, this means that the founding fathers wrote a constitution so that the elected representatives of this nation could not just go ahead and do what they wanted with complete disregard to the most basic law of this country - its Constitution.

The *democratic* ingredient of a constitutional democracy is *representative democracy* and, as noted previously it has to do with who holds and thus has the right to exercise authority on behalf of the governed. It also describes how such authority is acquired and retained (elections, impeachments etc.). Additionally it prescribes that the representatives of the people are accountable to the people, and through elections the people can change the face of the government by changing the face of its representatives. -- i.e. throwing the bums out...

A *constitution* as noted above is a very important document in that it provides the opportunity to protect liberty and freedom beyond the lives of the founders of the government. For the United States of America, its Constitution is the *supreme* law of land. Thus, it is of higher importance and takes precedence over all other laws of society. In fact, all other laws, to be valid and enforceable, must be written in accordance with the superior law of the Constitution. Thus, in recent years, a number of cases, in which laws were passed about matters of great importance such as abortion, have been appealed to the Supreme Court of the U.S., the court of last resort which determines whether laws pass the constitutional sniff test.

When the laws do not pass the test or when the political makeup of the court sees things in a different light, laws created by the states and by the federal legislature are not upheld. Thus, they cannot be enforced. On April 16, 2007, for example, the Supreme Court chose to uphold a law that banned a type of late-term abortion, a ruling that many believe portends enormous social, legal and political implications regarding this very divisive issue. Considering that the nine members of the court itself were sharply divided (5-4) could prove historic. Political analysts suggested at the time that it sent a possible signal of the court's willingness, under Chief Justice John Roberts, to someday revisit the right to abortion which heretofore had been guaranteed in the 1973 Roe v. Wade case.

No branch of government is exempt from following the Constitution. In the U.S., every law enacted by a legislature and every decision or action of an executive office or agency must pass the constitutional test. Not all laws that may be unconstitutional by definition if well examined, however, are challenged in court. For a law to be reversed it must be appealed and can be appealed as many times as needed until it may reach the Supreme Court of the United States. If the governmental decision or law or action in question is found by the courts to be contrary to the Constitution, the court system will uphold the Constitution and set aside the unconstitutional decision or action of the legislature or of the executive branches.

Each state in the Union of States has its own constitution thus giving the 50 states a notion of semi-autonomy (partly self-governing). These states comprise the federal union. The US Constitution guides the operation of the national government, and establishes its formal power relationships between the national government and the 50 semiautonomous states as well as the formal power relationships among the principal organs, or institutions, of the national government. You would not want this left to folklore or to memory alone as it is far too important. Thus it is written.

The U.S. Constitution is in fact, a single document consisting of the seven original articles drafted by the Federal Constitutional Convention of 1787, which were eventually ratified by the 13 original colonies (states), plus there are 27 amendments that have been added to the document during the 200+ years that have elapsed since ratification and adoption of the Constitution. The first ten of these amendments are known collectively as The Bill of Rights.

The US *constitutional system* consists of the power relationships among the principal branches of government resulting from the constitutional division and distribution of political authority among them by the Constitution itself. It defines the roles in the governing process played by each of the principal governmental institutions defined within the Constitution.

This is very important for Americans in that the Constitution provides the following attributes of government on our behalf:

- Divides and distributes the authority of government between the central government over the whole nation and the governments of the member-states of the federal union
- Assigns certain governmental powers to the states, while denying them certain other powers
- Assigns certain powers to the national government and expressly prohibits it from exercising certain other powers,
- Assigns the powers delegated to the national government to the principal entities of that government (the U.S. House of Representatives, the U.S. Senate, the President of the U.S.A., and the U.S. Courts). This is a key ingredient and serves the need for major checks and balances of power and it assures that the government does not run away from the people to begin to govern independently. Each entity has its own power, a strong incentive, and a legal right to oppose, block, check, and restrain the other entities of government if they get off track.
- Prescribes certain limitations on both the central government and the states by guaranteeing *civil liberties*, i.e., the basic rights and liberties of the individual citizen.

The U.S. Government has been set up to be constitutional in character. However, it does not necessarily follow that all branches of government will adhere to this precept and by neglect or by the political process, facets of the constitutionality of the government can be overridden in fact if not in deed. The US government must comply with two fundamental legal requirements to remain legitimate

- The government must operate in accordance with the provisions of the Constitution
- The government must not exceed the authority granted to it by the Constitution.

As much as we like our political representatives, we do not want them taking more power than we are willing to give them. When you read the Constitution it is clear how insightful were the founding fathers as they built the essential features of constitutionalism into the framework of the US government. The government's compliance with these two basic legal requirements are essential to its legitimacy.

So if we were to summarize the central purpose of constitutionalism it is to protect ourselves from our too-far-reaching neighbors who become politicians to promote their own welfare. The notion of limiting governmental power as dictated in the Constitution checks and restrains the persons who hold public office and exercise political authority. And it is up to us as a wary and watchful society that this government does not get out of control -- and hopefully this book will help us in this regard.

Therefore, we cannot watch as our democracy is shattered and the rule of law provided by our constitution is abrogated or abridged for political expediency. The rule of law strongly implies that there are limits to political authority, that there are limits to the power of any governing elite to rule society. The people own the government - not vice versa. All the entities of government-- the legislative and executive branches, and the administrative agencies under control of the President, and even the courts of law--are all required to observe and operate according to the law of the land.

The protection of individual rights and liberties is a major tenet of the rule of law. The people permit the laws to be enacted and enforced and the law guarantees each individual citizen certain rights and liberties and protects them from arbitrary interference or deprivation by government officeholders. The Constitution and the rule of law are vital to preventing a runaway government like we find in many other parts of the world, such as Russia, Cuba, and Venezuela.

The government cannot legally deprive a person of life, liberty, or property without due process of law. That is, the government, in taking punitive action against a person, is required to act in strict accordance with legally established procedures. The government caretakers (our elected officials) cannot, without violating the law, arbitrarily execute or imprison an individual or confiscate his property, disregarding the established rules of procedure. It does not matter whether the special interests would applaud such behavior, the rule of law is not intended to benefit the special interests and the elite ruling / Ruling Class. It is for the people.

What If the Founding Fathers Formed a Different Kind of Government?

The founding fathers could have made George Washington the King instead of the first President. However, they had already had enough of King George III and another King George would not have set well with them. Thomas Jefferson made his point with just these few words right on point: "An elective despotism was not the government we fought for." Jefferson and the founding fathers could have given George Washington dictatorial powers if they chose, but what if George decided things about America that were good for George and not good for Americans? What would be their recourse under the law? None -- nada, zilch, squat... and thus this was not a good system to choose and it was not chosen. If you'll pardon me for saying it, in a dictatorship, they'd have had to "let George do it."

The fathers could have formed a constitutional Oligarchy instead of a democracy. This basically is a system in which there is no representation and the few rule the many under the rules of a Constitution. The good news in this approach is that there is typically a body of law - the constitution. The bad news is that laws can be created or taxes imposed that can negatively affect the people with no recourse but to accept.

Considering that the major squabble with England was about taxation without representation, it would have been unlikely for the founding fathers to fight a revolution that would not provide for individual rights and liberties through a representative form of government. The constitution was written to assure these benefits and to keep the politicians from taking the country in a direction contrary to the will of the people, which they seem to have done anyway.

If it were not that political power, as in the notion that the political class is comprised of politicians, with the assent or tacit acceptance of all three branches, can in fact be wielded against the population, the issues of government today might be as minimal as in the late 18th century after independence was gained.

However, "grabby" politicians separate themselves from the people so they can serve others and the Founding Fathers did not have a remedy for lobbyists or real term limitations other than through the voters who today are too busy to pay attention and thus are easily duped by the politicos into electing the same bums each time their terms are up.

For its part even the Supreme Court has its political motivations and sometimes its actions are questionable. Clearly there are those who believe that George Bush would not be President if it were not for Sandra Day O'Connor and the other four Justices of the US Supreme Court. And, a new notion of eminent domain recently was determined by the court that permits political agents to confiscate your land and property for the good of someone else.

Many, and I include myself among them, believe this latter idea goes so far beyond the intentions of those who drafted the US constitution that it is actually humorous - but in a sick way. It needs to be overturned.

So, our Constitutional Democracy is pretty good, but it is far from perfect, mostly because it is administered and interpreted by human beings who have natural bias.

-- End of This Civics Lesson --

Sources

http://www.washingtonlife.com/backissues/archives/99nov/honorables.htm

http://www.proconservative.net/CUNAPolSci201HOutline.shtml

Chapter 4: Taxes, Taxes, and More Taxes

Everything Costs Money

You make it. They take it! Most of our representatives, who are good at their trade (politicians), never met a tax they didn't like. Nobody can deny that there is none better at bringing in the big ones than the current president of the US. He took the money and nobody even knew it came from them. Yup! It came from you. The many ingenious types of taxes we find throughout the U. S. prove that a motivated politician is as clever at least as the U.S. Chief Executive and surely as prolific as a con man in figuring out how to remove dollars from your wallet and place them in the government treasury.

After all, only with lots of tax revenue can politicians become folk heroes by taking some of this plunder and "creating jobs" or giving grants to other government bodies or corporations to strengthen their reelection opportunities. They thrive on income redistribution. Yours becomes theirs. They have just two goals:

1. Continuance in office (reelection)
2. Opportunity for a better office

In the first year of Obama, the government seemed not to care where he big payoffs would have to come from. But, now, of course we know what is coming. No matter what they appear to be working on, taking your money is their prime mission in life. Keep this in mind: Politicians serving as our representatives will not be denied their share of your income. It enables them to achieve their two major goals.

Of course there are good, God-fearing people serving as representatives and they are not all bad when they get elected. Some stay good but it sure seems that today they are in the minority. When the clock says there is just enough time left to get elected, that's where they focus their energies. Whether it serves us or not, reelection and the chance of a higher office trumps anything the represented may have had on their minds.

Government's Share of Your Income Is Increasing

According to The Tax Foundation, a nonprofit group whose mission it is to keep taxes to an absolute minimum, in 2007 Americans worked longer to pay for government (120 days) than they did for food, clothing and housing combined (105 days). Since 1986 taxes have cost more than these basic necessities. In fact, Americans have to work longer to afford federal taxes alone (79 days) than they do to afford housing (62 days). And, of course, that's not even counting state and local taxes! But, we are about to count them, literally, because they count big time.

US Citizens are sometimes asked to pay up -- to three or four and perhaps more intertwined levels of government. For example, United States taxation most certainly includes local government. Local Government on the other hand, refers to one or more of municipal, township, district and county governments. It also includes regional entities such as school and utility, and transit districts. Oh, did we mention the state and federal government? Having a closed wallet or purse in these modern times is tantamount to teasing the government. And when they find out... well...

We'll put off our discussion of Federal taxes for just a bit since most taxpayers already feel its sting and understand it in many ways. Besides, the Federal Government and its "honorable representatives" do not have to be as ingenious to bilk their constituencies out of the fruits of their labor. By the way, that "constituencies" word, that means us...

So, is there anything we can do about it? Oh, yeah there is but nothing happens overnight. The first step is being aware. The second step is making sure you read the rest of the book.

Heading off to Peoria

Some, especially retirees and the plain old rich, are so fed up with the state and local tax situation that they admit that they up and go "shopping" periodically for a new state or locale in which to live. Their motivation is nothing more than to pay less taxes. Most of us may go to the mall for a break while these of us head for the Interstate Highway System, only to find that the Federal Government has permitted the states to make them toll roads. So, on the trip to financial freedom, their wallets must open to pay the "road use tax."

Maybe Peoria is not the right place and maybe it is. The facts are that in 2010, just seven of the 50 states have no state income tax. Yes, we'll tell you who they are -- Alaska, Florida, Nevada, South Dakota, Texas, Washington and Wyoming. Hey, there are two others, New Hampshire and Tennessee, who tax only dividend and interest income. Such a deal.

Una fortuna, for most of us, the choice of where we are going to live the rest of our lives is often decided when we buy a home in our favorite city and we live in "our town" for enough years to make it home if it wasn't always home. And many of us, still live in our home towns. While this get-up-and-go notion may be fine for some, the burden of taxation is so imposing that there are others who don't care what the cost may be to get out, they are highly motivated to keep their income or their retirement from the grasp of greedy politicians, who are always ready to grab it. Those who do not feel a major loyalty to a particular state, simply take off and find states where the tax burden is lighter -- or so it seems at least.

If you are inclined to travel to keep more of your wealth, it pays to examine the tax burden you'll face when you arrive in your new state. State taxes are increasingly important to everyone, but retirees especially have cause for concern since their income in many cases is fixed. In a land of rising, punitive taxes, the future actually looks dimmer and dimmer. While you sleep, in addition to a number of other self-serving plans, your "noble" representatives are plotting to find new ways to get your last dollar. If they can do it with chicaneries, without your being aware, their thrill of victory is even sweeter for them -- but for you the bitterness endures.

The retiree is a special case since their incomes are fixed and whimsical taxes can play a big part in how much is left when the day is done. Many planning to retire and ready to use the presence or absence of a state income tax as a litmus test for a good retirement destination. This may be a very serious mistake since higher property taxes and sales taxes and nuisance taxes such as in the lists below can more than offset the lack of a state income tax. The point, of course is be careful if your car is warming up outside.

Though it is a definite plus for a state to not have an income tax--especially if the first letters of your states name is as follows:

C-A-L-I-F-O-R-N-I-A: there are other reasons to stay away from certain states, especially if your state's name is C-A-L-I-F-O-R-N-I-A. At 10.3% for the highest bracket, this tax is punitive. New York State and NY City together are about 10.3%. So, the left and right coasts are pretty tough on the wallet. The highest state income tax, however is neither of these. The price to play in balmy and beautiful Hawaii is 11% max rate. These state taxes, of course are on top of the Federal Income Tax and the Payroll Tax (FICA and Medicare). It's a big load to carry.

If you escape high state income taxes, you still must be careful on your journey to low taxes. It doesn't necessarily ensure a low total tax burden. When you see this exhaustive but still incomplete list of tax titles, it will remind you that states raise revenue in many ways including sales and property taxes for sure but also with penalizing excise taxes, license taxes, intangible taxes, estate taxes and inheritance taxes. Moreover, you can bet there would be taxes on taxes (the infamous taxtax) if your hometown or state rep could get away with it.

Depending on where you live, you may end up paying all of them or if you are lucky, just a few. If you are planning to take up your cot and move out of town, the message is that you better be right.

We pay Uncle Sam the same no matter where we live, but property, gasoline, tobacco, sales and state income taxes are all over the map in the fifty states and again, they are not inconsequential. What should you look for if you hope to better yourself by moving or what should you look for so that you don't get snookered by politicians in your home state by staying the course? Let's start by looking at a number of the known ways that politicians obtain more revenue. (And, of course more revenue means you pay more taxes) What are some of the major types of taxes that state and local politicians have come up with since the Founding Fathers enjoyed the Atlantic Sea Salt in the tea of Boston in 1773?

You might be surprised but then again, you might not be. Take a look at these lists. This will get you agitated so be careful that you don't read more than 10 of these twisted con artist tricks at a time. Whether it agitates you or not, hold on to your purses and wallets while you check out the following income redistribution schemes that we can credit only to our "trusty" representatives:

Common State Taxes

- **Cigarette Tax**
- **Fuel Tax**
- Inheritance and Estate Taxes
- **Personal Income Tax**
- Property Tax
- **Retirement Income Taxes**
- **Retired Military Pay**
- State Income Tax
- **State Sales Tax**
- State Unemployment Tax

Less Common State Taxes

Though less common, these potentially substantive taxes, depending on your lifestyle, include the following:

- Alcoholic Beverage tax
- Alternative Minimum Tax
- Air Emissions Fee
- Auto Rental Tax
- Casino Gambling Taxes
- Charity Gaming Tax
- Consumers' Compensating Use Tax
- Contamination Tax
- Contractor Registration Fee/Tax
- Controlled Substance Tax
- Corporate Income Tax
- Corporation Registration Fee
- Deed Tax
- Dry Cleaner Fee/Tax
- Drug Stamp Tax
- Drug Tax Stamps

- Environmental Protection Charge
- Estate and Trust Tax
- Financial Institutions tax
- Franchise Tax
- Fur Clothing Tax
- Gross Receipts Tax
- Household Hazardous Materials Fee
- Household Hazardous Waste Fee
- Hotel / Innkeeper Tax
- Insurance Tax
- Jock Tax
- Lawful Gambling Tax
- Landfill fees
- Mineral Tax
- Mobile Home Tax
- Motor Vehicle Use Tax
- Mortgage Registry Tax
- Ocean Marine Profit Tax
- Oil Inspection Fees/Taxes
- **Other Tobacco Taxes**
- Parimutual Tax
- Personal Property tax
- Real Estate Transfer Tax
- Riverboat Admissions tax
- Riverboat Wagering tax
- Special Fuel Tax
- Sports Bookmaking Tax
- Underground Storage Fuel Tax
- Unemployment Taxes
- Use Tax
- Water quality tax
- Wind Energy Production Tax
- Use Tax for individuals
- Utility Receipts Tax
- 911 Special tax

Local Taxes

- Amusement Tax
- Building Permit Tax
- Businesses License Tax (*many types of businesses*)
- Emergency & Municipal Services Tax (*Once called the Occupational Privilege Tax*)
- Earned Income Tax
- Cities & Municipalities Tax
- School District Taxes
- Mechanical Devices Tax
- Mercantile Tax
- Per Capita Tax
- Personal Property Tax
- Occupation Tax
- Health Permit Tax
- Jock Tax
- Parking Tax
- Parking Ticket Tax
- Real Property Tax
    County
    City
    School Districts
- Realty Transfer Tax
- Restaurant License Tax
- Taverns License Tax

Federal Taxes

- Alternative Minimum Tax
- Bulk Alcohol Taxes
- Beer Taxes
- Liquor Tax
- Cigarette Tax
- Corporate Income Tax

- Estimated Tax
- Federal Income Tax
- Federal Unemployment Tax
- Fuel Tax
- Highway Tax
- Internet Tax (When they think it's safe)
- Medicare Tax (FICA)
- Personal Income Tax
- Social Security Tax (FICA)
- Telephone Tax
- Tobacco Tax
- Wine Tax
- Etc. (I am getting tired)
- Yes there are more in each list

Recent Taxes Related Just to Obamacare

- **$123 Billion: Surtax on Investment Income – Capital Gains**
- **$86 Billion: Hike in Medicare Payroll Tax**
- **$65 Billion: Individual Mandate Excise Tax and Employer Mandate Tax**
- **$60.1 Billion: Tax on Health Insurers**
- **$32 Billion: Excise Tax on Comprehensive Health Insurance Plans**
- **$23.6 Billion: "Black liquor" tax hike**
- **$22.2 Billion: Tax on Innovator Drug Companies**
- **$20 Billion: Tax on Medical Device Manufacturers**
- **$15.2 Billion: High Medical Bills Tax**
- **$13.2 Billion: Flexible Spending Account Cap – aka "Special Needs Kids Tax"**
- **$5 Billion: Medicine Cabinet Tax**
- **$4.5 Billion: Elimination of tax deduction for employer-provided retirement Rx drug coverage i**
- **$4.5 Billion: Codification of the "economic substance doctrine"**

- **$2.7 Billion: Tax on Indoor Tanning Services**
- **$1.4 Billion: HSA Withdrawal Tax Hike**
- **$0.6 Billion: $500,000 Annual Executive Compensation Limit for Health Insurance Executives**
- **$0.4 Billion:**
- **$ Negligible: Excise Tax on Charitable Hospitals**
- **$ Negligible: Employer Reporting of Insurance on W-2**

Send In What You Want?

If I tried to tell you how the Federal Government was ripping you off on a system of income taxes that encourage cheating and assuming you are honest, you would be upset. I won't say that. But, one thing seems for certain, the Federal Government depends on the majority of its citizens to be honest and that is how they collect their tolls. What would be the alternative? Well, no politician on record has yet suggested that we just let it up to the people how much they choose to send in as their fair share just because they are honest.

The 2009 Soda, Drink, Juice & Milk Tax

Just when you thought you were safe from more stupid taxes because they got them all covered, our Federal lawmakers figured out another one. This one is a tax on soda, drinks, juice, and even flavored milk Obviously the makers of all these items as well as consumers have lined up against this tax and because President Obama did not get his healthcare bill passed in the summer, the US may have escaped this tax for now. But, now that the tax man has discovered it, watch your juice budget.

I know you think it is already too ridiculous but putting a ridiculous tax to fund a ridiculous healthcare package so that ridiculous behaviourists can cause Americans to behave the way they would like is simply ridiculous, but true, nonetheless . Yes, a tax on sugar-sweetened beverages, including flavoured milk, was in the initial list of revenue options released on May 18, 2009 by senators Max Baucus and Charles Grassley, chairman and ranking republican, respectively, on the Senate Finance Committee. .

While they did not specifically give a tax rate, the speculators have looked at various options and costs. . A tax of 3¢ per 12 fl. oz. for example could raise as much as $50 billion over 10 years to fund an overhaul of the nation's healthcare system, according to a congressional estimate. The Milk people who try everything to get kids to drink milk in any from rather than junk are outraged as one would expect. You may be able to slow the tax man, but sooner or later, the tax man cometh.

Chapter Summary

To get a better perspective on a number of the state and local taxes brought forth, check out the Civics lesson at the end of this chapter. Because you never would have bought this book if it were just a Civics Lesson, not all of the above taxes are presented. However, because I am most interested in your having a good feeling for how our representatives have betrayed We the People, I offer commentary along with the Civics Lesson on those that you may agree are worth discussing. And if you are convinced that all should be described in the Civics Lesson, feel free to take the title of the particular tax mentioned above and place it in Google or another search engine window, and you will have your fill of explanations for and against that particular tax. Rest assured, I am against it!.

The major point of this chapter is that all "representatives," and since we are all friends now, we can call them politicians, advocate the two question simplified tax return that was credited on the Internet at the time to the Clinton

Administration -- but it applies to all at all levels. The return was simple and after it assured who you were, it had just two questions about income:

1. How much money did you make last year?
2. Send it in!

The United States has over 7,000 different taxing authorities at the state, county, and city levels. You can run but you can't hide. There are more taxing authorities than the size of some of the cities in which we live.

Considering that all levels of government are taxing agencies, the question arises as to whom you should send all of what you earned last year. The answer is simple: Send it to them all. If you can't figure out how to do that and it is pretty simple in theory, try to figure out how to pay your fair share of all of the many taxes that we explored in this chapter. And when you are done doing all that, if you even think you can run away from the IRS, then you may be liable to pay the Jock Tax, one of the silliest taxes of all time, if your quest for tax freedom takes you across state lines.

Chapter 5   Civics Lesson: Lots of Taxes -- Explanations

Taxes Arrive in Somebody's Cookie Jar

W. C. Fields once said to "never give a sucker an even break and never smarten up a chump!"   I will repeat this quip in this book because it helps to remember politicians don't want you to be smart. Are we all suckers or are we all chumps? One way we can all help ourselves is by paying attention to what they are doing. If we are looking at them, when they have their hands in our cookie jars, our pockets, and our wallets, it will be more difficult for them to get away with fresh baked goods or cold hard cash.

So, let's put some text behind a few of these taxes now so that when the revenuers come visiting, you'll at least know about what they are asking.

There are a number of good Web sites and other sources available for you to find out the specifics of the various taxing states in this nation (in other words, all of them). The Web sites listed at the end of this chapter are among those that can help you in your quest for additional information. If you're curious, take a run to the end of the chapter now. Most of the URLs are short and the others can be easily found by typing the words in a search engine rather than using the long URL.

Amusement Tax
If you are amused but also sedentary, you may not owe this tax. This is a tax on the privilege of engaging in an amusement. Since politicians do not see (we think at least)

what happens after the front door closes, they charge nothing
for things like sweeper use, Swiffer use, pot use (cooking),
watching others work, etc. etc. etc. Technically it is a tax
levied on the admission price to places of amusement,
entertainment, and recreation such as State Fairs, craft
shows, bowling alleys, golf courses, ski facilities, or county
fairs, etc. The message from your representative of course is,
"Just don't be too amused or we'll get you!"

Cigarette Tax

Many states are continuing to raise excise taxes on cigarettes
and other tobacco products in order to increase revenue and
"cough cough" encourage the inflicted to go on to alcohol or
another abuse that won't cost the state as much. Right now,
Chicago is the most expensive place to buy cigarettes. When
you add the city tax, the Cook County tax and the state tax,
the total tax is $3.66 per pack. Light 'em up! Smoke 'em if ya
got 'em. The smoking lamp is lit on all authorized stations...
Hopefully, cigarette tax revenue is being put aside because of
smart representation for other things that can help the people
-- yeah, right!

By the way, states lead the way on tobacco taxes. The
American Lung Association gives the federal government an
"F" for its lack of political will to impose greater taxes on
tobacco. For each 10% increase in price, cigarette smoking
drops by about 4%, experts say. So, why would any state
look for this as a revenue source?

Earned Income Tax

Honesty has no play in this tax so if somebody says they paid
it to you by giving you a W-2, you do not have to sign an
affidavit that you actually earned the income. In
Pennsylvania this tax is levied at the state and the
municipality and the school district level. The state for
example is a flat rate 3.07 and my city is 2.5 and my school
district is .5 = an amount in total greater than 6%. New York

state and other states have graduated income taxes as do certain cities such as, you guessed it, New York City. If you can figure out how to have revenue, but no income, I'd say you are on to something.

Emergency & Municipal Services Tax
Prior to the last ten years, this tax was often called the Occupation Privilege tax in certain states. It was a tax on the privilege of working. Only the non-workers are exempt. But, if there were a rebate on this tax, your elected would make sure the non-workers got some of your tax money "back." Wanting a means of grabbing more than the $10 or $15 this tax once generated, public servants caucused and found a much more "appropriate name" for a higher tax and in PA for one, the rate was raised to $52.00, as the maximum amount by law.

Excise Tax
Excise taxes are the government's way, without even having to accompany you on your fine dining jaunts, to know that you have it too good and it's time to share your excess with your fellow man. Technically excise taxes are general taxes paid when purchases are made on a specific good, such as gasoline. There is no emotion in that definition. The emotion comes about when you find that it is you who ultimately pays the tax. Unlike the Jock Tax, the best part is that you don't have to keep track of these nasty taxes. These are sneaky little (maybe big if you drive an SUV) taxes that your friendly representative thinks you will blame on some "Taxing Authority" but never on your friendly representative. Collecting these taxes is simple it is almost always included in the price of the product such as in gasoline at the pump. There are lots of excise taxes because your "representatives" don't want to do anything that you will attribute to them and the notion of an excise tax sets them free from your retribution.

Fuel Tax

Try to find a state that does not collect "excise taxes" on gasoline, diesel fuel, gasohol etc., And you are destined to a continuous run through all 50 states. Enjoy the vacation. Some states charge such a high rate for fuel that when the Federal Government gives its rebates on the federal fuel charge, the politicians go out on holiday. Considering that the federal excise tax on gas is 18.4 cents and it is 24.4 cents for diesel fuel, this is more than the full price of gas was when I began to drive.

Sometime in 2008, this tax was supposed to triple, but, with the tax rebates, this idea may be dead for another year or so. When (not if) this is enacted, this increase will drive gas prices close to $4.00 per gallon. Additionally, as of now, there are nine states that, on top of the state gas tax, actually permit cities or counties to impose a local tax on fuel. What a bonanza? And you thought the oil companies were pigs?

Inheritance and Estate Taxes

If you are not rich, read the next item... Just kidding! An inheritance tax is an assessment made on the portion of an estate received by an individual. That individual may be you and that is why this entry is important. It differs from an estate tax which is a tax levied on an entire estate before it is ever distributed to individuals. Eleven states still collect an inheritance tax. They are: Connecticut, Indiana, Iowa, Kansas, Kentucky, Maryland, Nebraska, New Jersey, Oregon, Pennsylvania and Tennessee. Connecticut will be phased out after 2005. In all states, transfers of assets to a spouse are exempt from the tax. In some states, transfers to children and close relatives are also exempt. Pennsylvanians are hoping that the Connecticut residents spared from the tax will send their savings to Governor Rendell.

As for estate taxes, in 2001 the Feds phased out the federal estate tax and it should be fully repealed in 2010 unless our representatives, and the new President find a reason to keep it a bit longer

Jock Tax

The ultimate poorly conceived tax is the "Jock Tax." This is a term that describes the original purpose of the tax. Once there is an opening for a new tax, tax authorities (a term contrived to separate our esteemed representatives from blame for their role in raising taxes) go after these new "lucrative sources" with a fervor to match a politician running for reelection.

So, why the "Jock Tax?" Quite simply, like the hotel / innkeeper tax, it seemed like an easy way for the "authorities" to cash in on what otherwise might be left to a jock / athlete to spend. And, the implication of course is, "What do they know?" In this case, it is an old tax but a new victim. States or municipalities with jock taxes noticed that traveling business professionals, particularly visiting professional athletes seemed to have some success marketing or playing basketball, football, golf, tennis etc. in their locale. So they decided to relieve them of some of the monetary reward of their success -- but just that proportion of their income earned in that state or locale.

Then, one day some politician, serving triple duty as a representative of the people and as a legislator decided that all traveling professionals should pay income taxes in every state in which they earn income or have an economic presence - regardless of how infrequently they may visit the state.. So, now certain states, and more to come assess jock income taxes to visiting musicians, lawyers, skateboarders, and even touring troubadours. Home state does not matter. These "jocks" pay their own state tax and they don't need the burden of this lousy tax. Jock taxes are unfair for sure. They represent the ultimate in poor tax policy -- poorly targeted, arbitrarily enforced, and plain greedy. Why not a tax just on politicians?

The jock tax is hard to calculate. Who decides who owes what? Can you imagine asking businessmen to justify why Cleveland should get X and Des Moines should get Y. Message to the Jock Tax aficionados, "you made a mistake. It's not a good tax." Can you imagine a salesman trying to do income tax returns for 50 states?

Mechanical Devices Tax

For those companies who choose to offer a service but yet do not offer the service via human beings, this tax applies. So, maybe now you will consider getting your own washing machine and drier rather than use coin-operated machines such as jukeboxes, pinball machines, video games, and pool tables. Maybe coin-op washing machines and driers are not eligible in all states. Maybe so? The tax rate is set as a percentage of the price to activate the machine. To avoid this tax, do not activate...

Mercantile Tax

Don't plan on selling anything to local customers or you'll pay dearly. The mercantile tax is levied on the gross receipts of local businesses selling to local consumers. Sometimes this tax is known as the business gross receipts tax, or business privilege tax. It's really not that the business pays the tax. They collect it after they raise prices to cover the tax to maintain their profit margin. Only people who never buy anything like taxes like this.

Occupation Tax

The occupation tax finds roots from England during the seventeenth and eighteenth centuries. Occupations often were a form of property which could be bought and sold, much like real estate. The tax is levied on the value of residents' occupations, as determined by the assessors office. The occupation of school bus driver may have an assessed value of $25, for example, while that of a lawyer may be $290. The school bus drivers in this case, though seeing the caste system at work in the basis for his or her lower tax, does not typically complain about the inequity.

Per Capita Tax

Only headless are exempt from this tax and so on All Hallows Eve, tax collectors have no need to visit Sleepy Hollow to capture the headless horseman. If you have a head, and you are an adult, quite simply, you pay this tax. All adults pay the same amount and knowing the mindset of bureaucrats, you probably would not be permitted to pay for more than one head.

Personal Property Tax

The ultimate gotcha is when you think they'll let you alone if you choose to do nothing and you go on a hunger strike. They will find your fine china and assess the personal property tax even if you are not using it. This tax is similar to the real property and occupation taxes in that it is levied on the value of property owned by residents. The property it taxes is typically intangible personal property, such as mortgages, other interest bearing obligations and accounts, public loans, and corporate stocks. The personal property tax has sometimes been called an honesty tax because the only way a "taxing authority" knows the value of a taxpayer's personal property is if that taxpayer is honest enough to report it. And thus, most counties and other taxing authorities are willing to get rid of it since the reporting in this age of anything goes is a challenge.

Real Estate / Real Property Tax

This tax is a tax on the value of your real property, such as land, buildings, and other improvements, that are owned by you, making you the taxpayer. If you let the property get run down and dilapidated, your representatives will give you a tax break. But, if you use Kohler plumbing and have walls without holes, prepare to pay a big stipend to the taxing authority. What is this message?

The amount of real property tax a taxpayer owes depends upon the value of the land / improvements and the tax rate for the taxing district. Property values for tax purposes are determined by an assessment process conducted by the level of government collecting the tax though sometimes just one level does the assessment and the other levels piggyback with different rates. These assessed values are typically very different than the actual market value of the properties. Thankfully most often they are lower. So, don't use the assessed value as your appraised value.

Realty Transfer Tax

Don't even think of selling your house to put your kids through school cause they got you covered there too. The realty transfer tax is a tax on the sale of real estate. The maximum levy is whatever they decide. In PA it is 1%. PA politicians want to be fair so if both the municipality and school district levy this tax, both must share the 1 percent. Don't worry by the time you read this, the "representatives" will have plugged this loophole.

Social Security and Payroll Taxes

Since most taxpayers are tuned into the issues with the Social Security System, there is no big civics lesson associated with that topic in this book. It takes over 7% from most and 15% from the self-employed so it is a force to be reckoned with regarding budgeting and your gross pay. Economists suggest that those not working for someone else (not self-employed) pay the full 15% tax by getting lower wages. Don't worry with the hordes of illegal aliens being paid under the table, they aren't contributing so, along with falling birthrates and rising numbers of retirees in the U.S., the future of Social

Security is described by our representatives at best as "uncertain." But it really is certain. It is doomed unless a few more Warren Buffets surface and they choose to donate to the cause.

Over the years, tax economists have published many studies exploring Social Security's financial problems and outlining possible reforms to help restore the system to long-term solvency. Since our "representatives" do not have to pay heed to sound recommendations, the problem has gotten worse and unless we change the makeup of our government, it will get even worse. Besides all that, our representatives have permitted stealing from the fund to pay other bills over the years and that has made the situation even more difficult because none of the borrowers at any level of government have paid anything back.

State Sales Tax

All states except Alaska, Delaware, Montana, New Hampshire and Oregon, collect sales taxes. But to go there just for that might be too expensive. Maybe it is a good deal if you're thinking of buying your next yacht. OK, no more dreaming. Some states charge one percentage rate throughout the state though most states permit local additions to the base tax rate. No locations as of today have offered deductions. States with no local add-on include Connecticut, Hawaii, Indiana, Kentucky, Maine, Maryland, Massachusetts, Michigan, Mississippi, New Jersey, Rhode Island, Vermont, Virginia, and West Virginia. The Big sales tax state is California (7.25%). Mississippi clocks in with New Jersey and Tennessee and Rhode Island at 7% while Minnesota and Nevada at 6.5% are waiting for the Taxpayer Foundation to go on vacation to get their rates to the top. Cash registers calculate this stuff so easily that "representatives" will figure out how to take a tax over the years that is already too much and make it render even more. . And, you know where that all comes from -- right?

Sources:

- Federation of Tax Administrators;
  http://www.taxadmin.org/
- MSN Money "The Best and Worst States for taxes";
  http://articles.moneycentral.msn.com/Taxes/Advice/The
  BestAndWorstStatesForTaxes.aspx
- National Conference of State Legislatures;
  http://www.ncsl.org/
- Retirement Living Information Center;
  http://www.retirementliving.com/RLtaxes.htm
- Sales Tax Clearinghouse http://thestc.com/
- State Tax Handbook; http://www.amazon.com/State-
  Tax-Handbook-Timothy-Bjur/dp/0808015362
- The Tax Foundation; http://www.taxfoundation.org/
- U.S. Department of Commerce, Bureau of Economic
  Analysis; http://www.bea.gov/
- Various state tax and revenue departments; Use search
  engine

Chapter 6   Americans Are Overtaxed

Representatives do not do their jobs

We are taxed more than ever before today and just as in 1776, there is no sign of real representation. We go through the motions of holding elections regularly but then those who occupy the highest government offices choose to represent themselves and their families rather than the people of the US.

The spirit and reality of representative government that once enlivened this country following the American Revolution has all but eroded into what we see today: an ad hoc litany of superficial homage to the discarded bedrock of what was once the very foundation of this great country.

I wrote this book because our representatives in the House, the Senate, in state legislatures and city councils have forgotten their duties as representatives of the people. Additionally, the president, the governors, the mayors, and other prefects of the people in the executive branches of governments across the land have conveniently forgotten that the primary fundamentals of our representative constitutional democracy (republic) begint with representation.

No single branch of government can claim immunity in the sale and resale of the United States to outside interests and American corporations. Each knows no moral bound or impediment to the gluttonous drive to perpetuate its self-serving two-party system. Even the judiciary is more caught up in preserving the two-party system than permitting deserving independents their opportunity to run for public office.

All of the candidates running for president in 2008 called for big changes. They were all right. They struck a chord with the American people on "hope" and "change" but none offered specifics. Barack Obama came from no-place to be the cheerleader in charge and now, eight years later it is clear that he has moved the country so far to the left that the center is barely visible.

Nobody seemed to know what was on Mr. Obama's agenda. But we all learned fast enough with Obamacare as his top issue along with its big mess of poor options, higher fees, higher taxes, and poor medical care that we were in trouble as a nation. The preponderance of thought was that the President's to-do-list was created by his Chicago cronies, including Reverend Wright, Father Pfleger, and the followers of the master of indoctrination and quiet insurrection, Saul Alinsky.

As we emerge from the 2016 election cycle, we find that Hillary Clinton has promised four more years of Barck Obama's policies and more of Alinsky. Saul Alinsky has been Hillary's favorite prophet from back when she was a kid and George Soros is her favorite benefactor.

How Bad Can it get?

Right now, at the termination point of Obama's eight very long years of OJT, as sad as it may be, it looks like we are still headed like a missile down a road from which we may not be able to return. There is an assault on individualism, the Constitution, capitalism, and democracy itself, in favor of socialism and perhaps even Marxism (Bernie Sanders) and non-violent Communism. We need only look to England in colonial times to see how bad it can get in all aspects of life— at least for freedom lovers. Keep your muskets loaded at night for sure.

The irony of the last two elections before this one, is that as the people asked for real change, they counted on honest and skilled people, not self-centered ideologues to get the job done for them. We reap what we sow. Many today admit that they sowed poorly in election choices.

The greatest enemy of a skilled corrupt politician is an informed public. Therefore it is always time to learn, learn, and learn! This is a good book to begin your efforts. After what we have seen in the last few years, an informed public would be very careful about putting a skilled corrupt politician in any position of consequence.

Despite our best efforts, we were duped about political intentions in 2008 and again in 2012 because the "free press" is in the hip pocket of at least one of the political parties. The press is free to be corrupt and lie about whatever it likes. One day, we will learn not to pay any heed to their message.

We went to the Senate and it seemed out of 100 people, all anybody could find were Hillary Clinton, John McCain and Barack Obama. Did we really think the Senate was doing that great a job for us to pick our president from its "esteemed membership?"

The final Democrat (Obama) and Republican (McCain) were already in the symbolic House of Lords. Americans choose to call it the Senate, but it has become the House of Lords once again, and nobody from this body should have made it even to the candidate stage. They are the elite establishment and they have chosen no longer to represent the people.

Choose carefully when you vote

Representation at all levels for the most part is non-existent and yet we are being taxed more and more. If we do not change our government now, there will be little chance for better representation until 2020. Sending corrupt Senators

back to office or rewarding them with a better position
(Presidency) is not the right thing for Americans to do.

Our representative democracy and its Constitution together
are known as a republic form of government. A republic has
nothing to do with *Republican* other than the first eight letters.
Living in a republic however does not make any of us
Republicans. A republic is simply a representative democracy
with a set of rules known as a Constitution so that the
politicians cannot decide to enrich themselves instead of
taking care of the people.

In the 2008 election season, from which we are still
recovering, there were few Americans who had not tuned
into the problems we faced. Yet, we were not looking to
overthrow or republic with a dictatorship. We should have
taken more time figuring out who the candidates really were.
This change has cost us dearly as the status quo was clearly
better for us and our children before the "big change."
Unfortunately, unless this change is reversed and soon, things
will get a lot worse and may never get better.

We have had eight years of an unresponsive presidency with
a weak-kneed Congress. They gave us unprotected borders
and an unprotected America vulnerable to terrorist attacks at
a terrorist's whim. In all of this we have a President
apologizing for America all over the world for upsetting
terrorists.

Our Congress is dysfunctional as the Democrats want to
destroy America and the Republicans just do not want to be
blamed if the Democrats succeed. The whole scenario in
Washington – the guys we sent to represent us—is still
fraught with infighting, back-stabbing, and blame games
seemingly peeled from the script pages of a discarded low-
budget sitcom, except for one thing.

After we got the change "we can believe in," most can't
believe we got this kind of change. The economy went right

into the toilet and it has been there for eight years. Freedom is being attacked on all fronts, more than any time ever in most of our lifetimes.

The result of wishing for, and getting this new administration to exert its change on freedom loving people would be funny if it were not so dire in its implications. For years many of the older generation would joke when somebody would complain that Congress and the administration had gotten nothing done. Their quip was always: "Good." In the Bush years nothing done was the modus operandi.

In the Obama years, it is actually scary how quickly the President ushered the entire country into the poor-house. We have become well-taxed and poorly represented, and simply poor. Some joked in the Bush years that it was good that nothing was getting done since at least it meant that the corporations weren't getting any further ahead of us.

With Obama mowing people down regularly wherever he is deployed, finding big government as his only answer, we may be soon longing for the days of plain old corporate dominance.

Things Have Not Been Going Well for US

The report card is already in on the current executive and legislative branches. It is definitely not good. We should not be sending any one of them back to do anything "for us" ever. For the last ten years, our country has been sold out.

Actually, it's a lot more than ten, from Obama back through Bush past the Clintons to the last Bush. For twenty plus years there was no real progress for the good of the people while the establishment and the elites became more entrenched and harder to unseat. Additionally, the state of affairs has gotten substantially worse. Government become even more dominant, corrupt, and downright neglectful and disrespectful towards the people.

Those in power need to be held accountable: No repeat performances and no repeat performers. American prosperity has been sold down the tubes as jobs and national secrets and intellectual property have gone overseas and labor arbitrage (get to the lowest wage quickly) is the order of the day for non-union workers at home while union jobs move overseas.

There are few ordinary citizens better off today than the day Ronald Reagan left office. This country does need change. It must be a change for the better. Your author in this book outlines many areas in which we all can make big improvements. Step one of course begins with full government accountability and an untrusting public.

Though charged with the duty to represent the people, public servants are so overwhelmed with self-interests, special interests, the interests of corporations and the interests of other countries that they have no time to work for the people. When you finish reading this book, you will see that the "honorables" are not serving America honorably.

Taxation is OK with with representation

"No taxation without representation" was the catch phrase in the period of 1763-1776 to summarize the major grievance of the American colonists in the Thirteen American Colonies, incipient kernels of what would later become the United States of America.

When King George III of England and the English Parliament began to impose new taxes on the colonists (Stamp Act, Intolerable Acts, etc.) without their concurrence, Reverend Jonathan Mayhew of Boston coined this term during one of his sermons in Boston.

Another Bostonian, a politician by *the speak of the day,* James Otis, changed this just a bit and he is well known for the phrase, "taxation without representation is tyranny." Tyranny it was and in this book, you will see that tyranny it surely is again.

In 1773, American Colonists violently opposed the tax on tea imports at the most celebrated Tea Party of all time. The Boston Tea Party is recognized as the first experience in which the colonists acted against the Crown. Of course, the British could not accept this "illegal act" as they saw that it would undermine the authority of the Crown and Parliament. When the British Government began to crack down on these "illegal activities" as performed by the colonists, the colonists chose to defend themselves in case the British Government did not hear their pleas to correct the abuses.

Though today the tea still may be gone from the ships in Boston Harbor, millions have expressed outrage for the government. Just a few years ago, the notion of the Tea Party was used to show the rage. This was a national movement.

Conservative Americans from all over the country held tea party rallies in protest against the American government and rampant corruption in Washington. The corrupt press maligned the conservatives who joined in these rallies and nobody talks about tea anymore yet the same spirit is there. Bernie Sanders and Donald Trump have awakened the spirit of "NO" to a government that thinks it owns the people of this great country.

Why no Representation?

Just like the British Crown, today's Parliament and the Crown (Congress & the President) have demeaned the efforts of the new colonists (We the people of 2017) to get their word across the nation. The demonstrators of the new millennium may not have thrown real tea in the ocean but they were all nonetheless maligned as Astroturfers and simply an "angry" mob by the Queen of Mean, House leader Pelosi, and the President himself. The people are very unsettled.

So, in addition to all the ills suffered under Bush, who pretended to be conservative, the elected change to Obama as the chief executive brought forth government attacks on free speech and individual initiative, and freedom itself. The people are not about to let this stand.

Where are our representatives? One would believe they are hiding as they are spotted only rarely at election time. Regardless of Party, they all seem to have joined to be in unison with a president who has no respect for Americans. The representatives of the people have committed acts against the people by supporting the perverted Obama agenda and they show no remorse. This is unprecedented in history. It is time to send the representatives packing on the next train out of Washington.

Colonists & Regular People—Tough Indeed!

During the revolution, the brave colonists, not willing to be taxed without representation, formed militias and took control of each of the thirteen colonies. They armed themselves and expelled the Crown-appointed governors and they began an independence process for the new states of what would become the United States of America.

I am not suggesting that a revolution is now in order but it may be time for actually dumping a spot of tea in Boston Harbor or a harbor near you. Perhaps a few teapots worth of brew would symbolize that it is time to take America back from the political class, the establishment that Donald Trump has so incensed, and from those corrupt politicians who do not respect our democracy.

Patrick Henry, Ben Franklin, Thomas Jefferson, George Washington, John Adams, John Hancock, Paul Revere, and many other brave Patriots helped create a more perfect union of states despite the personal hardships they endured and the major risks that they took.

The cry of the colonists against Great Britain was not that high taxes were being exacted. Actually, the taxes were minimal. The issue was the fact that the taxes and everything else about the colonies were decided in London, and there were *no representatives* of the colonies permitted to be heard.

This is in so many ways the cry from the Elites and the establishment from the blood lines in Washington to give up the country to those who have ruled quietly behind the scenes. Maybe if these "quiet" rulers actually wanted what was best for the people, the people would not object. But there actions are not for the people. They are for their own selfish selves. It is amazing that when the people called for a Trump, the moneyed class said "NO," and yet somehow, with no money, the people won. When the people pay attention, we cannot be beaten. We have the votes.

And, so, it can be said that it was the pure desire for full freedom, and the annoyances from a lack of representation from the elected constabulary, that was the big issue for the colonists. We have the same issues today. It is not the taxation. It is the lack of representation. The people no longer feel that we can trust the government and we no longer trust that our representatives work for our best interests.

After the revolution, George Washington accepted British General Cornwallis's surrender and the congress wanted him to be King. During the Revolutionary War, the Founding Fathers ran the affairs of government using the Articles of Confederation while they were working on a better way—the Constitution.

When the representatives of the thirteen colonies of the United States put together their beliefs about how things were to be in the future, this august body codified their thoughts into one of the most wonderful documents ever written. As we all know, this almost-perfect document is known as the Constitution of the United States of America. It was put forth in order to create a *more perfect* union of the states compared with the Articles of Confederation, which was their first try.

The Constitution itself as difficult as it is to believe has been attacked by the Obama administration on numerous occasions.

The Constitution of the United States delineates that the purpose of the government is to be--by, for, and of--the citizens of the United States. Corporations are not mentioned in the Constitution as citizens or unfeeling creatures or entities of any kind. Why? It was simply because the colonists and the Founding Fathers had great disdain for corporations. The last thing on their minds was to build a new government to please these huge fictitious abstractions.

Representation of the people was paramount in the founders' minds. These were the framers of the Constitution. They decided that the country would be formed from three separate branches of government—executive (President), legislative (Congress), and judicial (Supreme Court and the normal Judiciary). This form of government under the Constitution has endured to this day but it is definitely having its challenges, as the men / women in the official roles do not seem to respect the precepts that the founding fathers had ordained.

With 5 million people living in the colonies back then, it would have been difficult to fit all 5 million into the same church basement or town hall to conduct the needed affairs of the government. So, a strict direct democracy was not feasible, and the form of our government became a representative democracy with a governing set of rules known as a Constitution. As noted previously, this is the definition of a republic.

As you read this book, you will find a number of identified Civics Lessons, which provide the reader with the knowledge to see how our government was formed and how it operates and how it taxes. The lessons also demonstrate how our Congress and our President have been changing it de-facto to suit their needs. Their methods would be declared unconstitutional if brought before an unbiased court that was truly interested in adjudicating grievances according to the law and not according to their biased ideology.

Influential corporations, the President and too many other politicians are now playing on the same team against the people. Corporations act together in an organized way so they can buy a Congress and buy public opinion.

They are out actively buying up enough of both Congress and public opinion to serve their own selfish interests. Notice how wages are falling and jobs are disappearing and yet the political class and the press parrot that things are better. The elite business class and the Congress, which they control, have been systematically lowering wages and blaming circumstances beyond their control. Since they own Congress, and the media, it has been very easy.

If it isn't our Senators and House members and the President who have betrayed us, then who is it? Our leaders have forgotten that they work for the people and not vice versa. You can see the signs of a government unresponsive to its people in regards to a number of major issues such as the unbridled rise of corporate power, the rise of government power, Obamacare, the giveaway of American jobs to those in other countries as well as jobs for legal and illegal foreign nationals, undefended borders and the intrusion of illegal aliens into all aspects of American life and the associated costs to the citizenry.

The logical conclusion is to throw the bums out or else we will get the government we deserve as we brought them in.

Chapter 7   American Fight for Liberty & Representative Government

Representative Democracy Revisited

Most Americans have a great feel for the notion of representative democracy and the sense that we elect representatives of the community to handle our affairs in the governing of the nation. We do not have a direct democracy in that we don't conduct the activities of government; instead we choose representatives among us to get the job done. Our representatives determine how much taxes were owe.

After Chapters 1, 2 and 3 of this book, there is a good chance that your notion of the purity of the act of representation may now be tainted. Something sure went wrong with the intention of representation from the Founding Fathers to what representation means today. Something went way wrong sometime between 1492 and the present day but the evidence suggests that the problem began closer to the year 2000 than to the year 1500. That's not to say that all was hunky-dory in the 1500s and onward. Let's look at how this all started to set the stage for an explanation.

Columbus, Vespucci, de León , & Cabot

After the first voyage of Christopher Columbus in 1492, the Navigator Columbus and his small cast got credit for being the "Old Worlders" who had discovered the "New World." But did he really discover the American mainland? If he did not, is it really such a big deal? Historians seem to agree that on his first two voyages, Columbus discovered Cuba, Puerto Rico, Jamaica, etc. It was not until his third try (1498) that he reached the mainland U.S. Thus, the claim that Amerigo Vespucci, a Spanish seaman, had reached the continent the year before Columbus may very well be valid. And, considering that the U.S. is part of the Americas and not the Columbias leads one to conclude that the Amerigo claim had enough merit when the naming was going on that he got the name.

Some historians argue that neither Columbus nor Vespucci discovered America. They say it was Juan Ponce de León who, ironically, considering that Columbus founded Puerto Rico, was Puerto Rico's first governor. They have him pegged as the first documented European to set foot on mainland American soil when he arrived in Florida in 1513. As you know, he is purported to have discovered the *Fountain of Youth,* the legendary spring that, so they say, restores the youth of anyone who drinks of its waters

Reasonable people have concluded that since there may not really be a Fountain of Youth, de León may not have discovered it. But, he surely discovered a nice state with some real nice warm weather on the mainland. Florida of course continues today to be an exceptional vacation spot. Don't write the name "de León" down on your pad in permanent ink yet as the first guy on the mainland from the Old World, since there are still other historians who suggest that he was in fact preceded by John Cabot to the US mainland in 1497. I am so glad that this is not a history book and we are not here to argue these points. Our point is that neither de León, nor Cabot, Columbus or Vespucci, are at fault for the failings of U.S. representative government since they predate even the "Founding Fathers."

A Few Hundred Years Before the Revolution

So that we all have a good idea on how the great experiment with democracy and constitutional representation began, let's take a look at how the states were organized originally and how they ultimately were able to form a government. Just like the discovery of America, this is not a fully clean story as historians continue to argue about what is actually what. For example, two of the original states were governed by a notion called self-government but later they were classified along with Massachusetts in a category known as "Corporate." But, the thirteen colonies, regardless of these classifications, were ultimately the land bodies that became the first Unites States of America.

The thirteen colonies of England were founded 100 + years after Columbus, with Virginia the first in 1607 and Georgia the last in 1733. Among the things we can be sure of as we look back to these colonial days, nobody from 1607 to 1733 created the current confidence problem in U.S. representative government, and they did not create a huge national debt for us, though our current "honorable representatives" might like to suggest otherwise.

These thirteen colonies were organized into two to three varieties depending on your historical perspective. The original three forms were known as (1) the Charter form, (2) Royal form, and (3) Proprietary form. Later these were combined into two forms, known as the Corporation (formerly Charter) and the Provincial (formerly either the Royal or Proprietary).

So, the individual colonies, did not each have the same exact form of government but ultimately they all reported to the Crown. The Corporation form included Massachusetts, Rhode Island, and Connecticut, though Rhode Island and

Connecticut were also, "self-governing." The provincial forms included the former proprietary colonies of Maryland, Pennsylvania, and Delaware as well as the former Royal Colonies of Georgia, New Hampshire, New Jersey, New York, North Carolina, South Carolina, and Virginia. By the way, these colonies stretched from Main to Georgia and that is the whole Eastern US seacoast other than Florida, which for the longest time was under Spanish dominion.

Even during this period, there was confusion and pressure as to which form a particular colony would take. For example, some of the Royal colonies became Proprietary colonies and vice versa and thus the notion of the term Provincial came to describe what today in our political system would be called the flip-flopping colonies... though their flipping and flopping was hardly voluntary.

The Governmental Form Was Similar

Most of these colonies had the same form of government consisting of a governor, appointed by the English Crown or by the proprietor(s). Additionally, they each had a council that also was appointed by the Crown. The most important body to the colonists was an assembly, which was known as the *house of representatives*. This body was elected by the people. These three bodies took on a governmental shape very similar to the king and the two houses of Parliament. Thus, in many ways the government of the colonies resembled the British government, and you can bet that was its intent. Though the English argued that this was a representative democracy, it is easy to see the failings in this notion when the "Crown" appointed the most important ruling bodies - the Council and the Governor.

The Governor

The Governor directly represented the Crown or the proprietor, who had already paid "allegiance" to the Crown.

Now, with that the case, it meant that the Governor did not represent the people per se. His loyalty was clearly to the Crown and/or the proprietor. To be successful, however, in governing the people, he owed a duty to the people over whom he was placed so it was nice, though not necessary that they liked him. As you can easily conclude, the interests of the two parties were so conflicting as to keep the Governor in a constant turmoil. Perhaps this is where the temperament of the politician as we now know them, would have served best. But, the notion of the politician as we know it today, would not arrive for a few more hundred years.

The Governor had immense power in his territory. He could convene, discontinue, postpone or even dissolve the legislature, and he had veto power over all of its would-be laws. He controlled the state militia, and he was the grand miffintiff (Big Boss) who appointed the important officials, such as judges, justices of the peace, sheriffs, and any others of authority. The one thing the Governor could not touch however, was the public purse, and this soon became a cause of lament for the British.

Though history suggests there were many kind and benevolent Governors, there were also those who took advantage of the fruits of the spoils system and they even sold some of the offices at their disposal to the rich in the community, thus affecting their own personal purse in a positive way. Unfortunately many of these men, and there were no women, cared little for the welfare of the colonists.

The Council

Typically there were twelve men in the council, though in Massachusetts there were twenty-eight. In Maryland, there were only three. Council members needed to possess certain attributes to retain their positions. For example, they had to be residents of the colony in which they served, and they needed to be men of station and wealth. The Crown or the proprietor appointed the council so the normal conflicts arose and they were settled in the normal way -- in favor of the Crown or the proprietor. Council had three major functions:

- Advise the governor
- Provide the "upper house" of the legislature (Lords)
- Serve as the highest court in that particular colony

In Massachusetts, after 1691, the council was elected by a joint ballot of the legislature, called the General Court. In the other colonies it was by appointment of the Crown or the proprietors.

The House of Representatives

Then, there was the lower house which was elected by the people and whose mission in life was to represent and theoretically support the people. It was the body of the legislature that actually made the laws. The innate power to make laws is a big deal in any form of government. So, the people did not get to elect the governor, nor the council (also served as judges) but the subjects of the crown actually were permitted their own house of representation to the Colony and ultimately to the Crown through the Council or the Governor.

Now, that's fair, right? Unfortunately, something happened on the way to real fairness. The laws/acts passed by this lower house could be vetoed by whim of the governor, or be set aside by the Crown within a certain time after their passage for any reason whatsoever. In other words, if Alf were to materialize as a friend of the Crown, and he did not like some legislation about cats that was introduced, just by having the ear of the Crown or the proprietor or the council, the legislation to protect cats could be defeated -- all because of Alf or perhaps it was really a guy named Gordon Shumway. Additionally, the Tanner family would have no standing in the matter.

The assembly had something that the Crown really did not want to give up but it already had. The lower legislature had the power of taxation. In retrospect, the Crown must have viewed this as a major faux pas.

Since the Assembly had the right of taxation and the Crown did not, the normal and natural governance of the colonies seemingly was in control of the colonists -- other than the veto power etc. of the other loyal bodies. Historians might even claim that the colonies were self-governing, and they should have had no concern for their liberties as long as they and they alone could retain this sole right of taxing themselves. We'll see how this notion plays out later in this chapter.

For the British, this did become a big problem. Not having any say in controlling the purse strings (tax coffers) of the colonies was a big issue that kept getting bigger as American wallets, made of the finest British leather, got fatter and fatter. The poor Brits had not given themselves an easy way of siphoning off a few pence for the Crown. A faux pas indeed!

This representative system of government, though obviously flawed, was common to all the colonies, but It did not enter the sphere of influence in Georgia until 1752. The notion began in Virginia in 1619; as noted previously it made it to Massachusetts in 1634, and it hit Maryland in 1639. The system of representative government was allowed by the Crown, but not required, by the early charters. After it had begun almost spontaneously in a number of colonies, it became a big part of a number of the charters. The people loved it.

The Problem with Colonial Suffrage

The one little piece of the fight for democracy puzzle that we
have intentionally left out so far was that there was no colony
in which universal suffrage was to be found. How about
that? It was a piece of democracy in which the people had to
first be anointed. Sounds like cause for a revolution -- but we
are moving too quickly. The notion of "who was able to vote"
gave back a bit more power to the Crown than otherwise
might have been noticed.

The people of the colonies had lots of concerns and reasons
to fear for many reasons, most importantly, for their lives.
For example, there were these guys known as Native
Americans, colloquially described as "Indians" in colonial
times. These folks were not as some may think, a western
U.S. phenomenon and only a major nemesis of cowboys. In
fact, at the time, there was no western U.S. So, the people
needed as much help as they could find to guard against the
Indians and the wild animals and other fears. Moreover, the
people wanted the right to attend their own churches so they
could talk to their maker without interference and they
wanted to have a safe trip each Sunday.

The Towns

Knowing that to be alone in this semi-wilderness was at best
an at-risk notion, they settled in small, compact communities,
or townships. They called them simply towns. In these times,
The town was a legal corporation, a political unit more or
less, and in the big scheme of colonial life, it was represented
in the General Court or another governing body.

It could be argued that this whole notion (if we take the
Crown from the Picture) was a democracy of the purest type.
The people met (adult males) and discussed the issues of the
day; they created taxes for the common good, and they

created laws to make it more simple to put the bad guys away. How could anything be better?

Colonialism and its pluses and minuses is not the matter of which this book is focused. So we won't take this notion much further. In this section, so far, we recounted a number of things you already know from the beginning of colonialism to the period of time right before the revolution. In all of the notions that we just discussed, I am unaware of any that suggested that the public representatives of the time before the revolution until at least the year 1750, were working for anything other than a better town or community. Yes, there was taxation, but, there was also some form of representation.

Of course, that is not how it is today and as we move forward through this chapter, we hope to identify the roots of the change and carry that into the representative pandemic from which today we suffer. If you were alive in 1750, then you know what I am talking about but if you came shortly after, you may have to take my word about a number of these very important events.

Today we know the democrats say red and the republicans say blue, and 47% of the people feel one way and 47% feel the other way and of course, there are six percent in the middle who are for something else. If we were to put a few names on that something else, on a perennial basis, the names might be spelled, "Ron Paul" or "Dennis Kucinich." The latter six percent are known today by the media as undecided. The 1750 crowd never knew it was going to get like it is or they would have done something about it to prevent it.

The Colonial "Democracies" were NOT like the state governments or the Federal Government that we have today. The "voice of the people" was often artificially limited -- at times just to property-owning white men. Suffrage was not a big deal since men and mostly rich men, were more tuned in than anyone else. Women were simply denied the right to vote, and there were few discussions about that.

On top of all the natural potential for corruption before 1750, the structure made it real easy. The colonial governors in some cases did have autocratic powers, and could act accordingly, despite the democratic aspect. If they decided to take more power than they were entitled to have, nobody was powerful enough to answer back. Some of these governors, as noted in prior comments, were appointed by the Crown back in England. Even those that were not Crown appointees could not be overruled by the representative legislatures.

England Dominated the New World

As the most successful imperialist nation of the day, Britain won control over American lands during the 16th and 17th centuries. Its control of the seas and its notion of colonial representative government were major factors in its ultimate success. The English nation of yore had a keen ability to recognize a good deal when it had one coming its way. The European countries such as England, Holland (Dutch Republic), Spain, France, and Portugal developed colonies in the Western Hemisphere for many reasons, but primarily the reason was to bring in more revenue. Though the English were late arrivals, they ultimately took all the spoils. The colonies were a great source of raw materials for trade (e.g. furs and precious metals) and they served as ready markets for finished products.

The Spanish, French, and Dutch had small settlements in what is now the continental US for a long time before the English got fully involved. But, none of the settlements were of major consequence. As the thirteen colonies began to grow with immigrants pouring in from a number of different countries, these settlers liked the English system much better than the authoritarian systems on the other countries. When England made its moves to capture these colonies as well as

Florida, not one of the original thirteen -- formerly dominated by the Spanish, they did so with ease. The settlers in many ways were happy to move to the more representative system of government, though as noted previously, it was not perfect.

The success it had in the continual conflicts between the European countries and England -- especially the conflicts with the French, culminating in the French and Indian War (1754–1763) positioned the English to dominate the new world. The French and Indian War was the North American front for a war going on in Europe at the time known as the Seven Years War, in which most of the European powers and England were battling.

France Was the Big Loser

The North American name for the war comes from the two major enemies of the British in America, namely the French and the various American Indian tribes. England emerged the big winner in this war, resulting in its conquest of all of what had been labeled New France (French claimed land east of the Mississippi) in addition to Spanish Florida.

The French were big losers on both fronts in this war. In fact the combination of the French and Indian War and the Seven Year War in Europe ended France's position as a major colonial power in the Americas. The losses were huge and the French were left with little more than French Guiana, Guadeloupe, Martinique, Saint-Dominguez, Saint Pierre, and Miquelon. To pay off the Spanish for its support in the war and Spain's loss of Florida, the French ceded control of French Louisiana (West of the Mississippi). Perhaps more devastating to France was its demise as the leading power in Europe. It sustained such heavy losses in the war that it was not until the French Revolution that France again became a major force in Europe.

American Leaders Understood British Govt.

Getting back on point in this Chapter, nothing that the English or the French or the Dutch Republic or the Portuguese or Spanish did during this pre-revolutionary period caused the current lack of faith in representative government as exists today in the United States. This lack of confidence in the motivation of duly elected representatives who represent special interests and themselves today rather than their constituencies was not a phenomenon of the 18th century.

In fact, as noted, the ultimate takeover of the colonies by the British in many ways was welcomed by the settlers because the British offered the concept of self-government, whereas their European counterparts were autocratic and authoritarian in dealing with the residents of the New World. This notion of self-government and representative government marked the colonies' early political development and this notion continues to exist today, though admittedly today in the U.S. it is in need of a bit of tuning.

All good things must come to an end, or so it seems. The rise of self-government in the colonies was a direct result of the fact that many of the English colonies were created as private corporate enterprises and as proprietary ventures. Additionally, a good number of the English colonists were knowledgeable of government and had in fact participated in government at home. So, they carried this tradition with them to America. They knew a good deal from a bad deal.

As noted previously, England was a bit late to the colonial party. It was not until the 17th century that the English Parliament, the legislative branch, began to stretch its own powers at the direct expense of the English Crown. These internal English "constitutional" struggles were not lost on the early Americans. In fact, most of the English in America supported the Parliament and the notion of representative government. In the British colonies, this was marked within

the three original types of colonies, which we examined
earlier in this Chapter: Royal colonies, Proprietary colonies,
and Charter colonies.

The Seeds of Revolution

The beginning of the end of this love affair of the colonists
with English-style government came about when the English
government began to impose direct controls on the settlers.
The French and Indian War had given England control of the
thirteen colonies plus other American territories. It seems
that the British snatched defeat from the jaws of victory as
they seemingly could not stand their own success and they
began to behave badly from an American colonial
standpoint.

In the 1750's some historical estimates suggest that the 13
colonies had about 5 million people. The "benevolent" King
of England at the time (Not King Charles and Queen
Camilla), King George III had concerns about how to protect
so many people from invaders, be they American Indians or
other European powers. He chose to do so with a British
army of 10,000 men stationed in America for the "protection
of the colonists." Though some objected to a standing English
army in the Americas, many others did not have an issue.
But, then, King George III decided he did not really want the
Crown to pick up the tab for all of the soldiers so he figured
the colonists should pony up to pay the bill. The colonists
obviously thought otherwise.

Illegal Taxation

King George saw himself as the ultimate ruler and so he
imposed a tax on the colonists in what was known as the
Stamp Act of 1765. Just a few years after defeating the
American Indians and the French across the globe, the
British could not wait for the lower house in the colonies to
tax themselves for the support of the British standing army.

They imposed it. This tax was to be paid by having tax stamps placed on newspapers, licenses, calendars, playing cards, dice and other items that were frequently purchased in the colonies.

Think of the word "impose" and then think of how you feel when someone else's will is imposed on yours for any reason whatsoever. Think of the Cap and Trade and the major healthcare debates of 2009. Likewise, the colonists were enraged at the King and the Parliament since they felt the British had violated their own constitution. Only the lower assemblies as elected by the colonists were permitted to decide which taxes should be levied, how much, when they were to become effective, and who was to get the cash. The protests began immediately and in 1766 the colonists appeared to have gained a victory as the British government gave in and repealed the Stamp Act.

Another nasty little Act that was imposed on the Colonists at about the same time was something called the Quartering Act. Under this law, American colonists had to provide housing, candles, bedding, and beverages to the British soldiers stationed in the various colonies.

Again the British were looking for a means to pay for their empire defense costs in America following the French and Indian War and another little war known as Pontiac's War. Not that it has major ramifications regarding representation in the US but a number of American Indian tribes at the time were understandably upset when the British and French stopped their war and the British were declared the victors and the Native Americans were left out of the deal. Pontiac's War was named after the Ottawa Tribe Chief Pontiac, who was the most prominent of the many native leaders (Indian Chiefs) involved in the conflict. Ultimately the British finished them off.

In the same vein as the Stamp act of this same year, the various Acts presented a big problem. After all, the uninvolved can easily see that the whole thing was just an uninvited assertion of British authority over the colonies. It completely disregarded the fact that troops had been financed for the prior 150 years by representative provincial assemblies rather than by the Parliament and Crown in London.

Americans Despised the Quartering Act

Locations which quartered more than their fair share of British soldiers, such as New York, resented the act even more-so and they were outwardly defiant. The problem at this time was that there was no way that the British were about to go away empty handed. They began to dig in more and more to protect their perceived "right" to get at the purse of the colonies through direct taxation.

The British determination was felt as they exercised their strength in ways that the colonists had never before witnessed. Because of the resistance for example of the Quartering Act, they almost immediately instituted the Suspending Act. This was insult to injury as it prohibited the New York Assembly from conducting any further business until the colony complied with the financial requirements of the resented Quartering Act.

When things did not look good, the British always seemed to do something to make matters worse. For example, they also initiated another act that has been called the Townshend Act in which duties were imposed just as in the Stamp Act. This time the taxes were noted as Townsend duties and were applied to lead, glass, paper, and tea and the tax was payable at colonial ports. After a reprieve from the Quartering Act, in 1770, the colonists found themselves suffering from an additional quartering clause, which was included in the Intolerable Acts of 1774. The American Revolution was getting closer.

The Honeymoon Is Over

The British government's honeymoon with the American colonists was well over but many colonists felt that it would be better to just act like it was OK. Yes, there were appeasers even back in early America. Think of the situation Britain found itself in. Unlike the Dutch and the Spanish and the French, their ruling style was not authoritarian and they had given the colonists the right to decide to whom they paid tribute. After all that fighting with American Indians and French and others, the British felt they had a right to something out of the deal. Where were their spoils?

Perhaps with diplomacy, the British Parliament could have convinced the lower assemblies of the colonies to see their ways. They also could have used some pressures from the governor or the council and court system to gain the will of the colonists so that they would agree as a group to be taxed to support the army and keep the British Army nice and cuddly.

One thing is for sure, the way it went down, the Americans were not ready for an imposition and the British were not ready to make America a loss-leader "possession." Parliament was not about to give up. They showed their resiliency to play another round by finding other means of taxing the colonists. Their next try was an import tax on everything. The colonists did more than offer objections. Checkmate for the colonists when they boycotted all imports from England. After a few minor scuffles and 18 months of time, Parliament dropped the tax on everything but tea and the British ships sailed away from Boston Harbor.

In 1773, the British were back and at it again hoping that knowingly or unknowingly they could get the colonists to buy teas with the tax buried in the price. Shiploads of tea from India were of lower cost and they sold it so low that even with the tax included, many of the Colonists, who enjoyed the English tea customs from the old world, could not resist purchasing it. However, there were many others who resisted and finally they took action to stop the sailors from unloading the tea.

Just a little reminder of the fact at this point in the story that the royal governor of Massachusetts, who happened to be Thomas Hutchinson, reported to the Crown and not to the people. Hutchinson decided to use his power to muster the British Troops and have the ships unloaded under their protection. As most Americans well know the story, the Bostonians disguised themselves as Indians, snuck on the ships and dumped about 340 tea chests into the sea. It was the *Boston Tea Party* and quite a party indeed.

This may be noted as this book's first lesson in representative government. "No Taxation without Representation." And it certainly demonstrates how clever the constituency can become when made angry of taxes imposed by a body not representing the people. Shall we take lessons?

Most Americans from grade school through high school learn the principles upon which this country was built and along with that the notion of representation. Looking back at the Boston Tea Party we can ask ourselves again the question of which this book is all about: "Who is it that our elected officials represent - a combination of special interests and themselves or the people? It seems that in recent times this answer is rarely, "the people." The British eventually learned its lesson well. U.S., state, and local legislators need to relearn this lesson or The U.S. may be looking at some more Tea in Boston and other areas of the mainland some time soon. In 2009 as we have seen Tea Parties are making a comeback.

Just as the tea tax upset the settlers, the tea party made the British furious. Not really to be taken lightly, the British brought their ships back into Boston harbor and they imposed a blockade until the colonists agreed to pay for the spoiled tea. With the port of Boston being a major point of commerce in Massachusetts at the time, the colonists had little choice but to give in or face financial ruin. But, their message was well delivered if not well taken.

Figure 7-1 Boston Tea Party

"The Destruction of Tea at Boston Harbor." 1773. Copy of lithograph by Sarony & Major, 1846. -- National Archives and Records Administration

This activity of the British known as the "Intolerable Acts" led to the first Continental Congress, which convened in Philadelphia's Carpenters Hall on September 5, 1774 and it finished its work on October 26, 1774. It was a meeting of 56 delegates from 12 of the 13 colonies. Major historical figures such as John Adams, his cousin Samuel Adams, Patrick Henry, and George Washington were present when this first meeting of the united colonies was held. Only Georgia, the newest colony at the time, was absent from the meeting as its English-controlled Governor ordered its delegates not to attend.

The Congress met until late October with its major function to affirm the right of the colonies to life, liberty and property and to assure that they would meet again the following year. Among their work was a letter to the King of England demanding an end to the blockade, and the Congress also approved resolutions for the people of Massachusetts to arm themselves and to stop trading with Britain.

Figure 7-2 The First Continental Congress - Carpenter's Hall Philadelphia

Two principal accomplishments of the Congress were the formation of a Continental Association as well as the Declaration of Rights and Grievances. The Association set up a boycott against importing British goods to the colonies. The teeth of this boycott was its enforcement by community groups and small committees.

The Declaration of Rights and Grievances was the formalization of the letter to King George and it called on the Crown to disband its army, cease and desist in the enforcement of its "Intolerable Acts," adhere to the right of **no taxation without representation**, and to recognize the right to liberty of the American people as protected by the common law of England. The Declaration also called on the King to restore the benefits of the existing English statutes at the time of their colonization. Just as these protected the English in England so also, according to the Declaration should they protect the English Colonists in America.

This was a major operation on the part of the colonists by rejecting the "Intolerable" Acts and it specified the only acceptable basis for a continued relationship between England and America. Though polite, it was a forceful document. Article Four of this work was authored by John Adams. This article is fundamental to the notion of representation as fostered by this book. It states that representation of the people in their legislature is a fundamental English right, essential to free government. Moreover, it acknowledges that colonists could not be and were not represented in Parliament, and thus it concluded that that body (Parliament) had no control over them.

It went on to inform the King that only by consent of the colonies — which America cheerfully granted — did Parliament have a right to regulate trade. In a powerful assertion, it concluded that such regulation by the Crown, must not have as its purpose the raising of any kind of revenue. No representation = no taxation and they delivered the words plain and simple.

This was not the beginning of the revolution per se and America had not declared independence as of yet but one could sense that the winds of war were in motion. There was some real hope that the formal written plea to the King would work but, just in case, the colonists put together a plan to elect delegates to a Second Continental Congress to deal with the possibility that the King would simply dismiss their concerns. King George III for his part was enraged at what he viewed as an "illegal" and treasonous document sent by the colonists and he was not moved to corrective action.

The Beginning of the American Revolution

In preparation for a potential war with the Crown, the colonists began to train and gather arms and ammunition. This was well noticed by General Sir Thomas Gage, the Commander in chief of the British forces and he became very concerned. Feeling that this was a plot of treason against the Crown, he planned to take action.

On the night of April 18, 1775, his troops seized some of the supplies and according to some accounts, they planned to arrest two of the militia's leaders, Sam Adams and John Hancock. Other accounts suggest that Gage didn't order troops to arrest John Hancock and Samuel Adams in Lexington on their way to Concord and as we have learned, such historian disputes almost never really get resolved. After Gage's papers were reflected in history, it is clear that a number of patriots thought that the capture of colonial leaders was probably the British column's mission, and they prepared accordingly.

But, the facts indicate that was not really Gage's plan. Nonetheless, you can feel the type of tension that was growing between American Patriots and the British Army.

Paul Revere had been a hero in the pre-revolution period in his ability to bring needed communication among the colonies about very important matters. Thanks to his warnings that the British were coming, as well as those of William Dawes, Joseph Warren, and others, the militia was waiting for the British and thus the American Revolution began the next day.

Paul Revere and the other Patriots rode from Boston to Concord through the dark on the eve of April 19, 1775, to warn as many families and country folk as they could of the danger about to come. The next day war broke out in the battles of Lexington and Concord. The revolution had begun. The unprepared and disorganized British ultimately had to retreat. The Minutemen prevailed and put the British on the chase. History will never forget the day.

Ralph Waldo Emerson, in his Concord Hymn described the first shot fired by the Patriots at the North Bridge as the "shot heard 'round the world." The clear irony of this shot however comes about because nobody knew then, nor is it known today, who it was who actually fired that first shot of the American Revolution.

No Taxation without representation, the rationale for freedom, was a major cause of Americans joining in for the fight for liberty. Today, without bloodshed, the battle of the Whigs and the Tories continues in the halls of Congress while neither seems to care about the will of the people. Unlike the late 1700's this new group of "representatives" does understand the value of public opinion and so these esteemed representatives in the U.S. in the latter part of the 20th century and until today seem much more ready to manipulate public opinion than to work to fulfill the public will.

Second Continental Congress (May 10, 1775, to March 1, 1781)

The Second Continental Congress met for the first time on May 10, 1775, during the war, on a day, which incidentally was the same date as the American capture of Fort Ticonderoga.

The American Revolutionary War continued with battle after battle. George Washington was appointed Commander of the troops even before the Second Continental Congress. The militias had gotten the colonists through its first battles of the war with England and with Washington leading an Army of the United Colonists, the superiority of numbers represented by the more than 5 million colonists was ultimately going to mathematically eliminate the Old World British from having its way in America. The more skill Washington gave the American forces, along with the more effective leadership he provided, the more it reduced the American casualties and it helped give the troops the stomach to see the Revolutionary War to ultimate victory. Somebody thought so much of his work in this regard that they elected him the first President.

It's time to remind the readers again that this is not a history book and so there is lots missing from the fantastic story of the American Revolution. Information is readily available on the Internet as well as in many wonderful books that give accounts right from the journals and diaries of the soldiers themselves on both sides. If you like this story about how Americans obtained their freedom, and this has given you a new interest in those subjects that may not have been quite as interesting in school, know that your needs for knowledge can be easily met on the Internet. The Internet can also direct you to some wonderful books on the subject, including those used in K-12, colleges and universities.

Putting Freedom in Perspective

During the trauma of the revolution, the bravery and direct suffering of the colonists to insure for Americans the rights to life, liberty, and the pursuit of happiness surely puts our freedom in perspective. Many of these brave souls died to preserve our right of representation, and it is that right that is under attack again today, though in a much more subtle way.

As noted above, while the American Revolutionary War was in progress, on May 10, 1775, as directed by the First Constitutional Congress, members of the Second Continental Congress met at the State House in Philadelphia. Again there were major historical figures in their membership including John Hancock from Massachusetts, Thomas Jefferson of Virginia, and Benjamin Franklin from Pennsylvania.

The New England battles were still fresh in the minds of the representatives and the colonial militia were still outside of Boston working to drive the British from the area. The Second Continental Congress gave the preceding events an air of legitimacy and established the militia as the Continental Army to defend the thirteen states from the only known enemy of the day, England. With Washington anointed as the Commander in Chief of the Continental Army, the colonists meant business.

As upbeat as the delegates were to the Second Continental Congress, many expected at the outset, that the issues between colony and mother country would be healed. This was not a congress whose mission it was to sanctify a revolution. Additionally, even though the delegates themselves believed they had no legal right to govern, since they were all still part of the dominion of the Crown, they went ahead and did so anyway since there was little choice.

They did have the ability to ask the "states" to provide money, supplies and men for the war effort, but just as the request was without authority, the answer if positive was purely voluntary. The states were free to accept, reject or modify these requests. This Congress knew that to make the war a success, it needed a stronger central authority. If you remember the last big 4th of July fireworks display you saw. It memorializes July 4, 1776, when the Declaration of Independence was drafted, signed by John Hancock, and sent to the printers.

The Second Continental Congress put forth the work to create the United States of America (though no states at the time were actually ratified) as an independent country. The matters of work put forth by this Congress are noted below:

Matters of the 2nd Congress

The Congress accomplished many tasks related to the new government and related to the growing war with England from when it convened to its conclusion on March 1, 1781. Among these are the following:

Figure 7-3 Second Continental Congress

Second Continental Congress at the State House in Philadelphia

"State" Governments: On May 10, the Congress adopted a resolution that urged the colonies to form their own independent governments to replace the all-but fully defunct royal governments. Once the "state" governments were seized by the colonists, there were no colonies anymore and the term state in the unofficial sense (not ratified) began to be used to refer to the original thirteen.

Military: On June 15, Congress assumed control of the Continental Army and appointed George Washington as commander-in-chief.

War Justification: Congress approved petitions such as Dickinson's *Olive Branch Petition*, a statement of abiding loyalty to the king, but disapproval of the actions of his ministers and Parliament. Congress also approved a much stronger statement titled: the Declaration of the Causes and the Necessity of Taking up Arms. This second document suggested that if America's rights are not restored, independence will be sought.

War Financing: This Congress issued certificates and borrowed from colonial and foreign sources. Financing was a major problem which continued for much of the war.

Independence: By July 2, the Congress was accepting that colonial rights were not going to be granted and it passed Richard Henry Lee's resolution of June 1776, that promoted the notion of independence. Lee's resolution of independence was adopted by Congress (12 colonies -- New York abstained). Jefferson's Declaration was completed after many revisions by Ben Franklin and others on July 4, 1776. John Hancock, President of Congress and Secretary Charles Thomson signed the original document and sent it to the Printing Shop of Charles Dunlap, just a few blocks away. The formal signing on a huge parchment was effected by 50 delegates on August 2, 1776. Some signed this original document later. Several hundred copies were sent to various governments across the world, reflecting the seriousness of the matter.

Independence Humor: President John Hancock signed the declaration's parchment, laid down his pen (quill) and said to the body in a very serious tone: "We must all hang together." Benjamin Franklin, upon hearing his comment replied: "Yes, we must, indeed, all hang together, or most assuredly we shall all hang separately."

Diplomatic Channels: The Congress needed world recognition and allies for its independence undertaking. They dispatched Silas Deane to France and later with the help of Arthur Lee and Benjamin Franklin, they concluded the Franco-American Alliance (1778).

Laws: The Congress still did not have authority to pass binding legislation on the states but did approve a number of non-binding resolutions. The technique was to ask the states to provide resources, including fighting men, for the war effort. Thankfully, in most cases, the states agreed.

To gain the authority needed to win the war, the Congress sought to make itself a stronger central authority. The July 1776 proposal called the Articles of Confederation, was intended to do just that. Upon introduction, however, the ambivalence of some of the delegates sparked a lengthy debate before the articles were adopted in November 1777. Ratification of the Articles by the states was not completed until 1781. As they say in Scranton, the rest is "history."

Cornwallis Surrenders

Washington made significant progress prosecuting the War of independence. When the Continental Army arrived in Yorktown on September 26, 1783, the French Fleet, was in firm control of the bay. The French operating under the Franco-American Alliance offered substantial assistance to the new United Sates. They had Cornwallis pinned in. With about 20,000 troops from state militias combined with troops from France, the American forces had stymied the British who were being led by General Lord Charles Cornwallis. Cornwallis's troops were taking heavy casualties from a constant bombardment.

Figure 7-4 Surrender of Cornwallis

Surrender of Cornwallis - The End of the American Revolution.

Cornwallis was the 2nd General in Command in the Americas, and to put it frankly, when reinforcements from New York, sent by the top General Henry Clinton, did not arrive in time to be of use, he knew he was licked and he surrendered on October 19, 1781. This was the de-facto end of the war though skirmishes continued for several years. In December 1783, George Washington made the end of the American Revolution official when he resigned his commission to Congress. The revolution had ended. America had achieved its independence and its representative democracy was about to get even stronger.

Chapter Summary

The government in the colonies was formed very much like the government in England. The Governor, the Council and the Representatives of the people made up the three branches. The Governor and the Council had their allegiance to the Colonial Proprietor or the Crown. Only the representatives could levy taxes.

When the French and Indian War and the Pontiac Wars concluded, the English Crown was looking to America to pay it back for its war costs and to pay it back for the 10,000 strong English standing army residing on American soil. Instead of doing things by the book, the English were impatient and began to directly tax the colonists but this was forbidden by the English Constitution and the Americans were subjects of the Crown.

Beginning with the Stamp Act and moving to the Intolerable Acts, it was a cat and mouse game of England taxes, Colonists complaints, England concessions, until the taxes were too many to take away. The English had the strongest Navy in the world but they had just 10,000 soldiers compared to the 5,000,000 colonists.

Soon the Colonists had had enough and the thirteen colonies formed the First Continental Congress and sent King George a note of demands called the Declaration of Rights and Grievances, hoping he would lighten up. Instead the King dug in. At the Second Continental Congress the war had already begun and the delegates fashioned the Declaration of Independence as well as the Articles of Confederation upon which the Constitution was built.

George Washington was appointed commander in chief and he and the army of the new U.S. won many battles and finally in 1783, the British General Cornwallis surrendered to Washington. The U.S. came into being and was commissioned as a free country and for years the country was bound by its Articles of Confederation until the drafting and ratification of the Constitution.

The Government of the United States

America's founding documents tell a tale of the character and temperament of the men who are now known as the

Founding Fathers. They represented the best that America had to offer. When the Articles of Confederation was introduced, it sparked lengthy debate before adoption in November 1777. This was the beginning of the government of the United States of America. The forming of that government of the people for the people, and by the people is fully treated as the subject matter of Chapter 5.

Sources:

http://www.archaeologyonline.net/artifacts/who-discovered-america.html

http://www.ngallery.org/united_states.html

Citizens' Initiatives Amendment to Improve Congress and Check its Excesses
http://www.cusdi.org/

Jamestown et al: http://usinfo.state.gov/xarchives/display.html?p=washfile-english&y=2007&m=March&x=20070309143325GLnesnoM0.5810663

Constitutional Democracy:
http://www.proconservative.net/CUNAPolSci201PartTwoD.shtml

http://www.usahistory.info/colonial/government.html

http://www.frontiertrails.com/america/americanrevolution.html

http://www.ushistory.org/carpentershall/history/congress.htm

http://memory.loc.gov/learn/features/timeline/amrev/rebelln/rights.html

http://boston1775.blogspot.com/2006_06_01_archive.html

http://www.kidport.com/RefLib/UsaHistory/AmericanRevolution/SecondCongress.htm

Articles of Confederation: http://www.ushistory.org/documents/confederation.htm

2nd Continental Congress: http://www.u-s-history.com/pages/h656.html

http://www.americanrevolution.com/SurrenderCornwallis.htm

Declaration of Independence: http://www.u-s-history.com/pages/h670.html

http://www.youtube.com/watch?v=ofYmhlclqr4

Chapter 8   The Forming of the United States Government

Representation at All Levels

One of the first documents on the way to the Declaration of Independence and the Constitution was the *Declaration of Rights and Grievances*. It was a product of the First Continental Congress. It was the first formal request of the "United States" to England for a return to representative government. Though nothing close to a constitutional democracy, the Colonists under English rule enjoyed representation in the lower house of the colonial governments. There was no union of colonies or states at the time and had the English kept to themselves and not levied taxes directly on the colonists, Americans today would be much more interested if Camilla is really ever going to be the Queen.

With a careful reading of the Declaration of Rights and Grievances, one can get a quick sense of what the colonists wanted from the Crown. It was simply, "no taxation without representation," and all of the many positions this plea represented. It was the first major document of the new government of the United States, though it occurred at a time when the states were not actively seeking independence from the Crown.

The expressed purpose of the First Continental Congress held in 1774 was:

"That a Committee be appointed to state the rights of the Colonies in general, the several instances in which these rights are violated or infringed, and the means most proper to be pursued for obtaining a restoration of them."

The committee was constructed and the declaration was drafted and it was read on September 22nd and the draft of the grievances was read on the 24th. The members of the First Congress debated the drafts on October 12 and 13, and after a final draft was produced, it was agreed on Friday, October 14, 1774.

Several days later on October 20, the Congress passed the Articles of Association. This declaration was addressed to King George III. In essence, it was a formal agreement of the colonies themselves to work together as an association of states with common purpose. It was basically a union of protest and boycott as many of the articles outlined the specific actions that the colonists were to take regarding the export and import of goods. When you read these articles, you can't help but notice the elegance and forethought in the draft. We are a fortunate lot indeed to have had such fine and capable, and yes, honorable men, representing America in those days.

Since life had not improved and the British, after initially backing off, began to impose its will on the colonists, The Second Continental Congress started on May 10, 1775 and it went on until March 1, 1781. The delegates of each of the 13 colonies gathered in Philadelphia to discuss their next steps in dealing with England. This Congress met at the State House in Philadelphia as the American Revolution began in earnest with the shot heard round the world still ringing in their ears. The militia was still engaged in Boston while the Congress was using its powers to formally establish the militia as the Continental Army of the United States with George Washington as the Commander in Chief. This marked another stage in the formation of the government of the U.S. The government would continue to evolve and after Independence was gained, Washington would again become

Commander in Chief when he was elected First President of the United States.

Sixty-five representatives appointed by the legislatures of thirteen British North American colonies accomplished a body of work that is historical in nature. At the time it formed the basis for the new government. The Declaration of Independence was the first well-known historical document produced by this Second Congress. The second was the Articles of Confederation, which was the pre-cursor document to the United States Constitution. The text of all these historical documents ae available online. Just search for the document name.

As noted in Chapter 4, the Second Continental Congress was begun during the American Revolutionary War. It served as the de facto U.S. national government. This Congress assumed power and raised armies, directed strategy, appointed diplomats, and it made the government formal while producing the two most fundamental and historical documents to American freedom.

United States Declaration of Independence

Some dates one never can forget. The Declaration of Independence as noted in Chapter 4, written by Thomas Jefferson, as put forth and approved for printing on July 4, 1976 did exactly what it purported to do in its title. It declared independence from Great Britain. It was not Pennsylvania, or Massachusetts or Virginia that declared this independence and this is a key point. Instead, it was all of the states in unison as they had chosen to assemble and join in a union to create a new federal government that would be known as the United States of America.

Once independence was declared, America began to legally operate fully independent of the Crown with its own government. Considering that the colonists were in revolt and war had commenced, it is an understatement to suggest that the colonists were not operating independently prior to the declaration. The declaration formalized their union of independence. The states were declared to be free and independent and "all political connection between them and the State of Great Britain, is and ought to be totally dissolved." The formal title of the document ratified on July 4, 1976 is "**The unanimous Declaration of the thirteen United States of America**, but to Americans it is known simply as the Declaration of Independence. This was the formal end of the thirteen colonies.

In addition to declaring independence, this document gave justification for the separation from the Crown in sufficient detail that the King and Parliament could not misunderstand its purpose and from whence it came. Since the colonies were no more, historians consider this Declaration as the founding document of the United States of America. In his Gettysburg Address of 1863, at the beginning of his address, President Lincoln memorialized the founding of the United States in these words:

> *Four score and seven years ago our fathers brought forth on this continent, a new nation, conceived in liberty, and dedicated to the proposition that all men are created equal.*

As we know from our knowledge of American History and from the recount of the Revolutionary War in Chapter 4 of this book, there were a number of battles until the Americans prevailed in the war with England. After the Declaration of Independence, the Second Continental Congress stayed in session passing laws and drafting documents that ultimately would define the new nation as the United States of America. The next major document in the formation of the government of the United States to be considered is the Articles of Confederation.

Articles of Confederation

Just as the Declaration of Independence is short for a longer title, the "Articles of Confederation and Perpetual Union" has been shortened to be the Articles of Confederation. Some say that the Articles of Confederation represent the United States of America's first Constitution. This document was the work of the Second Continental Congress who drafted it in 1777. The Articles established a "firm league of friendship" between and among the 13 states.

After having been subjected to the wiles of the strong central government of the British prior to the War of Independence, these Articles reflect a sense of the wariness by the states of a government that would not provide them with their God-given rights. The Articles are the agreed-upon remedy for the concerns of states' rights and for individual rights. Ever fearful that a government of the future might not have the right measure of concern for their individual needs if it were given too much power, and that abuses such as the Intolerable Acts, may again be the result, the Articles purposely established a "constitution" that vested the largest share of power to the individual states.

Under the Articles of Confederation, each of the states retained its "sovereignty, freedom and independence." The preamble of the US Constitution drafted in 1787 and ratified later by the individual states one at a time, sets its purpose as "in order to make a more perfect union." The government recognized that there were flaws in the Articles and the Constitution was its way of correcting those flaws and correcting the notion of a constitutional democracy for the United States.

There was a permanent institution called the Congress formed in the Articles as a national legislature comprised of representatives of the states. The Congress was responsible for conducting foreign affairs, declaring war or peace, maintaining an army and navy and a variety of other lesser functions. The Articles did not call for the separation of powers with an executive, legislative, and judicial branch. The Articles did not permit the delegates **to collect taxes, regulate interstate commerce and enforce laws.** Under the Articles of Confederation these important functions could only be performed if the states agreed.

Though the Articles had shortcomings, the document provided the guidelines for the United States government and it was the only real law of the land until the Constitution was adopted. Eventually, the shortcomings were addressed and this lead to the adoption of the U.S. Constitution. The beauty of the Articles of Confederation was that it provided a workable framework during those years in which the 13 states were struggling to achieve their independent status.

Considering that the Constitution itself is under fire today by those who would like it constructed in ways that were not necessarily intended by the Founding Fathers, from November 15, 1777, when adopted by the Congress, the Articles of Confederation did their job to keep the Country in good stead. Nothing in life worth having is easy. On March 1, 1781, the Articles became operational when the last of the thirteen states signed the document.

The Constitution of the United States of America

The Articles were an imperfect constitution for the newly formed union. The phrase "a more perfect union" in the Preamble notes the imperfections in the document and it introduces the rationale for the drawing of the Constitution. The U.S. Constitution (and its 27 amendments) has survived for over two-hundred years testifying to its perfection as the basis for the constitutional democracy of the United States as introduced in Chapter 2 of this book.

From the National Archives:

http://www.archives.gov/national-archives-
experience/charters/constitution.html

> The Federal Convention convened in the State House
> (Independence Hall) in Philadelphia on May 14,1787, to
> revise the Articles of Confederation. Because the
> delegations from only two states were at first present, the
> members adjourned from day to day until a quorum of
> seven states was obtained on May 25. Through discussion
> and debate it became clear by mid-June that, rather than
> amend the existing Articles, the Convention would draft an
> entirely new frame of government. All through the
> summer, in closed sessions, the delegates debated, and
> redrafted the articles of the new Constitution. Among the
> chief points at issue were how much power to allow the
> central government, how many representatives in Congress
> to allow each state, and how these representatives should
> be elected--directly by the people or by the state legislators.
> The work of many minds, the Constitution stands as a
> model of cooperative statesmanship and the art of
> compromise.

The Law of the Land

As noted previously, the Constitution of the United States
comprises the primary law of the U.S. Federal Government.
It also describes the three chief branches of the Federal
Government and their jurisdictions. In addition, it lays out
the basic rights of citizens of the United States. The
Constitution of the United States is the oldest federal
constitution in existence and was framed by a convention of
delegates from twelve of the thirteen original states in
Philadelphia in May 1787.

The Constitution is the landmark legal document of the United States and all other laws are tested against its specifications.
To give the reader an appreciation or a reminder of just how significant the Articles and the Amendments of this document really are, I am including this brief summary below:

Preamble

> We the People of the United States, in Order to form a more perfect Union, establish Justice, insure domestic Tranquility, provide for the common defense, promote the general Welfare, and secure the Blessings of Liberty to ourselves and our Posterity, do ordain and establish this Constitution for the United States of America.

Article I: The Legislative Branch: Consists of 10 sections and defines:

(1) All Legislative powers, (2) Composition of the House of Representatives, (3) Composition of the Senate, (4) Holding Elections, (5) Congress sets its own rules by House, (6) Compensation for Senators), (7) Revenue Bills originate in House, (8) Congress can lay and collect taxes, (9) Defines states rights and taxes (10) State treaties.

Section 9, Clause 8 of the Constitution of particular interest to this writer as noted in Chapter 2 with the automatic conferring of the title, the Honorable. Please look at what the founding fathers thought of such titles:

> Section 9 Clause 8: No Title of Nobility shall be granted by the United States: And no Person holding any Office of Profit or Trust under them, shall, without the Consent of the Congress, accept of any present, Emolument, Office, or Title, of any kind whatever, from any King, Prince, or foreign State.

One of the first constitutional loopholes was the notion of the giver being the King, Prince, or a foreign state. There is nothing here unfortunately about taking the title for oneself or having it granted via obscure rules of etiquette that have never passed the test of law.

Article II: The Executive Branch: Consists of 4 sections and defines:

(1) Executive Power and President, (2) President as Commander in Chief, (3) State of the Union & Information Requirements, (4) Rules of Executive Branch impeachment

Article III: The Judicial Branch: Consists of 3 sections and defines:

(1) Judicial Power, (2) Laws and Trial By Jury, (3) Treason

Article IV: Relations Between States: Consists of 4 sections and defines:

(1)Faith and Credit of State Laws, (2) Privileges apply to all in all states, (3) New States May be Admitted tot he Union, (4) Federal guarantee to defend states.

Article V: The Amendment Process: Consists of 1 section and defines the Amendment Process for adding / deleting from the Constitution.

Article VI: General Provisions, Supremacy of the Constitution: Consists of 1 section and defines the debt process and the requirement to support the Constitution

Article VII: Ratification Process: Consists of 1 section and it outlines the process for ratifying the Constitution.

27 Amendments to the Constitution

The Bill of Rights

Amendment I: Freedom of speech, religion, press, petition, assembly.
Amendment II: Right to bear arms and militia.
Amendment III: Quartering of soldiers.
Amendment IV: Warrants and searches.
Amendment V: Individual debt and double jeopardy.
Amendment VI: Speedy trial, witnesses and accusations.
Amendment VII: Right for a jury trial.
Amendment VIII: Bail and fines.
Amendment IX: Existence of other rights for the people
Amendment X: Power reserved to the states and people.

Later Amendments

Amendment XI: Suits against states.
Amendment XII: Election of executive branch.
Amendment XIII: Prohibition of slavery.
Amendment XIV: Privileges or immunities, due process, elections and debt: Consists of 5 sections and defines: (1) Citizenship (2) Apportionment of representatives among the states, (3) Rules for being a Senator or Representative, (4) Validity of the public debt, (5) Congressional Enforcement of this Article.
Amendment XV: Race and the right to vote.
Amendment XVI: Income tax.
Amendment XVII: Senator election and number.
Amendment XVIII: Prohibition on sale of alcohol
Amendment XIX: Gender and the right to vote.
Amendment XX: "Lame duck" session of Congress eliminated.
Amendment XXI: Repeal of Article XVIII.
Amendment XXII: Limit of Presidential terms.
Amendment XXIII: Election rules for the District of Columbia
Amendment XXIV: Taxes and the right to vote.
Amendment XXV: Rules of Presidential succession.
Amendment XXVI: Age and the right to vote.

Amendment XXVII: Pay raises and Congress

Amendments Never Ratified

Besides the above summary of the constitutional body of law, six other amendments have been proposed to the constitution that have not been ratified and thus do not represent the law of the land.

What Does This Mean?

Here we are in Chapter 5 of a book about taxation and representation or the lack thereof, and the articles and precepts in the Constitution as the primary law of the land completes the historical section of this book, and we now have identified the major culprits to the dilemma, which is the main subject matter of this book -- Taxation Without Representation. Taxation was a major problem for the colonists and the representatives of the Second Congress, even during the war did not have taxing authority. There was no welfare state. Every buck that a colonist earned could theoretically be kept since the state's mission was not to provide for the welfare of others.

Figure 8-1 Colonial Currency

Types of New England currency, including a Mass. bill of 1690, earliest paper money issued in America.

Actually colonists did not get to spend bucks. The thirteen colonies retained the British monetary units: pounds, shillings, pence. Besides barter, the colonists also used foreign coins made of precious metals (gold, silver). These were in circulation in the colonies and their values were determined by the several colonial legislatures. The dollar coin (or buck as we call it) was used even before the Declaration of Independence.

The Congress had authorized the issuance of dollar denominated coins and currency. The term 'dollar' was a natural since the most commonly used coin at that time was something called the Spanish colonial 8 real coins also known as the Spanish Milled Dollars. Several different systems of money were proposed for the early United States. The dollar eventually was approved by Congress in 1786. The first US dollar bill was not printed as legal tender until 1862.

Though there is nothing in the Constitution about income redistribution, a basic tenet of our current welfare system, the Constitution is the document that we can credit or blame for giving the government the right to tax the people of their wealth. The Constitution is also the current body of law that gives us our constitutional democracy and thus with this democracy we have a representative government. The founders of the country had no idea that even with the three branches of government representing the people and serving as a system of checks and balances, there would be thieving and conniving representatives in all branches and levels of government who now have the authority to take as much as 1/2 of the income of a middle class American and even more if that American is self-employed.

Chapter Summary

In this chapter we walked through the early instruments of government from the *Declaration of Rights and Grievances* to the *Constitution*. This brief walk gives us a general perspective of how the government got to be as it is, and that's necessary as we discuss things that are wrong and ways that we can change it in the rest of the book.

As you read the Constitution, and I urge you to do this to be as informed as possible about the basic law of the land, make note that there is no Article or Section or Clause that provides an upper limit to what government can take. My classic book, the Constitution 4 Dummmies available on Kindle can help in this regard.

The idea of course was that taxation would be reasonable but putting politicians in control of the money supply in all three levels of government is certainly one of the weakest notions in the Constitution. Though the notion of a nobility is expressly forbidden by the Constitution, there is nothing that suggests that the representatives of the people could not behave nobly. History proves that the Founding Fathers were very noble and so they expected that those who followed them to office would also be noble. They may be honorable (See Chapter 2 for humor) but few are noble.

So, we can't blame taxation and poor representation on the boss-a-nova. But, we can blame it on the Constitution and the fact that it is just over 30 pages and not the several billion page book that would be necessary to keep everything on the up and up forever and ever. States also have constitutions and cities have charters, and all of these bodies can levy taxes and create more laws. So, it is no wonder, as this country grows, that the whole system gets more unwieldy. Maybe we can start again. Surely this will be an option we examine as we explore how to deal with an unresponsive government in the rest of this book.

Now that you have finished Chapters 4 and 5, if you are intrigued about the American Revolution, and the formation of our government, and would like to sit back and listen to some historical tunes, I've got just the URL for you:

http://www.youtube.com/watch?v=Q_TXJRZ4CFc

If you happen to forget this URL or you would like to access it on Google or another search engine, just type in Schoolhouse Rock Preamble. You will be pleasantly surprised. The lyrics to the song are on the Schoolhouse Rock site if you want to print them and sing along. When you play this video on YouTube, look on the right hand frame and you will find a number of other Schoolhouse Rock productions such as "The Shot Heard Round the World. It's both a fun and uplifting experience and for those who have not read Chapters 1 to 5, it can be a complete learning experience. Enjoy!

Sources:

http://www.kidport.com/RefLib/UsaHistory/AmericanRevolution/SecondCongress.htm

http://en.wikipedia.org/wiki/Second_Continental_Congress

http://www.ushistory.org/declaration/

http://www.archives.gov/national-archives-experience/charters/declaration.html

http://en.wikipedia.org/wiki/United_States_Declaration_of_Independence

http://www.earlyamerica.com/earlyamerica/milestones/articles/

http://www.archives.gov/national-archives-experience/charters/constitution.html

http://www.gpoaccess.gov/constitution/index.html

http://etext.lib.virginia.edu/users/brock/

http://en.wikipedia.org/wiki/History_of_the_United_States_dollar

Chapter 9   Essays of Thomas Dawson: Illegal Aliens and Immigration

Taxation and Representation

There may be some topics that you find in this book that do not seem to go with the theme of taxation and representation such as immigration. Wouldn't it be nice if our tax money was not used to lure foreigners to our shores and then pay their way? Would it not be nice if we had representation about whether we should support people from other countries before our representatives took what they wanted from our wallets? So, yes, immigration has lots to do with taxation and representation—or the lack thereof.

Surprise in Email

While I was researching the first edition of this book, I came across numerous anecdotes, many of which were nothing short of amazing and phenomenally insightful. One thing I have learned in my 68 years (my 69th Birthday is on its way) is that nobody knows it all and as a corollary, there is something brilliant that is ready to be discovered every day. I was so impressed with the writings of Thomas Dawson, both in content and style that I wrote him a few months before the first edition was completed, and asked if I could use his material in this book. At the time, I had intended to use some excerpts of his works in the main body of some of the chapters in which his insights applied. But, when I received

Tom's note right before I submitted the first edition, I had to make other arrangements.

I thought about an insertion here or there and then I decided that, since Mr. Dawson offered no strings on his granting permission for the use of his works, I would print them as his essays for your reading pleasure and give him the full credit he deserves. This was his note to me. I have never met him but you can feel the goodness of this gentleman in his words:

Mr. Kelly:

Sorry I couldn't get back to you sooner. You are more than welcome to use any of my material at your discretion, either in agreement with my thinking or in disagreement. You need not give credit. This old bumpkin will be delighted if you can encourage someone to think about the world in which the next generation will live. Provoke thought whenever possible.

I wish you personal satisfaction in your endeavors, and please inform me when your book is available.

With warm regards

Tom

How can you beat that. So I took the poetic license to provide four of Thomas Dawson's essays from 2005 from the American Chronicle. Please enjoy and encourage others to think about the world in which the next generation will live. Provoke thought whenever possible.

Difficulties Lie Ahead

These works of Thomas Dawson are really well done. I wish I can meet Mr. Dawson one day. He is a real patriot. They are good pieces for you to have in your personal library and there is good news. There are a number of other works by Thomas Dawson on the Internet available for your reading. They tell a story like mine about taxation without representation. Mr. Dawson granted his approval to offer a similar thought as his on the subject and he offered me the opportunity to take issue with him. Very gracious!

Obviously I wrote this book to point out the travesty and the reality of taxation without representation in the modern age. Topics from taxes to the fact that hizzoners, all over the U.S. at all levels of government, who are not representing the American people, make up the bulk of this book.

The culprit in most cases is the corporation in cohort with the government but with major complicity of our "honorables." If I were Thomas Dawson, I would have said that the purpose of this book is to "encourage someone to think about the world in which the next generation will live. Provoke thought whenever possible."

I predict these essays will be a treat for you to read. I love reading them. Dawson hits all issues hard but never below the belt. The issues in the essays as the issues raised in this book are no more solved because you will have completed this reading task in these few pages, than if you do not.

There are big problems to solve. Mr. Dawson points these out in his essays. We have a lot of work to do in helping our brothers and sisters in America take back control of our government. It won't be easy. But, with the risk of having Barack Obama, Nancy Pelosi, Harry Reid, and perhaps Hillary Clinton, in charge of our lives for eternity, we must take action now.

I will sign off my part of this chapter now, leaving you in the hands of Mr. Thomas Dawson. Know that the difficulties ahead are solvable if we watchfully pay attention to our government and call it to task on what it must do. I feel confident leaving you to these essays and then to yourself and all the other selves like you and I, and Thomas Dawson, an American Patriot.

God Bless You -- and our America.

Illegal Aliens and Immigration

By Thomas Dawson
June 03, 2005

We do not have an immigration problem with Mexico. We do have a border problem with Mexico. Without making more jokes about Homeland Security, borders are important. Wthout borders, there is no country…or security. Some public political debate has begun, but don't expect too much. The easiest way to win a political argument in today's world, particularly if your position is without practical merit is to confuse the issues.

The proponents of open borders, and there are many, use this method to make their arguments. They never use the correct term "illegal alien". They refuse to view these people as either illegal or aliens. The most that one can hope for, is that they will use the term "undocumented immigrants". You can bet that after one or two minutes of discussion the term will degenerate into just "immigrants". Without any qualifier, most of what they say is correct. Most importantly, whatever you say in their context sounds racist. Of course, we live in an age of labels and buzzwords. If you allow such people to get away with it, they will play the game of "gotcha" as they try to stick a label on you. Unfortunately, this is not a child's game.

If the media polls are correct, the American people overwhelmingly recognize the gravity of the situation and would like to correct it. We're not talking about Democrats or Republicans here nor Conservatives or Liberals. When we take the labels off, you'll find that most American citizens can and often do, think!

Alas, there is little hope for any real change to take place in the near future. There is a great and growing disconnect between modern politicians and the people they are supposedly representing. So there will be a great deal of gamesmanship or slight of hand to convince people that they are looking into the situation. In reality, the politicians will continue to stall any useful action for the sake of their "financial constituency".

Some discussion at the federal level has finally begun again, and a few really big political names are making a lot of noise. But in a typical stalling tactic, the discussion is not about closing the borders. The talk is about those illegal aliens that are already here and many more that will come, as we make plans for them. Their only concern is what will be the final criteria to make them underclass citizens? Discussions with this kind of detailed minutia can be dragged out for a very long time... and they will be. Meanwhile, Vicente Fox is sending us as many of his people as he can; as fast as he can.

The federal politicians are beholden to organized interest groups for financial support and really find it difficult, if not impossible to stand up for their people 'back home' on any major issue where a lot of corporate money is at stake.

Amnesty for Mexican illegal aliens was granted a few years ago, and since then the border control has been relaxed. Now we are being told that there is no alternative for a humane solution without again providing amnesty. Don't listen to the politicians; they have no intention of closing the Mexican borders until, and only if forced to do so. It is only a ploy to bring in more cheap labor for exploitation.

The failed corporate religion of Globalization in the name of 'free trade' is really a search for the cheapest labor available. Corporations have greased the wheels of government and momentum is steamrolling any public opposition.

Manufacturers are now allowed to 'globalize' by outsourcing their labor costs to the cheapest of overseas labor, and retailers can 'globalize' by purchasing the cheapest products they can find manufactured overseas, and thus they can both increase their profits. They can also claim increases in productivity in a single stroke as they reduce their costs. The question arises. Why should agriculture and service industries that cannot move overseas not share in Globalization? The simple answer is they can. Simply have the politicians "move the mountain to Mohammed".

Now that the government allows corporations to bring in really cheap "illegals" for the service and agriculture industries, they too are receiving the labor/cost benefits of 'Globalization'. Not to mention the hundreds of thousands of "guest workers" that have already been imported to work as engineers, IT technicians, etc which are hired at only 50% to 80% of the going rate in this country, thus holding down the wage scales of the middle class and increasing corporate profits. With a single stroke of the pen and government grease, anything can be made legal. Seems like a sensible way to reduce wages and push profits up.

To paraphrase Milton Friedman, "Corporate executives, provided they stay within the law, have no responsibilities in their business activities other than to make as much money for their stockholders as possible." Milton Freeman is absolutely right. A corporation has no responsibility to anyone. It is not a person. It is a legal animal (entity) created by the law of a country. It is an animal without social conscience or concern for anything except profits. If a corporation has any responsibility, it is only to the law of the country in which it operates. It is the duty of the country of origin to regulate and control its offspring. When a domestic corporation behaves badly, it should be disciplined. When a foreign company behaves badly, it should be disciplined and if it continues, refrained from doing business. Every country should set the rules for its own house.

If we allow "globalization" to wring out our middle class, we can easily lose the increased standard of living gained during the first quarter century after World War II. (Since then. our standard of living has gone nowhere. It has probably even declined a bit in the last quarter century.) Our problem is not with the natural ambitions of corporations. Our problem is with the deliberately calibrated reluctance of (the peoples?) representation in government to regulate with any care for or concern toward the public good.

In the long run though, the politicians at the state and local levels will have to face the reality of the economic situation. Continuing to assume low cost, near poverty level labor has a depressing effect on all wages over extended periods of time. Increases in poverty create demand for state and local services as well as lowering per capita taxes. Hospitals across the south to California have had to go into bankruptcy and some have closed because of expenses incurred by illegal aliens who are unable to pay.

Many immigrants and illegal aliens have earnings low enough to qualify for welfare assistance. At the same time, these states and local governments are experiencing lower per capita tax revenues as wages begin to drift downwards. The greatest increase in costs due to these illegal aliens and low cost immigrants is, of course education. Law enforcement and incarceration costs are also rising. It is estimated that in 2003, California alone, even after accounting for tax contributions from illegal aliens, the direct cost was more than $8,000,000,000 and total costs probably well in excess of $11,000,000,000. California can't even fix their roads, and this is just the beginning! All this is just part of the cost of subsidizing labor for the service industries.

As we erode the middle class and the consumer market begins to falter, the tax base will continue to shrink and tax revenues fall. After all, middle class working people pay the vast bulk of the tax burden. What will your town look like as state and local governments slash services by 15, 20, or even 25%?

Increasing numbers of illegal aliens and poverty level immigrants cause economic and social disruption. On the other hand, carefully managed legal immigration will contribute to the economic and social growth of the country. Bringing in large numbers of qualified people to fill jobs (at current rates of pay) where there are labor or professional shortages means more contributing citizens. Encouraging carefully managed increases in immigration is important to this country, both as an economic contribution and by increasing the population underpinning.

Do we have problems in agriculture? Certainly! How many people do we need to help us out? The government says that we already have between eight and a half million and eleven million illegal aliens. Others estimate between eighteen and twenty million. [Brian Kelly estimates 60 million.] The likely probability is that we have between twelve and fifteen million.

This means that the illegal aliens represent about four percent or slightly more of our population. This is about one out of every twenty-five people. Should we bring in more people for every crop and then let them melt into the general population and continue to grow a permanent underclass of cheap labor, undermining the wage base of the entire country? Of course not! There must be a constant, but controlled rotation of workers for agriculture. Perhaps permanent labor arrangements could be had with foreign labor at a slightly better rate of pay. Assuming we want to continue to subsidize agriculture with cheap labor, there are a number of possibilities.

Alternatively, we may want to consider taking the gratuitous profits away from corporate owners of our subsidized, socialized agricultural enterprises. Or perhaps even doing away with socialized agriculture and even corporate welfare entirely! I am sure that politicians would find this to be a national security issue far greater than merely open borders! But that is a subject for another day.

Even if we continue to subsidize agriculture with (dare I say dirt cheap) labor, this does not mean that every business should be entitled to hire at poverty wage levels. Inviting immigration at or near poverty level wages is not good for this country's public good. Let the service businesses pay a little more and charge a little more. We can pay more for the services or pay a lot more for the subsidies.

Workers in the construction trades have been a part of the middle class for the last fifty years. Now, with the strongest continuous housing boom and the highest prices for houses in our history, construction workers are experiencing falling wages and unemployment due to unemployed cheap and often illegal labor. It's past time to consider where we are heading.

It's also time to close our borders and then begin a serious discussion. In any case, any political talk about solving the immigration problem without first closing the borders is pure deception, and a sham!

Chapter 10   Essays of Thomas Dawson: All Immigration Problems Solved

By Thomas Dawson
June 11, 2005

A panel set up by the Counsel on Foreign Relations wants Americans to stop thinking of themselves as United States citizens and to think of themselves as just North Americans. The panel has published a report called "Building a North American Community" in which it proposes a single common border around the three countries. The purpose is to create a free flow of goods and labor between the countries. They hope to accomplish this over the next five years, by 2010.

It seems unfortunate that Asia is not adjacent to us so that they could provide even larger numbers of even cheaper labor for the corporate citizens of this new world order, that has now completely bought out our government.

In reality, this is just another salvo in the battle to create an aura of inevitability around the idea of globalization. The destruction of borders for the purpose of moving cheap labor is only one facet of this new deity. If we can be convinced that we are caught up in the inevitable tide of history, then the right to choose has been taken from us.

It has become the obligation of our highly paid government officials to prepare the middle class citizens for changes that their employers intend to make in this world. Certainly, if they can pull it off, this would be a great step forward toward globalization. In any case, these kinds of discussions create another great stall to keep the borders open.

Globalization, the idea of a 'One World Government" is not new. We fought WWII so that the world would not become fascist. We endured the cold war so that the world would not become communist. Since then we have worried that the UN would take over the world and form a world government. Now we find that the seeds of our cultural destruction are to be found in the very basis of our democratic free enterprise system.

This country has always indulged the corporate community as one of our children, giving it status, favoring it over any other public interest. We have asked little in return. We mistakenly assumed that in return for this favored status, these entities would naturally provide employment for our citizens with wages sufficient to sustain an improving standard of living in the long run. For the past thirty years we have considered failure in this regard as only a temporary setback. Now we find that sustaining a reasonable standard of living or even the continued employment of middle class citizens is not on the agenda, not even a consideration of the corporate community. Unfortunately, this unwritten contract or understanding does not exist in principle any more than it does in writing. What did we expect? We have failed to discipline this child of ours and now it has become a self-serving tyrant. You probably thought the "Robber Barons" were tough. I can assure you that, as Ronald Reagan would say "You ain't seen nothing yet!"

We are spectators to the birthing of this new world order called Globalization. Large international corporations, which even now are no longer responsible to, nor contributing to any public good, have high hopes of running the world as a single cooperative trading entity. The very concept of traditional nation-states will become irrelevant. Large trading companies will run this brave new world on an "as needed" basis. Nation-states will become reduced to mere cultural centers. These will become the transport systems of the trading companies, with which they will trade in people and goods wherever required. A managers' dream! Indeed, the managers are already, at this very moment, the aristocrats of our time. Globalization is to become the manifestation of their consolidation of power.

Managers have already replaced the capitalists and entrepreneurs in the world of international corporations. Only minor players and small companies are still willing or need to risk their money in today's environment. International companies do not invest in new enterprises or attempt to compete with other companies. They either buy out small companies that appear to be successful within a given market, or merge with their competitors. In either case, market share is increased and a secure established market is acquired without risk. Little is left to chance; they are managing everything; most especially the governments of the western world. Management has finally trumped leadership in business, as well as in government.

To be sure, at the moment they still need other companies with whom they can appear to compete. This is not an overt conspiracy. It is rather, a "gentleman's agreement"; an understanding, if you will. For the moment, at least, the illusion of competition must be maintained. But, consider that just this week, Toyota is taking the poison pill because they fear someone will take them over due to their recent financial success. In the dawn of this global environment, the realization of any entrepreneurial success will probably become sufficient reason for your immediate demise, as expanding international interests will try to gobble you up. Our enormous financial institutions will even provide money for little fish to eat big fish, providing the big fish have control over secure markets. Because of the low risk factor in these kinds of takeovers, these financial institutions only require a relative premium over the current interest rate.

The United States has been an easy mark for the globalization movement due to the close ties developed by corporations between themselves and financially dependent and greedy government officials, readily managed by corporate money. These corporations are, to our elected representatives, their "financial constituents". The pharmaceutical industry alone has two people lobbying on every congressman.

Asian countries may not be so easy; they only needed corporate connections with the west until they were locked into the relatively affluent western economies. They have the world's largest cheap labor force and are now graduating great numbers of highly educated people. They will soon have the largest and cheapest well-educated work force in the world. Their economies have gained momentum and as they grow, they become somewhat insulated and independent of western style corporate persuasion. They will appear to tolerate a certain amount of corporate "rule making" such as "intellectual property" only so long as it serves their interests. They understand the greed of our corporations and are happily building "feed lots" for them. When all is said and done, Asia will not view these international corporations as their own children, to be coddled and upon whom they will stake their future. When these corporations have been fattened and can no longer contribute to the national interest, their assets will be nationalized; gobbled up by some "really big fish" that are hardly manageable.

Chapter 11 Essays of Thomas Dawson: Labor Arbitrage? Better Known as Cheap Labor

By Thomas Dawson

October 12, 2005

It's time we stopped kidding ourselves! The continuation of the illegal immigration from Mexico is the direct intention of our government. When a government enforces a law, we are inclined to think that the enforcement is their duty. However, when a government does not enforce the law, we are inclined to think that perhaps it is their choice. It is not. Not when it concerns the security of our borders. Of course there are reasons for our government's overt support for the illegal immigration on the southern border.

Since the end of the 'Cold War', our international companies have turned their attention and swayed the attention of our government toward the domination of world economics without concern for the domestic consequences. This variation on the economic system is referred to as the neo-liberal economic system and is generally understood as globalization. It is part and parcel of the modern democratic theory as expounded by the United States and is to be imposed upon the rest of the world, by force if necessary. Even our children understand by now that globalization favors corporate profits above the common good, or anything else.

The most obvious example of the effects of globalization in this country is our relationship with Asia. Over the past few years, we have not only outsourced our jobs, but have moved our manufacturing to the Asian countries, especially China and India. Corporate money has influenced our government to allow the transfer of practically any business into these new rising economies at the expense of American jobs. There are two major reasons for this interest. First, Asia is seen as the future of economic progress because of their tremendous population and potential buying power. Second, labor and manufacturing plant is so cheap that exorbitant profits can be made when Asian manufactures are sold here; at American prices of course.

It is not difficult to understand that when the cost of plant and equipment is about half of the costs required in the United States, and labor costs are only 10% of the costs in the United States, corporations will naturally choose to manufacture in Asia. Our government officials are no longer concerned about the common good of its citizens; rather they are interested in their personal gain to be acquired through corporate influence.

At home, our service industries can only exist as long as there is enough money circulating among the middle and lower classes to support the consumerism. Our financial industry can only continue to exist as long as the asset bubble continues. Our only real source of income is our military weapons business. We supply most of the world's weapons. Where does the money come from to maintain our economy? It is the consistent growth of our national and personal debts that maintains the momentum of our economy. Our government needs to maintain that momentum for a while longer.

As far as our corporations are concerned, the writing is on the wall. Real, or long-term investment will be made in Asia where a huge population with rising incomes will eventually dominate the economic world. The unemployed population in China alone is greater than the entire population of the United States. As the income of the average American citizen continues to erode, we are viewed by the corporate world as a mature market. The United States is no longer a prime market for investment. It is time to reap the profits of past investments and maintain the cash cow as long as possible, or at least until a prosperous Asian economy can be built.

Unfortunately, it is obvious that our government supports this corporate view, regardless of what their lips tell us.

A few years ago, these investments would not have happened. There were laws against unfair trade, concerning environmental issues, unfair labor practices, and a plethora of other rules and considerations for the public good. In the past few years many of these laws have been expunged or relaxed in the name of deregulation to allow for the international exploitation of labor. This is our government at work in behalf of their corporate constituencies.

Lest they lose their corporate sponsors, our media is now blaming Asia and especially China for the loss of our jobs and their excessive use of 'our' oil. It is our own government that encourages companies to invest in foreign countries, even to the point of awarding tax breaks for doing so. It is our own government that is encouraging the displacement of American workers with cheaper foreign workers. China is not the villain here. It is our own government encouraging and aiding international corporations to move their business overseas in search of that Holy Grail, profits.

What about corporations that are not international in nature? Our government is doing its best to take care of them as well. It has deliberately brought in well over twenty million illegal Mexicans to work at menial wages and continues to dilute the work force. Of course, the government will explain that farm labor is still in short supply and we need more workers there. It seems that 'illegals' don't want to farm either. They are coming in faster than the great immigration of the late nineteenth and early twentieth century. To be sure many of them eventually earn more than minimum wages. However, they can secure few, if any rights and are treated poorly. They do not generally get health benefits, nor do they get retirement benefits. Just as the international companies can exploit cheap labor, a similar arrangement has been made for the national companies. Labor is arbitraged just as any other commodity.

Our population is estimated at somewhat less than three hundred million people. If we have only twenty million illegal immigrants, it means that one out of every fifteen people in this country is illegal. It is a significantly higher portion in the work force.

Notice that even in the rebuilding of New Orleans, the prevailing labor rates will not be paid to workers. The contracts will be generally given out without competitive bidding at cost plus, to insure corporate profits to preferred companies. Restricting labor expenses will be the only means to hold down costs. For some strange reason there seems to be a shortage of workers. The government is bringing people willing to work from Central America. Is this because construction is just one more type of work that Americans won't do? Many of them will probably remain in this country to further dilute the work force. Meanwhile the poor of New Orleans have been dispersed around the country and will probably not be heard from again.

Reducing labor costs is the mantra of our time. This first attempt to dismantle Social Security is only the beginning. Many of our corporations are hiring illegal immigrants and do not pay any benefits. Other corporations will soon be crying that they cannot compete if they have to pay for health benefits or pension plans or perhaps even paid holidays. Our government intends to get cheap labor for their corporations by leveling the labor of the world at the expense of the American citizen. We have embraced a Darwinian system of economics to the detriment of our citizens! Or is this the Intelligent Design at work? In either case, it looks like plain old government sponsored greed.

Chapter 12   Essays of Thomas Dawson: Coin of the Realm

By Thomas Dawson

November 14, 2005

Since World War II our political entanglements with the rest of the world have been increasingly, rightly or wrongly, intended to secure or engender the business interests of our corporations. Suddenly our international companies are enamored with the opportunities to move labor-intensive segments of their business to foreign lands. They now view the United States as only a temporary cash cow; a mature market to be used until faster growing markets can be developed elsewhere. At the same time, the interests of these corporations, who indirectly control our domestic economy, are often at odds with the welfare of our middle class. Corporate America has bought and paid for the influence of our politicians and since the end of the "cold war" they have been systematically reducing their liabilities and responsibilities with respect to the people that work for them in the quest for greater profits.

The primary and driving force of corporations is profit and this is as it should be. These corporations make up the engine of the American economy. However, the continued displacement of middle class jobs, which are flowing out of the country at alarming rates, and the eroding standard of living, are the result of this same kind of thinking, and is encouraged by our present political structure. But, lest we forget, these United States were not intended as a land "of the corporation, by the corporation and for the corporation".

The national debt, trade deficits, middle class wage erosion, immigration problems, health care costs, and a plethora of other national problems are all related to the political reality of "American style free trade" expanding throughout the world in the last quarter century. We are told that these are normal, sequential economic changes taking place within our political system. Not so. The primary causation of most of these changes is the direct result of political pandering to corporate interests by our elected officials. Legislation should have some consideration of the "people" mentioned by our founding fathers.

The standard of living for the middle class in this country has not improved in the last quarter century. In fact, it has declined for the vast majority of Americans. Real wages have fallen more than 6%. Yet the GNP really is up! Because our (domestic?) companies are really making record profits! Our corporations are awash in money. At the same time the country is currently acquiring nearly THREE BILLION dollars of new debt through the trade deficit every day! Consider the National Debt. Disgraceful, and dangerous! A lot of other things are also going on here. This is a direct result of political pandering for corporate money. Politics is a very lucrative "profession". (Hardly anyone is doing this as a public service)

The truth is that politicians cannot survive without hoards of money. Ask anyone who has ever run for office how much it costs. Certainly the man on the street cannot support them. So where do they get it? Who has it? Only large corporations can make large contributions regularly over long periods of time. Most of it is given to the party's themselves so they can keep members in line through the use of the money spigot.

Not so long ago, this seemed like a reasonably good idea. Most of the large companies were entirely domestic and employed many people. The import/export companies were either bringing money into the country or buying products not available here. Many companies took on an international flavor while we were rebuilding Europe and Japan after WWII with their captive markets. Large amounts of money were acquired by American companies, along with a great deal of knowledge about other countries' economies and politics. Great sums of money were spent on R&D and any new technology from around the world was developed quickly by the large US companies. All this employment was one of the major factors in building the American middle class. "What's good for General Motors is good for the Country" seemed to be a pretty accurate phrase if not an accurate quote. A direct connection between domestic GNP and the domestic standard of living was just assumed to be the natural condition. Unfortunately, in a few short years, this assumption would be ruptured.

In the middle 50's and 60's we began to see some interesting changes. We began to increase the imports of foreign goods, and some of our companies began to build plants in foreign countries and even exported products back home. Volkswagen began to sell cars over here. We could now buy an English Ford. This was good business for everyone. Business around the world was heating up. Everyone seemed to understand the rules and we all did well. The Japanese suddenly burst on the scene. By the end of the 70's and into the 80's their quality cars were the best buy for the money. They had the best quality and Americans bought them. American car companies had manipulated the auto market for years for their own benefit and now the Japanese were encroaching on their very survival.

Fortunately, Reagan was made to understand that we could not just watch such a large section of the middle class workforce go down the drain. He effectively limited the number of Japanese imports. When the Japanese asked to build automobiles over here and employ Americans, he invited them in. It was not the corporation he was protecting, it was the middle class American workforce. (This ridiculous, Pro-American concern for the citizen did not go unnoticed by our growing international corporations and was soon to be changed.) The American manufacturers quickly improved the quality of their products and regained much of their reputation. Again, business was good for everybody.

Many corporations, especially those with international interests became extremely powerful as they did more business than many countries. It is only natural that they would want to extend their influence. For corporations this large, there is only one place of effective influence and that is the politician, domestic and foreign.

As large corporations are always looking for a profit advantage, they could hardly help noticing the disparity in wages between the developed countries and the under-developed ones. Japan has no natural resources and cannot compete with countries that do. They have to import, add value, and then export to make a profit. Business was so good that as their standard of living rose and they were over-employed, they "outsourced" the labor and for a few years had an enviable economy (read corporate profits). (Remember Japan bashing?) Other international companies soon began to follow when the "cold war" came to a close.

This kind of business was obviously not within the range of Reagan's pro-American thinking, but who cared? Corporations were making plenty of money and political contributions were rolling in! By the end of the 90's the world economy had so heated up that politicians easily convinced us that outsourcing cheap labor would not hurt the developed countries and that it would be of great benefit to the under-developed ones if only work rules, environmental considerations, and other regulations would be removed. (How benevolent they had become!) Besides, their corporate benefactors could make a lot of money. We were having a domestic technology boom not unlike the automotive boom of the twenties. The slow-down (recession) of the early 90's seemed like a blip in an ever-growing world economic boom.

To really make the corporations happy, the government got into the act with a bill to open so-called "free trade zones". And thus, NAFTA was born. This bill was sold as raising the Mexican standard of living and creating thousands of

American jobs. A win, win bill! No one seriously believed American jobs would be created! In just a few short years this labor arbitrage has reduced the average wage in Mexico to about half of what it was before NAFTA. Our corporations were doing very well, because now they had something just as good as or perhaps better than a free trade zone.

They arranged another form of arbitrage, outsourcing their labor to Asian countries. Why pay 50 cents an hour to a Mexican when the Asians will work for 25 cents? The politicians even found ways to pay their corporate benefactors to outsource, by offering them tax breaks for doing it! No one can compete with Corporate America! Certainly the American citizen can't!

Big farm Corporations have been trying to control congress since the 1930's. They have learned well and now other large corporations emulate them. All kinds of moneys are spent by the farm lobbies on strong incumbent congressmen and their families to "educate them" on the reasons for, and the importance of farm subsidies and other corporate interests.

Along with his family and personal 'educational' benefits, the incumbent congressman will often get considerable moneys as contributions to his election campaign. Even larger contributions are made to his party (both parties for control purposes); of which his share will trickle down to him from a number of sources as long as he does not depart from the party interests (read corporate interests).

It's not hard to get a Congressman from Iowa to support a farm subsidy bill. It's a little harder to get a Delaware or Massachusetts Congressman to support it. One might think that this would take a bit of doing, as many times the congressman must support those things that are a direct detriment to his voting constituents. Most of the time however, his opponent will not even challenge him on these highly financed issues because his own funds from the party are controlled at a higher level. This system works so well that even pharmaceutical companies now spend rafts of money to "educate" doctors and their families at various resorts around the country. Currently, the pharmaceuticals are even "donating" to the FDA (for our benefit, of course). Understand that politicians can and do pass laws to benefit themselves, this is all perfectly legal

At this point in time, the voter has been effectively disenfranchised. It is not that he does not have a choice; it is only that there is no choice. Whoever runs for office is beholden to the corporations for the money that is a necessary prerequisite to attain and retain the office. This, in effect, is the new democratic "one party" or "corporate party" system.

The politician and his family live in a world filled with both perks and promise. If he cooperates and is in office for any considerable length of time, he is practically guaranteed a plum lifetime job consulting or lobbying for these same companies and thus greasing the wheels of other politicians. (Responsible companies always reward their good soldiers.)

The heavy hand of corporate influence on the members of congress is not a new problem. It has been a festering problem since the earliest days of our country. When the great majority of citizens were farmers, it didn't seem that lobbyists could do much harm. As corporate America grew and farming became more efficient, the trend was for more Americans to leave the farms and become employees of these new corporations.

In the last part of the nineteenth century, thinking people were becoming concerned that the interests of Corporate America and the country as a whole were not of a like nature. There was much concern that corporate money was controlling the outcome of most of the laws in this country, and something should be done to curb this influence. In his annual message to the congress in 1907, President Theodore Roosevelt stated "The need for collecting large campaign funds would vanish if Congress provided an appropriation for the proper and legitimate expenses of each of the great national parties, an appropriation ample enough to meet the necessity for thorough organization and machinery, which requires a great expenditure of money. Then the stipulation should be made that no party receiving campaign funds from the Treasury should accept more than a fixed amount from any individual subscriber or donor, and the necessary publicity for receipts and expenditures could without difficulty be provided." This is an idea that is still mentioned from time to time.

Many, if not most of the legislation that is enacted helps one group of people at the expense of another. Such is the nature of laws. Laws against cartels and monopolies in favor of fairness to the other corporations and indeed the citizens are necessary and good for the health of our country, but only if the government chooses to enforce them.

Laws passed against the middle class Americans in favor of powerful corporations are not good for the health of our country. In theory, the elected officials are supposed to represent the voting public, not the corporate contributors. Passing legislation that will erode the middle class for the benefit of corporate profits is a crime against the citizenry.

You cannot blame a rat as a thief if you allow it to steal grain, nor blame a cat as a murderer if you allow it to kill rats. That is the very nature of these animals. You cannot blame corporations if you allow them to buy politicians. This is indeed the very nature of this animal. To paraphrase Milton Friedman, "Corporate executives, provided they stay within the law, have no responsibilities in their business activities other than to make as much money for their stockholders as possible." That is why we need laws and regulations, to determine exactly what is to be allowed. You can and should blame politicians for selling out their trust of the people. No longer does anyone except perhaps some relatives and political associates hold politicians in high regard. That is why we need laws and regulations, to determine exactly what is to be allowed and what is not.

You can and should blame corrupt politicians for selling out their trust of the people. They are committing overt crimes against the voters of these United States. Politics and Crime have become two faces of the same coin. Unfortunately, in the United States it has become coin of the realm.

Sources

http://www.americanchronicle.com/articles/534-- Illegal Aliens and Immigration, June 3, 2005

http://www.americanchronicle.com/articles/613-- All Immigration problems Solved, June 11, 2005

http://www.americanchronicle.com/articles/2884-- Labor Arbitrage? Better Known as Cheap Labor, October 12, 2005

http://www.americanchronicle.com/articles/3693 -- Coin of the Realm, November 14, 2005

Chapter 13   The Rise of Corporate Power & the New Robber Barons

The Union Is Not Perfect

Merriam Webster defines capitalism as an economic system characterized by private or corporate ownership of capital goods, by investments that are determined by private decision, and by prices, production, and the distribution of goods that are determined mainly by competition in a free market. In the "Logic of Action, 1997" Murray N. Rothbard defines state capitalism as consisting of

> "one or more groups making use of the coercive apparatus of the government... for themselves by expropriating the production of others by force and violence."

Today, Rothbard's groups are corporations that in one way or another have an unholy alliance with government and receive assistance or approval for their "work" from the government and they receive favorable legislation from our representatives.

And you thought this was going to be a fun book? One of the problems that we have today in the US, and one of the many in which our elected representatives have taken a pass is the increasingly negative notion of the corporation. At this point, I am not talking just about corporate greed.

Corporations Are Citizens

The theme of this chapter is much more basic than stopping corporate greed. A quick read of the Constitution and you will not see anything about Corporations as quasi-citizens or having any legitimate right to exist. The Founding Fathers hated the mere idea of corporations as they had seen the impact on England.

In their present form, there is so much abuse and potential for abuse that perhaps corporations should wholesale be eliminated. But, before they are fully gone, a citizens board needs to watch over their predatory actions against the population, and after they are gone, their assets need to be distributed to "companies" equitably, if that is even possible. .

So we are all on the same page, let's take a quick look at what makes up a corporation. What exactly is a corporation?

A corporation is a nonhuman entity. It is a fictitious citizen because it has no meat and bones, but it operates in most other ways as a citizen and it has some attributes, such as stock issuance that a citizen does not have or need. Investor Words provides us with this definition

> The most common form of business organization, and one which is chartered by a state and given many legal rights as an entity separate from its owners. This form of business is characterized by the *limited liability* of its owners, the issuance of shares of easily transferable *stock*, and existence as a *going concern*.
>
> The process of becoming a corporation, called incorporation, gives the company separate legal standing from its owners and protects those owners from being personally liable in the event that the company is sued (a condition known as limited liability).

Incorporation also provides companies with a more flexible way to manage their ownership structure. In addition, there are different *tax* implications for corporations, although these can be both advantageous and disadvantageous. In these respects, corporations differ from *sole proprietorships* and *limited partnerships*.

Before we begin to discuss the numerous reasons why corporations are built to get out of control and are absolutely out of control, let's take a few pokes at the government of the United States from more than 200 years ago. The first notion that helped corporations become implied citizens came about in the Marbury v. Madison case of 1803. Please note that the current Supreme Court and the Executive offices are not the first to have played with our Constitution.

This case established the concept of judicial review, which sounds like an OK thing but it tips the balance of power of the three levels of government to the Supreme Court. The founding fathers never intended a tipping of the balance. In 1803, the Supreme Court ruled that they were "Supreme" and the Congress at the time did not fully evaluate what this meant and the fools did not contest it.

This, in essence gave the Supreme Court the power to make law. Oh, they can't propose legislation and have it voted upon, but this small group of nine got the power from an unawake Congress to divine the "real intentions" of the authors of any law upon which they get to rule, even if the law had nothing to do with their divinations.

Using its power to divine intent -- even the intent of the Constitution, in 1889, in the Minneapolis & St. Louis Railroad Co. v. Beckwith case, the Supreme Court, in one of its worst rulings of all time, declared that a corporation is a person for both due process and equal protection under the process. Since Shakespeare's time It's been argued that "something is rotten in the state of Denmark." The 1889 Supreme Court decision helped begin the decay of the potential for the American dream, unless, of course, you have no flesh. And that, my dear readers is a travesty. The damage is done but it must be undone. Unless the Obama czars steal away our rights, the people still have the power, and we need to act judiciously through the Congress.

Money, Corporations and the Ruling Class

Because of all the money that passes through corporations, the Ruling Class through their corporate power, have more rights than the people. This commonly accepted notion of a corporation, that it is like a person, goes way too far and shifts the power from sovereign individuals. If we were a country in which ethics and morals were the guiding principles, this would not be such a bad deal for the people.

It was bad in 1889 with the "Robber Barons," but today, in the "me" generation, ethics and morals often are not even afforded lip service. Today in fact, the blatant greed of corporations and their owners is ever visible as one worker after another is losing his or her jobs to lower paid foreigners, and one corrupt corporate officer after another is being indicted for violating the public trust. In my home town of Wilkes-Barre PA, Pennsylvania judges and other politicos are going to jail after careers of stiffing the constituency. The fact that they have been indicted and have been convicted in many cases actually is a major sign of hope.

As hopeful as we may be, in the great bailouts of 2008 and 2009, the principle that a corporate entity might be too big to fail has become something of which to be concerned. Check the Constitution and you will find nothing that says the people are to bail out poorly run corporations merely because they can't make a buck in a free market. Yet, the government now owns General Motors and Chrysler and a good many of the nation's financial institutions. By not adhering to the principles of survival of the fittest, the action of our government has blessed a future in which these major corporations and others too big to fail have a built-in permanent weakness. They do not have to excel to exceed. They can actually fail again and use the people's treasury to bail them out while lining their pockets with cash. This means that the rich Ruling Class no longer have to risk their capital to succeed. They now risk ours as held by the US Treasury, and this must end now.

Exxon the Money Machine

By the way, in the 1990's IBM lost $13 billion. It was quite devastating for IBM and Mr. Akers, the Chair. Yet, it is nothing compared with Exxon's single quarter profits. In February, 2008 the oil giant made corporate history by logging in a sweet $11.7 billion for just three month's work. That is some corporate citizen.

The math majors quickly translated the Exxon profit news for the John Doe's out here by noting that its 2007 earnings could also be stated as $1,300 a second. Before the huge executive salaries payoffs and other company expenses were subtracted, the company grossed about $350 billion for the year.

$45.22 Billion Profit for 2008

In my wildest dreams when I wrote the first edition of this book, I could not see revenues topping $400,000,000,000 in 2008. Hey, as life got more miserable for the taxpayer, in 2008, the economy busting excessive gas and oil prices had a huge impact on Exxon. Even those who predicted good times, never saw how the corporate greed factor could ever pull in such unbelievable record revenue of $477,851,000,000 for 2008. In my humble opinion, these record profits began the economic downfall that assured a Republican defeat and assured Barack Obama's victory as change was definitely needed.

Corporations and Government Collusion

Though I listen daily as the new Commander in Chief appears even more petulant daily in the news proselytizing his agenda, I have heard nary a whimper on the evils of corporations -- oil or otherwise. Yet, I have seen much of the national treasury dumped out for those corporations that had no idea of how to be a success. If I were able to check further, I am sure I would find wads of cash from contrived payoff business deals heading for the treasuries of the corporations that helped the President get elected. Using the people's treasury to pay off huge corporations seems to be an acceptable practice nowadays, though it is blatantly dishonest. The wallets of the corporate titans are wide open and they are being filled.

In my IBM career, I recall that IBM once grossed more than Exxon. IBM is now about a $100 billion dollar company and Exxon is $477 billion. GE is in between these two now in revenue but its capitalization is through the roof -- # 1 -- maybe # 2. It is the most successful real company (not oil) in the world.

Way back when the government often worked for the people, it took it upon itself to sue IBM because it was a monopoly. Somehow as big as it was, it was OK for Exxon to acquire Mobil Oil and yet they still have not yet been tagged a monopoly -- and this is a democratic administration. What gives?

Exxon is the biggest of all of the modern day corporate Robber Barons for sure. Its history reeks of Robberbaranesque gains while the common people had no idea what was going on. But, they seemingly do not have to worry about anti-trust action because they helped President Bush get elected and reelected. He will be forever grateful. IBM could only wish that it were big and fat enough to be accused again of being a monopoly. So, now why, other

than not allowing any more oil drilling off coast is President
Obama so quiet about this oil monopoly. Is there oil money
in his war chest? It has been reported that in the campaign, he
got 20% and McCain got 80%. Who knows? But, we should
know in a "transparent" government.

The Robber Barons Are Back

There are many who believe in their hearts and many others
who have actual proof that the Robber Baron days are back
again but this time the human perpetrators are not being
identified since a corporate veil hides them from public
scrutiny -- unless they get too greedy. So, unlike the 1890s
we do not see names of heralded industrial leaders such as
John D. Rockefeller (pictured as King of the world in Figure
10-1 below courtesy of usinfo.state.gov.), Cornelius
Vanderbilt, Grenville Dodge, Leland Stanford, Henry
Villard, James J. Hill, and others who in the days before the
20th century got that nasty label, "Robber Barons."

Figure 13-1 Standard Oil Monopoly - circa 1890

These were rich and very enlightened people, yet they were cutthroat competitors operating as entrepreneurs with minimal restrictions. They committed thinly veiled acts of stealing to improve their resources at the expense of their customers and employees. This is the image of the greedy, exploitative capitalist that I want you to have as you consider that just like JAWS, they're b-a-a-a-a-ck!

There are some real bad guys today in corporations but the one, never convicted of any crime, who gets a lot of press for being a modern day Robber Baron is none other than the richest man in the world, William Gates III. Rudolf J. R. Peretz's online book for usinfo.state.gov, full URL shown in sources at end of chapter shows then Microsoft president Bill Gates testifying before the Senate in 1998, at a hearing on anti-competitive issues and technology.

Like Rockefeller before him, Gates was accused of running a monopoly - this time computer software rather than oil. Peretz notes that the distinction between a legitimate, if large, business and an impermissible monopoly is still a work in progress. The picture of Gates captured in his book is shown below in Figure 13-2. A second picture immediately follows.

From Yahoo Answers: *a robber baron is someone that uses unfair tactics for their personal gain they sometimes might use illegal business practices*

> "To some, Bill Gates has become the robber baron of the late 20th century (2) who engages in the classical monopolist behavior that the anti-trust legislation of the United States is specifically designed to prevent. In this view, Microsoft is gouging virtually everyone on the planet through artificially high software prices that it can enforce by intimidating peers and competitors alike.
>
> Bill Gates, well known for his competitiveness, has simply let success go to his head. His fears about non-existent competitive forces have made him paranoid.

To protect its dominant position and to maximize revenue and net income, Microsoft is stifling competition and software innovation.

In the robber baron view, the Department of Justice is right on target in its efforts to clip the wings of Microsoft and allow more competition into the world of operating systems and application software."

Figure 13-2 Bill Gates, Modern Robber Baron?

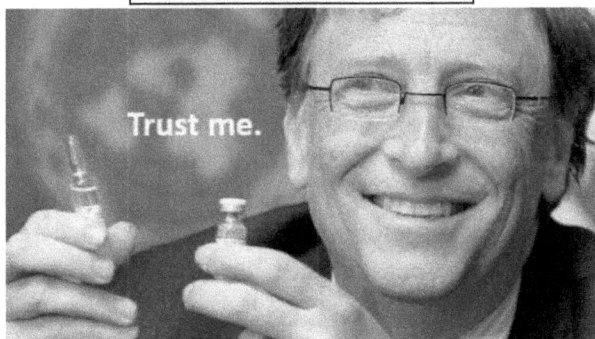

Trust me.

Arthur Anderson - The Bottom of the Rubble Pile

Recent history tells us that in the early 2000's, companies like Enron (not Exxon), Global Crossings and others made the news for their management's utter disregard for corporate or human ethics as they operated in a corrupt manner motivated by greed and then they lied to protect their gains. These corporate titans were made temporary heroes, but it was not that long that their actions put their companies out of business, creating havoc not just for the rich and the well-to-do but also for small investors whose entire pensions were eliminated. If today's overly greedy and corrupt corporate citizen's need a face, it's the face of Enron, or Global Crossings, and for good measure, let's throw in the worst face of them all, Arthur "trust-me, I'm an auditor" Anderson.

Bernie Madoff had not even been born yet. OK, he was but he had not yet been discovered by our billion dollar bank examiners. In the wake of the biggest corporate scandal of all time, in 2008, the banks were about to collapse, GM and Chrysler were about to go under and everybody's pensions made them look like they had chosen not to save for a rainy day. Could corporations have again been the cause?

Going back just a bit in time, but in the same spirit of a thief such as Bernie Madoff, Arthur Anderson, later reformed as *Accenture* after its scandal, attested to the falsifications of huge corporate clients such as Enron. Before its demise, Arthur Andersen Consulting swore on a stack of bibles that they did no wrong.

Still other companies such as Adelphia and even Martha Stewart Living found ways to stiff the public of its financial opportunities while they made or hoped to make a killing for themselves. Is Bernie Madoff serving time for all of the thieves in the banking industry? Why is he the only one there? Their greed created major hardships for many people and they too should do time with Bernie. They can make a movie out of it.

Call it "greed." And remember that the famous Philosopher Eric Fromm saw greed as "...a bottomless pit which exhausts the person in an endless effort to satisfy the need without ever reaching satisfaction." Sounds like Fromm had been talking to Twilight Zone's Rod Serling. With men and women of greed instead of creed in positions of trust, running the corporations of America, what better should we expect? In 2010, we notice a bit of a shift in power. The government has assumed all power, or so it seems. Government greed and the current Administration's lust for power is endless.

Corporations that played ball with the government in the latter part of 2009, were a phenomenal source of capital for the government and its minions -- or better yet, the corporate minions, and the government contracts they controlled. Can you imagine all that money that needed to be given. Though corporations have no hands, they were first in line t fill the company coffers with good old green government cash. Considering what has really happened, it is highly improbable that the change the young voters were looking for in 2008 has come yet or is coming any time soon. Greed as usual is business as usual.

In this corporate world, there is enough money at stake that the notion of "you lie and I'll swear to it" has taken root and is SOP. Consequently, there is always an abundance of liars to go around the corporate boardroom, devising and agreeing to schemes to bilk the unknowing of their hard earned income And, just like Arthur Anderson, now sunning in a new corporate form in Bermuda as Accenture, there are still enough swearers out there to match the liars. These complicit corporate auditing firms are willing to look the other way or give a customary wink and a nod in order to sustain and grow their own business opportunities. After all, who wants to lose a "client" on a technicality?

Time for a Structural Change

You don't have to look far anymore to find somebody out there willing to give up integrity in a heart-beat to increase their bank accounts. It is a real shame. Bob Yanelavage, a barber in Plymouth PA, runs his small business on Main Street. By all accounts, Bob thinks that people should be honest and that's that. Yet, Bob is a very smart guy and he knows that we are all hurting partly because our representatives are not honest. They hide under the radar and they are disinterested in the people's business.

Corporations exist because dishonorable representatives such as these, say they should!

The whole notion of corporations and the huge tractor trailer loads of cash they handle clearly provides more seedy opportunities than the normal executive or politician can resist. And so we, who elect those who give corporations their power, reap what we have sewn. It's time to demand a change. Go ahead and get a haircut to make your point.

And, when you go to Bob's shop, make sure you tell him thanks just for being a great American. He is a small businessman who thinks of people first, and profit second. Profit will come if the people see the quality and value in his service. So, why doesn't every politician have to be something else before they become a politician? And, I am sorry, community organizer does not fill the bill as a real job.

Some Attempts at Correction

There is some hope on the horizon. For example, the Sarbanes-Oxley act and other laws are written to minimize obvious corruption. Now, if only the bill could be properly applied to the actions of the legislature. Laws, such as Sarbanes-Oxley, have surely helped the situation by making it more difficult for corporations to cheat. But, the basic notion that greed trumps all is too much to expect that anything has really changed.

Boardroom operations have not magically become directed towards the good of the country or the good of the consumer or the good of the employees just because a few new laws are on the books. A few more prosecutions would help. In fact, a lot more prosecutions would help.

Name Some Names

Just as in the original Robber Baron days , we know who the
individual perpetrators are since their names are on the
indictments. If it were not for indictments, however, these
@$%^&%$#@ would continue to be anonymous, clipping
the fabric of the U.S.A. every chance they get and admitting
nothing.   You know that more are out there to be discovered
but they surely are busy covering their tracks.

In this age we have seen names like the late Ken Lay of
Enron and Gary Winnick of Global Crossings, both
associated with corporate corruption at its max. And, of
course the face of corruption in 2009, Bernie Madoff. Unless
caught, the Lays and Winnicks, and Madoffs, and the new
barons, still operating behind the corporate veil, are
unrepentant and continually in denial. We should deal with
them all by watching them even closer. Until we see a
paradigm shift in boardroom ethics, we should not expect
any better behavior. Why? Because the stakes are so high and
because we know from Eric Fromm that greed is bottomless.

Bernie Madoff is gone but his sins live on. Anybody can
become rich. The rich, who were taken so badly by Madoff
are not the corporate titans, impervious to a few rocks in the
market. The Madoff investors were not as sophisticated.
They reportedly were not well diversified. They trusted
Bernie. The earnings font appeared never ending. They
really got taken for a ride. They foolishly mortgaged homes
and properties for cash and converted other wealth to cash to
give to Bernie so they could be part in the Madoff "can't-lose"
Ponzi scheme. To them, It was a sure thing. They saw little
risk because Bernie would handle it. Yet most of these folks
who started with everything, wound up with nothing. And,
no friends in government lined up to help.

Bernie's clients took a bath and were not bailed out at all. The
big rich did not take care of the little rich. The corporate
moguls took care of themselves and let the little guys like

Bernie's clients take the full rap. AIG and Fannie and
Freddie and Citibank and Goldman Sachs initially took a
bath but their friends in the Congress of our United States
bailed them out. They were too big to fail. Stockholders were
bailed out and their executives still got their bonuses while
Bernie's people are now washing dishes. Corporations are not
fair but government is less fair.

My Friend, the Government

In his book, The Truth About the "Robber Barons," author
Thomas Di Lorenzo defines a *market entrepreneur* as a
capitalist who succeeds financially by selling a newer, better,
or less expensive product, on the free market, with no
government subsidies, direct or indirect. He must please his
customer to get the business since the consumer is the final
determinant as to who gets the sale. He sees a *political
entrepreneur* as one who succeeds primarily by influencing
government to subsidize his business or industry or to enact
legislation or regulation that harms his competitors.

In his book, The Big Rip-off: How Big Business and Big
Government Steal Your Money, author Timothy P. Carney
dispels the widespread myth that Big Business and Big
Government are rivals -- that Big Business wants small
government, a "level playing field" and a "bare minimum of
regulation." Carney says, "Not so," and he demonstrates in
his book how some big businesses, more than you may think,
together with elected officials of both parties, are doing
everything possible to replace America's robust free market
with a web of government handouts, stricter regulation,
higher taxes, and other special favors to stifle competition.
The losers: smaller competitors, less established businesses,
consumers, employees, and taxpayers. The bottom line losers
-- you and I. Has the Obama administration changed this
notion or exacerbated it?

So the modern Robber Baron, the corporation has a partner in crime, the US government. From our work in Chapters 1 through 9, we know that the Constitution does not deal specifically with the notion that government and industry would collude against the people. Who would have ever thought that such controls would be necessary?

The Founding Fathers could not conceive that the representatives of the people would sell out the people. Corporations were not a big part of the landscape in America in the 18th century, and the prevailing thought on the English corporations was disdain and contempt. One could extend, that if there were as many corporations as today, the Founding Fathers would have created a much thicker Constitution and corporations would be subjugated overall to the will of the people. .

America, long the land of the free and the home of the brave and the land of unlimited opportunity is becoming the land of corporate-only opportunity. Without working through conspiracy theories which I do not subscribe to, the facts show that regular Americans are under attack in our own country on many fronts. Our government, through our representatives, many of questionable character, has chosen to ignore the Constitution that we do have as it passes "illegal" laws that the legislators themselves often choose not to read.

Lap dog corporations seem to love lap dog representatives and they make a beautiful team. The friendly corporation meets the friendly representative. They take turns opening their wallets to receive their due tribute for services rendered. Corporations always stand ready to gain more power and influence and profit for the Ruling Class. With the vast resources corporations have, and the more they are given by our lawmakers, the more dangerous it is to be in their crosshairs by design or by accident.

Corporations have no reason to like you as a member of the
citizenry, and they don't like you, and they never will. In
fact, when they look into the mirror and see a soulless
nothing that takes and never gives, they do not even like
themselves. Even the corporate officers must get a little sick
to their stomachs thinking about their own personal greed
and selfishness. Yet, even in melancholy, the corporate titan
of yesterday or today is pleased to crush anything that
attempts to diminish its opportunity for more profits. If you
happen to be in its way, check your healthcare policy if you
still have one!

The Old-Time Robber Barons

The Robber Barons in their heyday were involved in lots of
big ventures. One such opportunity was the building of the
transcontinental railroad. Don't think for a minute that the
railroad barons used only their own money. What we know
today as corporate welfare was well practiced even in the
19th century. There were those at the time that felt that the
free market could not have come up with adequate capital to
create the railroad that crossed the entire continent.

The Union Pacific and the Central Pacific received subsidies
based on each mile of track laid. They received low interest
"loans" and big land grants to assure the right-of-ways. Other
large projects however, such as the Great Northern Railroad
were financed privately. Thus the Union Pacific and Central
Pacific railroads received welfare from the people and the
Great Northern had to do it by itself. It doesn't seem fair does
it? A wise man once said, "It isn't what you know, it's who
you know," and those with government connections, the
political entrepreneurs always have the edge on the market
entrepreneurs when competing for the same markets.

Figure 13-3 Good Old Fashioned Robber Baron Depiction (Web)

The smell of collusion was rampant in the building of the subsidized railways. For example there was a lot of politicking but Jay Cooke, an American financier who made a ton in financial markets used so much of his own money in the Northern Pacific Railroad, that he went bankrupt and sold his shares for pennies on the dollar. He was not too pleased that the Government backed the Union Pacific and Central Pacific as they built the first transcontinental railroad. Wikipedia chronicles the history of the transaction quite well on its site. Congress passed the necessary legislation and subsidies. Is GM the new Union Pacific and is Chrysler the Central Pacific? What would that make Ford—an American Car Company?

The railroad construction was planned by Theodore Judah. The Congress gave the OK in 1862 and some independent financing came from other magnates who participated in the building. They were known both as the Big Four and as the Associates. These four were Sacramento, California businessmen Leland Stanford, Collis Huntington, Charles Crocker, and Mark Hopkins. The group entrusted Crocker with the construction mission. Much of the labor was provided by Chinese workers, who like today's illegal foreign nationals, worked for a pittance.

Not only did these magnates make out on the deal, so did the politicians. Their perks included things that you don't see unless you pay attention. For example what looks like a railroad bed for industry may not really be so. The perks included separate rail lines besides those heading cross country. These were required to be built to serve communities represented by influential members of Congress even if those lines were uneconomical. How about a nice set of tracks right up to the side door of your home?

Railroads and Scranton, PA

There has been rumor in Scranton Pennsylvania (true or not?) for years that the coal baron family of former Governor Scranton had a caboose or two and an engine ready to go at the drop of a hat on their property in the event that the coal miners were to strike. Nobless oblige was not always the major concern of the wealthy. John Murtha is ready at all times to take off from the infamous John Murtha Airport and there is always a seat in the snack bar, the main concourse, the men's room, and anywhere else that you look. Echoes are also commonplace at the John Murtha International Airport, but there is nobody there to hear them..

The Robber Barons of the 19th Century had it all and like the corporate billionaires of today basically they could do whatever they wanted. They owned all of the means of production and they had full control over the components of production, material, labor, finished products, and even distribution. There was nobody to get in their way other than the government. Somehow during this time, the government, instead of monitoring and controlling, were colluding with and subsidizing Robber Barons, helping them get richer and richer while the poor were getting poorer and poorer. Workers had no voice. There were no really powerful unions. There were no laws to protect workers from abuse or assure their safety or to protect the environment from the waste that industry was producing.

The Robber Barons rewarded their political allies and like a 21st century video game, they tried to destroy their enemies. They were not beyond colluding with the government (our trusted representatives) or their competitors in restraint of trade so long as this aided them in their pursuit of wealth. They had little regard for the consequences of the acquisition of such wealth. They were as greedy as greedy could get and though they helped America achieve great innovations, they did so on the backs of the poor.

As Samuel Clemens noticed, America has the best politicians money can buy.

http://www.informationclearinghouse.info/article3925.htm

The Plight of the Worker

For the next 100 years after the Declaration of Independence, The United States was largely an agricultural nation. Unskilled workers fared poorly in the early U.S. economy. They received as little as half the pay of skilled craftsmen, artisans, and mechanics. Forty percent or so of the workers in the bigger cities, not involved in agriculture, worked for low wages. They served as general laborers, seamstresses in clothing factories, or other mass production undertakings.

In many ways, other than the general American opportunity, the common worker lived most always in dismal circumstances. With the rise of industrial factories, children, women, and an ever increasing supply of poor immigrants were commonly employed to run the machines. Is there any question as to why the Illegal immigrant of 2010 is well appreciated by the "Barons" of today.

Labor Arbitrage -- The Lowest Wage

As industry grew in the late 19th century and the 20th century, many Americans left the farms and small towns to work in these new factories. The factories were organized for mass production, and thus relied heavily on a ready supply of unskilled labor willing to work for the lowest wage possible.

During this period labor arbitrage, an ugly term at best, was quite prevalent. In the current day and for the past twenty years or so, the notion of labor arbitrage again has raised its ugly head as the motivation for off-shoring and outsourcing of jobs to the lowest bidder. Labor arbitrage was operating in the 19th century as the industrialists held all the cards. The well-known Robber Barons and later the Factory Barons in the new industrial age were so concerned about their business matters that the lowly worker was the last one considered.

The Barons were most concerned about the ultimate survivability of their enterprises but as soon as they knew they were going concerns, other important things, such as increased profits, and beating the competition at all costs quickly took the top listings on their agendas. If the worker had any place at all on their to-do-lists it was to convince the worker to provide their service for the smallest amount of pay possible. The story of the Unions role in labor arbitrage is given in detail in Chapter 11.

Though our elected representatives, throughout history, were to be serving the public and not themselves--and not the elite, it was the elite with whom they fraternized and it was the elite who provided them with perks they could never achieve being part of the John Q. Public fraternity. So, the thought of taxation without real representation was and continues to be a natural. The British pulled up stakes long ago and the French left without even saying adieu, yet normal everyday Americans again find themselves facing a world in which we are taxed and taxed and taxed and if there were another day of representation, it would be lonesome.

The citizens suffer from the Congress's preoccupation with the matters of big business and big people and the lack of concern for the voters (We the People) who put them in office. Thankfully, as in the cases of Ken Lay, (Enron) , Gary Winnick (Global Crossings), John Rigas (Adelphia), Martha Stewart, and of course Bernie Madoff, the new Barons care enough about the American judicial system at least enough to answer their subpoenas.

Corporations Have No Heart and No Blood

In his article of the unofficial history of America™, Kalle Lasn captures the essence of corporations from time immemorial at least from a U.S. perspective. He notes that there are official and unofficial versions of the fight against the crown. In his unofficial version he identifies a real and true perpetrator of far more consequence than the flesh-laden Robber Barons, but in the same ilk. These are the English corporations who operated in America during the pre-revolution days and who in many ways helped contribute to the colonists frustration with England and their desire to be free of the Crown as well as its corporate allies. Lasn writes:

> ... The unofficial history of the United States is quite different. It begins the same way -- in the revolutionary cauldron of colonial America -- but then it takes a turn. A bit player in the official history becomes critically

important to the way the unofficial history unfolds. This player turns out to be not only the provocateur of the revolution, but in the end its saboteur. This player lies at the heart of America's defining theme: the difference between a country that pretends to be free and a country that truly is free.

That player is the corporation.

The United States of America was born of a revolt not just against British monarchs and the British parliament but against British corporations.

We tend to think of corporations as a fairly recent phenomena, along with the legacy of the Rockefellers and Carnegies. In fact, the corporate presence in pre-Revolutionary America was almost as conspicuous as it is today. There were far fewer corporations then, but they were enormously powerful: the Massachusetts Bay Company, the Hudson's Bay Company, the British East India Company [numbered among their ranks.] Colonials feared these chartered entities. They recognized the way British Kings and their cronies used them as robotic arms to control the affairs of the colonies, to pinch staples from remote breadbaskets and bring them home to the motherland.

The colonials resisted. When the British East India Company imposed duties on its incoming tea (telling the locals they could buy the tea or lump it, because the company had a virtual monopoly on tea distribution in the colonies), radical patriots demonstrated. Colonial merchants agreed not to sell East India Company tea. Many East India Company ships were turned back at port. And, on one fateful day in Boston, 342 chests of tea ended up in the salt chuck.

... The Declaration of Independence, in 1776, freed Americans not only from Britain but also from the tyranny of British corporations, and for a hundred years after the document's signing, Americans remained deeply suspicious of corporate power. They were careful about the way they granted corporate charters, and about the powers granted therein.

... Early American charters were created literally by the people, for the people as a legal convenience. Corporations were "artificial, invisible, intangible," mere financial tools. They were chartered by individual states, not the federal government, which meant they could be kept under close local scrutiny. They were automatically dissolved if they engaged in activities that violated their charter. Limits were placed on how big and powerful companies could become. Even railroad magnate J. P. Morgan, the consummate capitalist, understood that corporations must never become so big that they "inhibit freedom to the point where efficiency [is] endangered."

The two hundred or so corporations operating in the US by the year 1800 were each kept on fairly short leashes. They weren't allowed to participate in the political process. They couldn't buy stock in other corporations. And if one of them acted improperly, the consequences were severe. In 1832, President Andrew Jackson vetoed a motion to extend the charter of the corrupt and tyrannical Second Bank of the United States, and was widely applauded for doing so. That same year the state of Pennsylvania revoked the charters of ten banks for operating contrary to the public interest. Even the enormous industry trusts, formed to protect member corporations from external competitors and provide barriers to entry, eventually proved no match for the state. By the mid-1800s, antitrust legislation was widely in place.

... The shift began in the last third of the nineteenth century -- the start of a great period of struggle between

corporations and civil society. The turning point was
the Civil War. Corporations made huge profits from
procurement contracts and took advantage of the
disorder and corruption of the times to buy legislatures,
judges and even presidents.

A larger excerpt of The Unofficial History of America,
is available on the Web for you pleasure at:
/www.informationclearinghouse.info/article3925.htm
   Looks like a good book to buy after you finish this
one.

Thank you Kalle Lasn for a great account of the early
corporations in the United States. Clearly the wary eye of the
government of the states was needed to keep corporate power
in check so that nothing like the British East India Company
could ever rise again to terrify the citizens of the U. S. A.
Unfortunately, through political greed and individual greed,
corporations have re-gained a foothold in the U.S. that will
be very difficult to un-foot. Looking back, one thing is clear.
Ours is not the first generation to have been exploited by
corporations in concert with dirty politicians and ours will
not be the last. But, it sure would be nice if we could do
something about it.

Brief History of Corporations

Joel Bleifuss in his article "A Brief History of Corporations"
In These Times magazine, February 1998 minces no words
as he outlines the issues with corporations and then speaks
about how ridiculous it is that we permit their very being:

To begin this retooling process, we need to expose the
absurdity of granting First Amendment rights to
corporations. We can draw our inspiration from both
the 17th-century English philosopher Thomas Hobbes,
who decried corporations as "worms in the body

politic," and from Hobbes' star pupil, King Charles II. In 1664, the owners of the Massachusetts Bay Company protested when Charles II tried to investigate their company's operations. The Crown responded, "The King did not grant away his sovereignty over you when he made you a corporation.... When his majesty gave you authority over such subjects as live within your jurisdiction, he made them not your subjects, nor you their supreme authority."

We should be as wise.

http://query.nytimes.com/gst/fullpage.html?res=9F02EEDE173 DF937A25752C1A96F958260&sec=&spon=&pagewanted=all

Peter F. Drucker died about six years after being referenced in a New York times article in the URL above. He is forever revered as the father of modern management. In 1999, he had a new message for corporate executives: "Find another line of work." In this book, for this insight and the hope that it comes true, we must say, "Bravo! Dr. Drucker"

Drucker saw the information and knowledge workers today as retreating from corporate culture and instead saving their best efforts for nonprofit social service organizations, where he felt that in the 21st century, they could make a bigger difference. In his words, "The 20th century was the century of business," he said. "The next century is going to be the century of the social sector." So, again there is hope... as long as it does not turn to full socialism.

Abolish Corporations ? -- An Opinion

http://ming.tv/flemming2.php/   show article/ a000010-000393.htm

Flemming Funch, perhaps a pseudonym for a guy who does not want to be identified offers a number of insights and caveats as to how to abolish corporations. He believes that the biggest obstacle blocking the emergence of a free and peaceful world is the legal concept of a corporation. He notes that the corporation as we have discussed is merely a legal fiction in the first place, and it is "not any naturally occurring 'god-given' phenomenon or right."

Corporations exist only because our representatives have made laws saying that they can exist and they have rights only because again our representatives in the legislature and in the courts have said they have rights. He recognizes that the notion of the corporation per se would be hard to eliminate because just like anything about to die, the corporation would fight like hell to survive and they would use their vast resources to protect and even expand their own power. Bribing our elected officials is certainly one of their favorite armaments.

> People should certainly be able to organize themselves and operate as a group or organization. But a corporation is something else. A corporation is allowed the rights of a natural person. However, it has responsibilities and liabilities less than a natural person. And it can live eternally.

> These things can be useful and sensible when it is a small group of people who are trying to operate a business activity together. The initial people don't have to be too worried about being personally liable for the potential failure of the business, and the business can open a bank account for itself, and it can be continued even if the original participants drop out for some reason.

> But when it grows bigger, there are certain key design features that start to become prevalent. A corporation is controlled by very few people, but the fuel is provided by a great many people, in the form of investments and manpower.

A large corporation might have the will of one person, carrying out one person's plans, and it has the legal right to act in most arenas as one legal person, but it might have the manpower of 100,000 people, and available resources bigger than those of a small country. All in the hands of a handful of people who don't have any personal liability for what the corporation does.

It is very difficult to successfully convey what a horribly bad idea that is. Most of us are so used to the idea of corporations, and most of us have bought the propaganda that they're inextricably linked to free markets. Nothing could be further from the truth. Large multi-national corporations are the anti-thesis of free markets. They are the communist revolution you never even noticed happening.

A big corporation is much like a communist state, or like an old-fashioned kingdom with a divinely ordained dictatorial ruler, if you like that metaphor better. If you are one of its subjects, it might take good care of you, feeding you and clothing you, and it might give you bonuses and parties and fancy titles. But you have to do what you're told, and you have to direct your efforts to the benefit of the will of your rulers. It is not a democracy in any way. You have no rights whatsoever in terms of influencing what it does or how it does it, other than within the confines of the job you've been assigned from someone higher up in the hierarchy. But as an employee it isn't too bad, just like it wasn't terribly bad for most people to live in a communist country. Your range of success is very limited, but you can feel fairly secure that you'll have a job if you continue to do what you're told, and you can be confident that it doesn't matter a whole lot what you individually do or don't do.

... playing in the market with large corporations is typically not fair. The CEO of a large corporation can

book every single billboard in town, pay for TV
infomercials, hire experts of all sorts, all to say exactly
what he wants to say, very loudly, so that everyone in
sight will hear it, again, and again and again.
...

Chapter Summary

The Robber Barons of old and today's corporations acting as
the new Robber Barons have too much in common. Using
excessive work visas of all flavors, off-shoring, and illegal
aliens, today's Robber Barons have figured out how to defeat
the unions and the workers at the same time through labor
arbitrage.

There are many opinions about how corporations came to
have such power. Though nobody appears to be taking
action to reduce corporate power, the scholars upon
examination of the facts and the fourteenth amendment have
been concluding independently that corporations were never
intended by the framers of the fourteenth amendment to have
gained super human power.

Though corporations may very well self-destruct over time,
the time has come to rein them in by bringing our
government back to the people and enacting legislation that
will eliminate the potential for harm by these too-well-
endowed corporations. And, please in the future when a
corporation is dying, do not offer it life support. Check its
living will as brought forth by the Founding Fathers. In other
words, let it die, and quickly.

Sources:

http://www.ratical.org/corporations/ToPRaP.html
"http://www.mises.org/story/2317
The Truth About the "Robber Barons"
By Thomas J. DiLorenzo Posted on 9/23/2006
http://www.thirdworldtraveler.com/Corporations/KnowEnemy_ITT.html
http://www.rumormillnews.com/cgi-bin/forum.cgi?read=111114
http://query.nytimes.com/gst/fullpage.html?res=9F02EEDE173DF937A25752C1A96F
958260&sec=&spon=&pagewanted=all
http://en.wikipedia.org/wiki/Central_Pacific_Railroad

Chapter 14   Countervailing Power: Unions Meet the Robber Baron Challenge

Power Meets Power

Whenever there is a void, there is an opportunity. The labor arbitrage of the late 19th century affected mostly unskilled workers but in reality, all workers. The greed of the Robber Barons of this era was so self-centered that they wanted to pay not one penny more than the most meager of subsistence. if they could get away with paying less, they would. In this environment, labor unions sprang up and gradually developed lots of clout. They offered a power of equal magnitude to the power of employer and they made the worker something that management had to consider if they wanted to be able to run their plants and factories successfully.

The general policy of early labor and trade unions was to rely on discussion and cooperation to secure good working conditions and wages for the workers but the biggest weapon was the strike and the threat of a strike. Later unions relied on arbitration and education as well as the legislature. At their meetings for example, they would pass resolutions to be brought to the representatives in the hope that legislation would be passed to solve some of the corporate abuses.

As an example of abuse, the work day in the beginning of the 19th century was 12 hours or more and often seven days a week. For all those hours the worker got just enough pay and sometimes not enough pay for a family to make ends meet. It is generally accepted historically that small, local labor unions had been scattered around the thirteen states for about a hundred years before the corporate abuses of the Robber Barons brought them into the limelight.

The early groups were mostly trade unions in which craftsmen joined together in guilds. The national labor movement in the U.S., however, did not really hit high gear until after the Civil War. The National Labor Union and the Knights of Labor were formed right after the war. The former did not last long (1873), but the Knights of Labor was a viable Union until the 1890's and it did not formally collapse until 1917.

The Rise of Powerful Labor Unions

By 1886, the Knights of Labor was losing its prestige for a number of reasons, such as union repression as well as the Knights having lost some key contract negotiations with the railways. Samuel Gompers was quick to step in to fill the void. He founded the American Federation of Labor (AFL) and he served as its first president until his death in 1924.

Prior to the AFL, Gompers had been a local and national labor leader, and with the AFL, he hoped to build the labor movement into a force powerful enough to transform the economic, social and political status of America's workers to more favorable conditions. Gompers was well on his way to achieving his goals for at the time of his death there were over 3 million members of the AFL. It was a very, very powerful union.

As a labor leader, Gompers learned that economic reform was longer lasting than political reform so unlike other leaders, with the AFL, he was not as concerned about getting legislation passed. Gompers had in fact used political clout in one instance in which he had two laws passed regulating what was called the tenement production of cigars.

Figure 14-1 Samuel Gompers, President, AFL

This law forbade workers in residences to make cigars. Obviously, the Union wanted them to be organized. When Gompers saw that he could get crafty legislation passed but the Supreme Court could just as simply overthrow the law, he began to focus his energies on gaining economic benefits through negotiations and contracts. He learned that which the state may give, the state can also take away but the benefits gained by contract are long lasting. Gompers was no pushover. One of the first acts, for example when he became the president of the AFL was to promote a general strike on May 1, 1886. Its mission was to support an eight-hour workday.

Strikes Often Turn Violent

Though he was respected by the captains of industry, nobody made his life easy. After May 1 for example, there were still companies insisting on more than 8 hours per day and Gompers insisted that all AFL workers not yet on an 8-hour schedule, were to cease work in a nation-wide strike until their employer would meet the demand. There was a mix of employers who met the demand and those that did not.

Haymarket Riot

There were strike actions all across the country. This was the first national strike ever called. 80,000 marched in Chicago alone and it was seen as the start of a possible revolution. It was taken quite seriously. On May 3, in Chicago, for example, there was a violent confrontation with police. On May 4, a labor meeting was called at a location called Haymarket to discuss the brute force of the activities the day before. History notes the meeting was not well planned or organized and the leaders were looking for speakers even as the meeting began.

Then about 100 Chicago police showed up to put down the meeting and have the crowd disburse. When the police showed up, a person, unknown to this day, threw a bomb among the police and chaos erupted. Nobody could see with the smoke of the bomb in the air and the police panicked. They drew their weapons and began to fire on the crowd. Several in the crowd were killed including a number of policemen. Only one policeman was killed by the bomb and the other dead police were presumed to have been killed by other police firing haphazardly. This event historically is known as the Haymarket Riot and like all good stories there are myths about this event floating around in Chicago to this day.

Rise of the AFL

By 1900, the AFL was booming with memberships and it was soaring faster than any other period in the US labor movement. The "Robber Barons," a.k.a. "Captains of Industry," however with their newly formed corporations did not take too kindly to this decrease in control from accommodating Gompers and his union. They were not accustomed to sharing power with anybody or anything. To combat the anti-union hostility of the employers, Gompers and the AFL were eventually forced to go back to a political strategy to seek protective legislation from angry employers who were, to say the least, not very nice.

Corporations Strike Back

To retaliate for their own losses, companies had begun to sue the unions using the same anti-trust laws that had been passed to weaken those very companies. Workers began to fear that actions could come back to bite them if each member were to be found liable for treble damages from the strikes and boycotts that they were so effectively waging.

The Union's New Friend - The Elected

So, guess who the unions had to become buddies with? Your friendly congressional representatives. In fact, the unions put forth union-friendly candidates for the very purpose of affecting their legislation. Considering that most of the voters were workers and not employers, it is not too hard to imagine that the union candidates at this time in history, with unions being so popular, had no trouble getting elected. Unions were in America to stay and they would never be less than a major force with which to be reckoned.

The CIO

Gompers' A.F. of L as it was called, had been mostly a craft union that had little to do with unskilled labor. Some think this had a lot to do with race as skilled workers were mostly white. Regardless of the rationale, the American Federation of Labor was reluctant to organize unskilled workers. Every void is an opportunity for someone. This someone was John L. Lewis, known for his work with the Mining Unions in the mid 1900's. Lewis created the Committee for Industrial Organization within the A.F. of L. in 1935. The A.F. of L. did not really like this and so Lewis took these unions in 1938, and he created a new organization called the Congress of Industrial Organizations. Thus, the A.F. of L. and C.I.O. had separate existences until an agreement was effected in 1955, which created what we now know as the AFL-CIO.

Figure 14-2 John L. Lewis C.I.O.

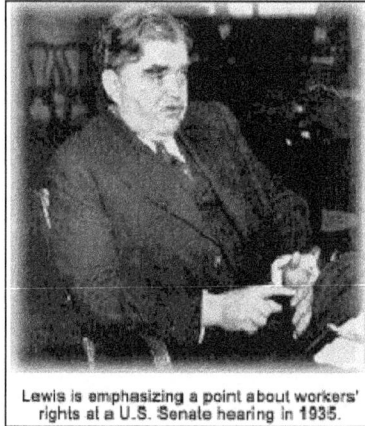

Lewis is emphasizing a point about workers' rights at a U.S. Senate hearing in 1935.

Labor Organizers like Samuel Gompers and John L. Lewis were brave and gutsy and in many ways arrogant. They had to be all of that to stand up to the powerful Robber Barons of the day. John L. Lewis for example pulled a power play on the strength of his Union affiliation back in 1940. He was a Republican, which was very unusual for a union man. Nonetheless, he had backed Roosevelt for several elections.

For his own reasons, he wanted Roosevelt out of the White House. So, he made a vow with the American people that if Franklin Roosevelt was elected president again, he would resign from his presidency of the C.I.O. The power-play did not work. Roosevelt was elected and, Lewis kept his word, and the C.I.O. Presidency passed to Philip Murray, who had been President of the United Steel Workers.

When Murray died in 1952, Walter Reuther, whose background was the United Auto Workers became the last president of the C.I.O before its merger with the A.F. of L. Clearly the AFL-CIO is the largest labor Union in America today at 13 million members. One of its fastest growing affiliates is the 1.4 million strong American Federation of State, County and Municipal Employees (AFSCME). Recognizing the importance of political affiliation, AFSCME hopes to be able to influence your representative for U.S. President and the Union went on record in 2008 to endorse Hillary Clinton for President.

However, when Hillary did not win the nomination in June 2008, the AFL-CIO endorsed Barack Obama and worked hard for his election. In support of the candidate Obama, the AFL-CIO launched a new website: Meet Barack Obama. In its endorsement statement, the General Board of the union noted that Sen. Barack Obama "has secured the nomination of his party in a campaign that has energized millions of Americans and spoken to the hopes and dreams of people from every corner of our nation." The Web site continued: "His leadership can re-engage disenfranchised Americans and bring our country together. Sen. Obama has advocated a change of direction for our nation that mirrors the priorities of the labor movement."

Chapter Summary

To answer the opportunity that arose when America's mostly unskilled laborers were subjected to starving wages, local unions formed to help pressure the Ruling Class into providing a better work environment. Over time, big national unions took over most of the small unions and today we find the AFL-CIO, and the Teamsters as two of the largest unions in the U. S. A. Unions provide a very important countervailing force against the power of the corporations who in many cases have colluded with government officials to gain advantages. There are very few companies today who like IBM in the 1970's and 1980's put the employee first and expect the employee to do their best for the company. Today, corporate greed is everywhere and it is seen more and more in the labor part of the equation.

The Ruling Class does not want to pay any more than the minimum and the workers want enough for subsistence and a level of enjoyment. Traditionally, since they gained power in the 1890s, unions have provided this for employees and this is why employees faithfully pay their union dues. The notions of offshoring and illegal immigration have posed big problems for unions, none of which it seems the unions have been able to solve. Offshoring as it is known today for professional jobs is not a loss for the unions since most professionals work directly for their companies with no union protection. The fact is that a worker has no employment rights at work unless he or she is part of a collective bargaining agreement. Why Unions are not making hay on this is a big question and for workers paying dues, it should be a big concern..

Labor Unions again are also doing poorly in terms of being a countervailing force for illegal immigrants taking U.S. jobs. Despite these shortcomings, organized labor is still a very important political and economic force today, but its influence has waned markedly. Manufacturing, where Unions once thrived has declined substantially, and the service sector has grown. Unskilled blue collar jobs are not as abundant as in the early 1990's. Unions have become very powerful in education and government under AFSCME and this is one of their major strongholds today. Overall the # of unionized workers in the US declines every year.

Sources:

http://www.aflcio.org/aboutus/history/history/gompers.cfm
http://www.kentlaw.edu/ilhs/haymkmon.htm
http://www.freerepublic.com/focus/f-news/1755355/posts
http://www.lawyersandsettlements.com/articles/01056/illegal_immigrant_crack down.html
http://www.fraudfactor.com/ffunionfraudintro.html
http://www.commondreams.org/headlines/021700-02.htm

Chapter 15   Worker Visas Take Many American Jobs

Onshore vs. Offshore

The big difference between losing your job to a person with an H-1B Visa and having your job offshored is whether the person who gets your job will be playing a home game or an away game. If they get to work in their own country, say India for example, then for them it is a home game. Your job has been offshored. If instead, they get an H-1B Visa, then they get to come to the U.S. to take your job. In the latter scenario, however, your company or the company that would have hired you first lies about your availability to work or they would not get the H-1B visa slot. The next lie is that they will pay the H-1B visa worker or any other work visa, the same pay for the same work you would have done.

Visa Alphabet Soup

We can always thank the Greeks for the alphabet, because overall, the U.S. visa problem is not stuck on the letters H-1B. There are several visa types for just about as many letters fashioned for us by the Greeks and Phoenicians many, many years ago. As you would expect, in addition to H-1B, there is an H-1A, and there are visa types that start with A and go to T with many variants within those letters. Right now, there are 81 different visa types, each promising somebody in the world the opportunity to come to the U.S. for one reason or another. I have reworked a table from a government site and it is shown in Table 7-1. To see the whole table, rather than type the four line URL, just type *Immigration Classifications and Visa Categories* into your browser and you can see the full chart and all of its meaning.

Actually there are so many visa types that foreigners interested in coming to the U.S. often use one type of visa that they can get rather than the type of visa that they actually should get for the type of work or study that they are hoping to do. It is a bureaucratic nightmare that only a desperate non-citizen or a lawyer could be paid enough to want to fully understand. That's why the latter make a lot of money on the former trying to squeeze them in.

Figure 13-1 Immigration Classifications and Visa Categories

	Nonimmigrant Classifications and Visas	Govt. Information
	Foreign Government Officials	
A-1	Ambassador, etc.	
A-2	Other foreign government official or employee, members of immediate family.	
A-3	Attendant, servant, employee of A-1, A-2, and members of immediate family.	
	Visitors	
B-1	Temporary visitor for business	
B-2	Temporary visitor for pleasure	
	Visa Waiver Program	Visa Waiver Program (Immigration.gov) Visa Waiver Program (Dept. of State)
	Aliens in Transit	
C-1	Alien in transit directly through U.S.	
C-1D	Combined transit and crewman visa	
C-2	Alien in transit to UN headquarters	
C-3	Foreign government official , members of immediate family, attendant etc.	
C-4	Transit without Visa	
	Crewmen	
D-1	Crewmember departing on same vessel	

D-2	Crewmember departing other vessel	
	Treaty Traders and Treaty Investors	Instructions for Form I-129: Petition for a Nonimmigrant Worker
E-1	Treaty Trader, spouse and children	
E-2	Treaty Investor, spouse and children	
	Academic Students	
F-1	Academic Student	
F-2	Spouse or child of F-1	
	For Foreign Medical Graduates	
	Foreign Govt. Officials to Int. Organizations	
G-1	Principal resident to organization, and members of immediate family.	
G-2	Other representative of organization, and members of immediate family.	
G-3	Same as G1 for non-recognized or nonmember government	
G-4	International organization officer or employee, and members of immediate family	
G-5	Attendant, servant, etc. G1-G4	
	Temporary Workers	
H-1B	Specialty Occupations, DOD workers, fashion models	Capped at 65,000 but has been as high as 180,000
H-1C	Nurses going to work for up to three years in health professional shortage areas	
H-2A	Temporary Agricultural Worker	
H-2B	Temporary worker: skilled and unskilled	
H-3	Trainee	
H-4	Spouse or child of H-1, H-2, H-3	
	Foreign Media Representatives	
I	Visas for foreign media representatives	
	Exchange Visitors	
J-1	Visas for exchange visitors	
J-2	Spouse or child of J-1	
	Fiancé(e) of US Citizen	
K-1	Fiancé(e)	
K-2	Minor child of K-1	

K-3	Spouse of a U.S. Citizen (LIFE Act)	
K-4	Child of K-3 (LIFE Act)	
	Intracompany Transferee	
L-1A	Executive, managerial	
L-1B	Specialized knowledge	
L-2	Spouse or child of L-1	
	Vocational and Language Students	
M-1	Vocational student or other nonacademic student	
M-2	Spouse or child of M-1	
N-8	Parent of alien classified SK-3 "Special Immigrant"	
N-9	Child of N-8, SK-1, SK-2, or SK-4 "Special Immigrant"	
NAFTA	*North American Free Trade Agreement (NAFTA) (see TN, below)*	
	North Atlantic Treaty Organization	
NATO-1	Principal Permanent Representative of Member State to NATO, family, staff	
NATO-2	Other Rep. Member State; Dependents etc.	
NATO-3	Official clerical staff accompanying Rep. of Member State to NATO or immediate family	
NATO-4	Official of NATO other than those qualified as NATO-1 and immediate family	
NATO-5	Expert other than NATO officials qualified under NATO-4, NATO employee, immediate family	
NATO-6	Member of civilian component etc.	
NATO-7	Servant or personal employee of NATO-1-6	
	Workers with Extraordinary Abilities	
O-1	Extraordinary ability in Sciences, Arts, Education, Business, or Athletics	
O-2	Alien's (support) accompanying O-1	
O-3	Spouse or child of O-1 or O-2	
	Athletes and Entertainers	
P-1	Individual or team athletes	

P-1	Entertainment groups	
P-2	Artists and entertainers in reciprocal Exchange programs	
P-3	Artists and entertainers in culturally unique programs	
P-4	Spouse or child of P-1, 2, or 3	
	International Cultural Exchange Visitors	
Q-1	International cultural exchange visitors	
Q-2	Irish Peace Process Cultural and Training Program (Walsh Visas)	
Q-3	Spouse or child of Q-2	
	Religious Workers	
R-1	Religious workers	
R-2	Spouse or child of R-1	
	Witness or Informant	
S-5	Informant of criminal organization information	
S-6	Informant of terrorism information	
T	*Victims of a Severe Form of Trafficking in Persons*	
T-1	Victim of a severe form of trafficking in persons	
T-2	Spouse of a victim of a severe form of trafficking in persons	
T-3	Child of victim of a severe form of trafficking in persons	
T-4	Parent of victim of a severe form of trafficking in persons (if T-1 victim is under 21 years of age)	
	North American Free Trade Agreement (NAFTA)	
TN	Trade visas for Canadians and Mexicans	
TD	Spouse or child accompanying TN-	
	Transit Without Visa	
TWOV	Passenger	
TWOV	Crew	
U	*Victims of Certain Crimes*	
U-1	Victim of Certain Criminal Activity</FONT< td>	

U-2	Spouse of U-1	
U-3	Child of U-1	
U-4	Parent of U-1, if U-1 is under 21 years of age	
	*Certain **Second Preference** Beneficiaries*	
V-1	Spouse of an LPR who is the principal beneficiary of a family-based petition etc.	
V-2	Child of an LPR who is the principal beneficiary of a family-based visa petition etc.	
V-3	The derivative child of a V-1 or V-2	
	Humanitarian Parole	
	Temporary Protected Status (TPS)	
TPS	Temporary Protected Status	

H-1B and White Collar Tech Workers

All of the visa programs have the opportunity for abuse, but none has come under as much fire as the H-1B Visa program. This is the first time I can recall that the government has invited foreigners to take the jobs of Americans. Displaced white collar workers from this visa program and from offshoring have been creating quite a stir about their government's acceptance of the job losses suffered by American citizens.

Corporations, who we know from the last two chapters we can trust implicitly, say they need H-1B visas to compete in the world market (meaning they want to pay lower wages). Just like George Bush says illegal aliens do work that Americans won't do, corporations say there are not enough workers to fill their high-tech jobs. There are about 300,000 high tech students that graduate from American Universities each year and yet there are only about 120,000 jobs for them to get. So, who is lying, the corporations or the statistics? I think we know.

The fact is corporations do not want to find Americans for jobs when legal foreign nationals will work for so much less. In fact the law firms are so sure they can get around the intent of U.S. law which is to hire American's first if available, have not only figured out ways for companies to prove that Americans will never be available, one firm was so bold as to explain their scheme on YouTube. Use your search engine next chance you have and type in YouTube H-1B and see what you get. On June 21, 2007, Computerworld did an expose on this scam. Here is an excerpt from that article:

June 21, 2007 (Computerworld) -- WASHINGTON -- That explosive H-1B YouTube video offering advice on how to hire foreign workers instead of Americans has gotten the attention of U.S. Sen. Charles Grassley, (R-Iowa), and Rep. Lamar Smith, (R-Texas), who called it evidence of abuse of the visa program. Both men want a federal investigation and are seeking answers from the law firm that posted the original video on YouTube.

In a letter to U.S. Department of Labor Secretary Elaine Chao, Grassley and Smith characterized the video as "exposing the blatant disregard for American workers and deliberate attempt to bring in cheaper foreign workers through the H-1B program." They also ... want the labor secretary to review the video and investigate "the law firm's unethical procedures and advice to clients."

In the video, a person identified as Lawrence Lebowitz, an attorney at the firm Cohen & Grigsby PC in Pittsburgh, explains how U.S. companies can avoid hiring U.S. workers. "Our goal is clearly not to find a qualified and interested U.S. worker," said Lebowitz in the video. "And that, in a sense, sounds funny, but it's what we are trying to do here."

Other Companies Help Take American Jobs

If an IT worker tries to get a job with one of the companies that like to spoof the system, the company, of course does not expect that the IT worker will complain because you don't have as many lawyers as the company does to figure out what is what. You see, if you are available to work and the employer of the person who gets the job ignores that fact and they hire someone from Bhopal or Japan instead, for example, they are not operating within the U.S. Law. But they don't care because their lawyers will solve it for them. Smart lawyers know how to get a good deal for their clients, and though you may wind up unfairly on the wrong side of the deal, the lawyers will sanitize it for the company so that it is as easy as clicking on Murthy's Web site.
http://www.murthy.com/h1bvisa.html

Here's a little bit of what they would find from the above click:

> What We Can Do For You : At the Murthy Law Firm, we can consult with you to determine that the nature of the position and the beneficiary's background are appropriate for the H-1B, and suggest alternatives if the initial proposal is not a viable option. We can advise both the employer and prospective employee regarding the H-1B documentation requirements and legal issues. We can also prepare paperwork and submit it to the Department of Labor and USCIS.

That beneficiary they are talking about is the guy from Bhopal. By the way, it helps in this light to know what a beneficiary actually is. I picked the definition that seems to me to best apply to the situation at hand. A beneficiary is:

> A person or entity who is the recipient of or will receive some or all proceeds of money or property held by the current owner upon a specified event or condition.

Trade Agreements Negotiated by Buffoons

Many remember the big hoopla with NAFTA and GATT. President Bill Clinton, Hillary's husband at the time, took many bows for completing these treaties. Guess what? Our negotiators locked in the minimum # of H-1B visas at 65,000 in exchange for the passage of the trade agreements. That means every year at least 65,000 new high tech workers from India or South Africa or some other location come to the U.S. and Congress's great trade negotiators took away our power to shut off the spigot. With the six year option, that is 390,000 new high tech jobs taken by legal foreign nationals every six years. Don't think they go ever go home!

Now, because the government saved money by not sending its negotiators to negotiating school, Congress no longer has the option under the agreements to ever reduce that number without violating the trade agreements. This is just another example of our friendly representatives working on behalf of special interests and corporations and not the people. Again there is a Clinton in the foray. This time it is Hillary who must think these middle class voters are Republicans as she is pushing hard in favor of the corporations over the U.S. middle class. Lou Dobbs called it like it is: "Clinton is "selling out our middle class on H-1B visas." Taxation but no representation. A mistake maybe, but a mistake that helps the Ruling Class and not the college graduate who just lost her opportunity for the American dream.

Chapter Summary

There are over 80 visa types. Only foreign nationals and corporate lawyers understand them all. They are the means that people from other countries use to get an extended stay in the United States. Many of the visa types permit the workers to have gainful employment in the United States. Others, such as the L1, H-1B, O1, etc. actually are the ticket for gainful employment and a reasonably long time period for U.S. temporary residency.

Visas are good for the U.S. in many ways. Unfortunately, opportunistic corporations and law firms have found a way to reduce company expenses by bringing workers in under these visas to replace American workers. Often the citizen must train the foreign national to do his or her job.

Congress has been lobbied profusely by the rich Ruling Class, especially Bill Gates of Microsoft, to do away with the caps (now back to 65,000 from over 200,000 in 2004) completely. Gates seems to be convinced that Americans either are not smart enough or want too much money. I'm thinking the latter. He suggests that business will be crippled if it must be limited to hiring Americans or permitting them to keep their jobs when foreign nationals who are either smarter or who will work for less can be available almost immediately

It's time to outsource guys like Bill Gates and other corporate titans and their henchmen in management to a country that will accept them. Then, we can go back to being an America for Americans. Additionally, there may be 435 representatives and 100 senators available for the trip overseas after the next election for the outsourcing pool if we are smart enough to do what is right.

Recent Update and Perspective on Trade

This piece is excellent. Buffoons negotiate for the US.

Free trade in an Unfree Trade World is Economic Suicide For the USA
Raymond Richman, 7/23/2015
http://www.idealtaxes.com/post3896.shtml

George Washington in his farewell address urged the US to "Avoid foreign entanglements". How right he was. US foreign entanglements began with a vengeance under

Presidents Wilson and Franklin D Roosevelt especially the latter. The Bretton Woods agreements which were negotiated by Harry Dexter White, as the U.S. representative, later exposed as a Communist spy, created the World Bank and the International Monetary Fund.

Benn Steil, senior fellow and director of international economics at the Council on Foreign Relations in New York, founding editor of International Finance, a top scholarly economics journal, in his book, The Battle of Bretton Woods: John Maynard Keynes, Harry Dexter White, and the Making of a New World Order (Council on Foreign Relations, (Princeton University Press, 2013), discussing the creation at Bretton Woods of the World Bank and the IMFwrites.

Together with the United Nations, they marked the beginning of Post WWII's march toward global government and simultaneously the march toward state capitalism, a political mixture of a powerful state, socialist enterprises, and state-dominated private capitalist enterprises. Mussolini, a former Communist, and Hitler, a national socialist were the first world leaders to recognize the power of the new economic system. Both freed themselves from the ideology of Marxism and both recognized how a socialist state could dominate private enterprises and bend their will to the service of the state.

New Deal innovations included the minimum wage and the Davis-Bacon Act, two laws to advantage labor unions, which returned blacks to conditions worse than slavery by denying Blacks equal opportunities for employment since the unions at that time were nearly all lily-white. Black rates of unemployed males are twice those of whites and in the 1st quarter of 2014 the unemployment rate of black male teenagers reached the astronomical level of 44 percent. Until 1950, blacks had lower rates of unemployment than whites.

Other innovations included the regulation of labor relations, the initiation of farm subsidies, the creation of the Social

Security System, the creation of the Securities and Exchange Commission (SEC) and the creation of the Tennessee Valley Authority and its network of electric utilities.

The U.S. in 1947 began the General Agreement on Tariffs and Trade, conducting eight rounds of talks during the ensuing decades The Uruguay Round, which was completed on December 15, 1993 after seven years of negotiations, resulted in an agreement among 117 countries (including the U.S.) to reduce trade barriers and to create more comprehensive and enforceable world trade rules. The agreement coming out of this round, the Final Act Embodying the Results of the Uruguay Round of Multilateral Trade Negotiations, was signed in April 1994. The Uruguay Round agreement was approved and implemented by the U.S. Congress in December 1994, and went into effect on January 1, 1995. This agreement also created the World Trade Organization (WTO) in 1995.

But all this globalization, initiated by the U.S., turned out to be an economic disaster for the U.S. U.S. manufacturers in droves moved their factories overseas and out-sourced production exacerbating the decline of manufacturing in the U.S. which is making the U.S. a second-rate economic power. Millions of well-paid manufacturing jobs of American workers were eliminated.

The U. S. continued with its free trade policy. Congress passed the North American Free Trade Agreement Implementation Act in 1993. Pres. Clinton, while signing the NAFTA bill, stated that "NAFTA means jobs. American jobs, and good-paying American jobs. If I didn't believe that, I wouldn't support this agreement." He may have believed that but he was wrong. The US goods trade deficit with NAFTA was $94.6 billion in 2010 and accounted for 26.8% of the overall U.S. goods trade deficit.

The trade deficits caused the U.S. to go from being the world's leading creditor before 1970 to becoming the world's leading debtor by 1985. The huge accumulation of U.S. Treasury bonds abroad has made the U.S. vulnerable to a collapse of the dollar as the world's medium of exchange, which now appears to be unavoidable. One possibility is that the dollar will be replaced by the IMF's Special Drawing Rights (SDRs) and a currency of the new international fund being organized by China and Russia.

Why didn't U.S. corporations move their factories abroad before the era of trade liberalization? Because their exports to the US would have been subject to tariffs. American firms open factories abroad to produce products to be consumed in the countries they invest in and to produce products to be exported to the U.S. and the rest of the world. The US trade deficits have been exacerbated by the imports from American companies producing their products abroad and exporting them to the U.S. The effect on American manufacturing has been disastrous for American workers. Millions of well-paid American jobs were lost as American manufacturing moved overseas.

A world free trade regime is only possible if countries retain the ability to impose the Scaled Tariff, a single-country variable tariffs, which we describe in our book Balanced Trade (Lexington Books, 2014). The single-country-variable tariff is indispensable to provide a tool for countries experiencing large chronic trade deficits, as the U.S. has been experiencing with China, Japan, and Germany, to compel balanced trade. Of course, if a country's total trade is in balance, it should not have the right to impose single-country variable tariffs. A world trade organization like the World Trade Organization has been completely ineffective, unnecessary, and costly.

The right to impose single-country variable tariffs is all a country needs to prevent other countries from employing mercantilist practices, tariffs, barriers to trade, subsidies, and exchange rate manipulation, to achieve a trade surplus, what Keyes described as a beggar-one's-neighbor policy. The

Greek Crisis could be solved and the Eurozone preserved if members of the Eurozone had the authority to impose the Scaled Tariff.

The number of international agencies has exploded since the end of World War II. The UN alone has created dozens, many of them anti-U.S., and including some inherited from the League of Nations. Most have outlived their usefulness, and many are counter-productive, but remain a burden on taxpayers around the world, particularly the USA.

The USA continues with its foolish trade policies, the latest being the fast-track Trade Promotion Authority requested by Pres. Obama. It is ludicrous to read the U.S. Chamber of Commerce pamphlet entitled "America Needs Trade Promotion Authority". It points out correctly that U.S. exports provide job opportunities for American workers but make no mention of the fact that increased imports, and the trade deficits, cause a net loss of millions of jobs.

The trade agreements not only have created trade deficits for the U.S. but encouraged American manufacturers to move production of their products abroad. Economists Justin R. Pierce, on the staff of the Federal Reserve Board, and Yale professor of economics Peter K. Schott wrote in 2012 that one result of the U.S.-China trade agreement of 2000 was a sharp drop in U.S. manufacturing employment after 2001 resulting from the elimination of trade policy uncertainty. As a result American companies produced their products abroad and exported them to the U.S. free of duty. The list of companies that moved their production overseas reads like a Who's Who in the US Chamber of Commerce.

--End of post--

Both comments on this post are also right on the mark.

Comment by M, 7/25/2015:

Boy, the way Glen Miller played.
Songs that made the hit parade.

Guys like us, we had it made.
Those were the days.
Didn't need no welfare state.
Everybody pulled his weight.
Gee, our old LaSalle ran great.

Those were the days.

And you know who you were then.
Girls were girls and men were men.
Mister, we could use a man like Herbert Hoover again.
People seemed to be content.Fifty dollars paid the rent.
Freaks were in a circus tent.

Those were the days.

Take a little Sunday spin.Go to watch the Dodgers win.
Have yourself a dandy day that cost you under a fin!
Hair was short and skirts were long.
Kate Smith really sold a song.
I don't know just what went wrong.

Those Were The Days!!!!!!!

Comment by Ray Tapajna, 1/23/2016:

Excellent article - However, even talking about our present
day free trade as trade has to change. Free trade is not trade
as historically practiced and defined. It is more about
dividing investments from production and moving
production anywhere in the world for the sake of cheaper
labor for the sake of investments. It does not work. Our
economies based on making money on money instead of
making things are burning out across the world.

President Clinton had to bail out the process in 1995 after more than 4000 US factories were moved to Mexico. He had to rush billions of dollars to Mexico to save the value of the peso and the Mexican economy. It was threatening international money values. So the first bail out went to a foreign nation and predicted the coming of the super bail out in 2008 by President Obama. However he only propped up the big money interests and not anything real. The value of workers and labor is a real money standard and must be in parity with the value of interests or everything will remain economically upside down. Presently, our economy is set in quick sand. http://tapsearchnews.filetap.com

Sources
http://www.idealtaxes.com/post3896.shtml
http://www.h1b.info/about.php
http://ei.cs.vt.edu/~history/Gates.Mirick.html#family

Chapter 16   Offshoring: Bad for You; Bad for Me; Bad for America

Foreign Nationals in Foreign Countries

After working our way through Chapter 13 as we ripped apart the logic for the U.S. Government to be advocating the replacement of American Workers in the U.S. with Foreign Nationals, like me, you are probably hoping that this Chapter brings better news of our representatives' service. I sincerely regret that I have no such good news. In fact, Offshoring, the topic of this chapter, may even be more egregious than the visa scam since it shows in spades the globalization strategy of corporations vs. an America first strategy. More to the point, it also regrettably shows the complicity of Congress in giving the country to the mighty corporations and the Ruling Class.

History of Outsourcing

Outsourcing has been with the world for thousands of years. The sale of food, tools, and other goods from one community to another is a form of outsourcing. If you don't grow your own food then you outsource its acquisition. As soon as small communities and societies began to form, certain people began to specialize in certain functions. The bakers baked goods; the candlestick makers made candles; the weavers made fabric; and the tailors made clothes. Eventually the specialized professions began to trade with each other for goods and services. In effect it can be said that each worker was outsourcing some activities to others.

There were companies in the 1800s and 1900s who were vertically integrated and they did it all. They took care of their own production, mining, and manufacturing from raw materials, building finished goods, shipping the goods, and selling the products in their own stores. Many of these companies even went so far as insuring themselves; handled their own bookkeeping and taxes; had their own lawyers etc. Some designed and built their own buildings as it was viewed as the proper way to expand their enterprises.

Eventually, it no longer was a matter of pride that a company did it all. Furniture manufacturers began to get their wood from loggers rather than maintain their own forests. Other manufacturers began to bring in raw materials that were in a more finished state from contractors -- steel sheets rather than iron ore.

This is how it began. As service companies began to emerge, the manufacturing companies found it more productive to do a number of things with these companies rather than require the in-house expertise they would otherwise need. In the industrial revolution there was a large growth in the service sector as manufacturers began to purchase needed skills such as insurance services, architecture and engineering services, and many others. At this time in the U.S., the companies doing the outsourced work were almost always located in the U.S., and most often in the same city, just like the customers.

Corporate Globalization Takes Outsourcing Offshore.

As the economy became more global as fast ships and large airplanes permitted people and goods to be moved rapidly from country to country, it became feasible to move activities that were once done on-shore in the U.S. to a foreign country. This process is known as offshore outsourcing or simply offshoring. At first it was an experiment but the ingredients of success were in the cards. As relationships were formed in developing countries, it became easier and easier for the next company to do the same thing.

Facilitator service companies emerged who would set up the whole deal for any company that did not know how to get it done. In the beginning of course, the outsourcing channels were not greased as well as today. In fact, companies of today ready to outsource no longer do the work themselves. They outsource to the facilitator companies to gain the outsourcing/offshoring expertise and there are many such firms that are now in place to expedite the entire process.

In the last ten to twenty years the notion of offshoring has become as commonplace as outsourcing on-shore had been and it has gotten more and more positive press in the business community. It has become very popular, especially in large companies in which the Ruling Class and the stockholders believe their company is as modern as the times permit when they are offshoring their work. In some ways it is a management status symbol besides a way of doing business. Unfortunately, though the corporate miffintiffs (Big Shots) would argue against this premise, it really provides little benefit for the sending country.

The first types of products to be manufactured overseas were the low-tech items such as toys, shoes and apparel goods. Eventually, higher value items like high-tech components, computer chips and wafers, and consumer electronics began to appear. There are no televisions or VCRs made in the U. S. and even the analog television faceplates, which were once made by Owens-Corning and later Techneglas in Pittston Pennsylvania are now made in Korea. So discrete manufacturing was the first activity that began to move to offshore destinations in the corporate quest for significantly lower labor costs.

Cheaper Wages in the South

In the early 1990's one of my first consulting clients when I retired from IBM was Muskin Leisure Products. They operated in the largest plant in my original home town of Wilkes-Barre, PA. They make above ground swimming pools and had been very successful through the 1980's. Muskin was originally an American company and was sold a few times and eventually the company was sold to Zodiac, a French company. Zodiac is a world leader in above ground swimming pools and pool care products. Muskin had established its own long tradition in the manufacturing and distribution of above ground pools and claimed Sears and Penny's and a number of American chain stores as its prized customers.

When the Union held out for higher wages, Muskin, a French company, a division of American Leisure, theoretically already offshored from France, would not budge. In fact, they wanted to lower existing wages. Rather than continue negotiating, when the workers went on strike, the company decided to do something very much like offshoring. They chose to move south to Georgia where wages were much cheaper. Many American companies had made the trip from the Rust Belt to the south for the very same reason. It was the corporate precursor to offshoring.

Muskin's own engineers, unfortunately for company executives, had designed and fabricated a number of the specialized machines used to build the pools and the parts that were not purchased. It was once a company competitive advantage. So, there were no machines in the Industry such as these so the company could not set up shop in Georgia and then move the company. It had to move the company and then set up shop. It was an all-or-nothing risky deal.

A number of the skilled workers and engineers stayed home, retired or got other jobs in Pennsylvania. They did not move with the company. Though the hourly rate was substantially less, after a few years of trying, the company could not make it in Savannah and so Zodiac shut them down. It would have been even more difficult to effect this operational move if the destination were a country half-way across the world. Yet, for those that fail, such as Muskin, at least in light manufacturing, most succeed.

In other parts of the country, companies were moving operations, just one plant at a time to offshore countries and it was working quite well. As more offshoring occurred and the infrastructure in the developing nations were built and were expanding, transportation and all of the logistics improved, and it became easier and easier to do. Costs were decreased and offshore manufacturing increased. Success breeds success.

The Textile Industry Wants to Stay in U.S.

There are currently about 600,000 jobs in the U.S. textile industry. This is down substantially from when the U.S. was a leader in textiles with mills all across the country.   As other industries such as electronics basically gave up and let it all go overseas, the U.S. textile industry actually invested heavily in itself so that it could compete in the world markets.

From 1994, the U.S. textile industry invested more than $33 billion in new plants and equipment and has increased productivity by just about 50% percent over the last ten years. This industry is now securely in second place ranking among all industrial sectors in productivity increases over the past ten years. That's not too bad in a country that is moving away from manufacturing.

The National Textile Association argues that the U.S. textile industry is a highly innovative, productive industry that can compete with anyone in the world. The problem is that the U.S. government (that's our legislators and bureaucrats folks) places them at a disadvantage by supporting a trade environment that favors overseas producers over U.S. manufacturers, in particular China.

China has a preference over our own U.S. textile industry despite the fact that 600,000 U.S. taxpayers depend on this industry. International politics is in play on this deal. China is now a member of the World Trade Organization (since 2001) and they are considered by the WTO as a developing nation. Thus they get the trade benefits associated with that notion.

The problem is that China is huge. It can buy and sell whole countries and can sell anything dirt cheap because of the conditions in that country. Moreover, they don't really play by the rules, and because they play around with their currency, they beat the U.S. and all others in the money game all the time, and we let them.

Despite the farce, American lawmakers approve agreements that hurt America and these permit the Chinese to dominate the textile industry. Congress seems pleased by its trade actions that cost U.S. business and U.S. jobs because it is complying with WTO mandates. China's success as a "developing nation" seems to be tantamount to U.S. success in its trade negotiations. But, in reality, China is the winner and the U.S. is the loser—on purpose. From the Congress's viewpoint, the loss could not be sweeter.

Since 2001, for example, the U.S. textile and apparel industries have lost 365,000 jobs, which is a highly significant 38 percent decrease in the entire workforce. In the single year from 2005 to 2006, the industry lost 44,500 jobs. North Carolina, which has traditionally been highly productive in the textile industry has been hit the hardest. Plant closures and job losses cost over 11,000 jobs in the last year, or 12% decrease of its entire textile workforce. Industry leaders have petitioned the government for help since they believe the current environment is not sustainable long term.

Nobody in this battle is naive enough to believe that the U.S. government has any real direct control over events in China. But, why our representatives permit aggressive "protectionism" on the part of China and choose not to defend American workers and companies is an enigma. Their posture is that Congress should defend this industry and its communities and its way of life from what they see as the Chinese mercantilist policies that exploit democracy and the free-market system for its own gain.

America is a big loser in trade-- free trade or otherwise-- all the time. The U.S. is the dunderhead at the trade table and everybody always walks away with something good when the U.S. brings its bag of goodies to trade. The U.S. bag is always empty when the negotiating day is done. When you give away more than you gain, how can that be good for the country? We get whipped on every negotiated deal and the American worker and the American economy pays the price.

If the U.S. were to engage another crackerjack trade negotiator tomorrow, he or she would be lonesome. If these agreements were good for America, why is it that we have such a huge trade deficit? Why have we suffered the loss of more than one and half million manufacturing jobs already in just this one industry?

The textile industry executives have done their homework and they have a right not to be happy with our representatives. They posture that there is a very real possibility that the Bank of China may soon have more control over our economy than the Federal Reserve and suggest that is what we will get if inaction and turning the other cheek is our trading style. They blame this on decades of do-nothing politics by the American government to help itself while we are being outwitted by countries whose leaders know how to do at least one thing -- beat the hell out of the U.S. in trade. Ask not which country can do better in trade negotiations than the U.S. If there were a scorecard, the U.S. would be dead last.

Colleges and Universities Should Step to the Plate

American Colleges and Universities are not helping much lately. Bill Gates thinks American Colleges and Universities stink! He thinks we should bring in foreigners because they know more. If that is not always true, he thinks the U.S. should give work to foreigners because they do it better, not just that they are cheaper. If it is true, how'd that happen?

The China example may prove Bill wrong but he's looking at the Masters level students in the U.S. who he thinks are not as good as their compadres in foreign countries. Why is that? I am not necessarily agreeing with the billionaire but US Universities do not foster the notion of striving for excellence. Being an Assistant Professor at a University and having taught adjunct since I was in my twenties, I have a few clues on this matter.

I am not suggesting Gates is fully correct as many students are bright and willing to be the front-runners. Let me just say that here are many ways American Universities can improve for the better.

University Accreditation: Good and Bad

In the U.S., the accrediting agencies rule the day. Without accreditation, an institution does not get any students. Without students, they go out of business. So, for a year or more before an accreditation visit (every ten years or so) the whole university is in a tether. Committee after committee recommend changes to help please the accreditation visiting team.

Some are good and some are just icing. Most of the good ones have been presented previously to university management who often choose not to implement. So, there is a rush to implement to please the agencies since survival is at stake every ten years. Once accreditation is renewed, these initiatives are again forgotten.

This is a management problem and there is also a problem with the university elites. For accreditation for example: The elites of one university are the visiting team at another. Therefore, they quickly learn what the documentation needs to be like in order to pass the inspections. Though good things do come about, it is mostly an exercise for show. Nobody seeks excellence. The desire is conformity.

Another problem with Academia is that in many institutions there is a lack of continuity. For example the fact that Academics have a pension plan called TIAA-CREF is a symptom of a problem of allegiance. This pension plan is designed so that it does not matter for which institution you work, the pension company is the same. This tends to magnify the fact that the academic elites are not necessarily loyal to their university.

Is Protectionism Good or Bad?

This time, regarding American jobs, we do need government's help or as the old prognosticator would say, "we're heading down the tubes." Our representatives need to act in America's interests instead of as puppets of the Ruling Class who would seemingly be just as pleased to have their corporate HQ in New Delhi rather than New York. Jobs for high skilled workers in our country must be protected while the industry sages figure out other ways to create openings for investment and advancement in the still-developing nations.

With the burgeoning use of the Internet and IT in all facets of business, Americans are no longer able to reap the rewards of their pioneering efforts in application programming. This is already a big problem. With the availability of cheap computer hardware, theoretically there should be no disenfranchised users. Yet somehow, a casualty of the pervasiveness of technology, we have the disenfranchised American IT worker.

Here we are in an information revolution, and our representatives along with the Owners Class are hell bent on replacing high paid and highly skilled IT workers in this country with foreign nationals in the U.S. or foreigners by taking the positions offshore. What is going on?

Here we are now licking our wounds as a nation as damage has been inflicted on the structure of IT services within this country. As the availability of the Internet spreads to other countries, so too does the knowledge required to create highly skilled IT workers. Where will U.S. firms find their talent when it is theoretically available every place else in the world at 1/10 the cost of an American.

So, no wonder that students in Universities have chosen a different major. They cannot trust the government and the Ruling Class for the opportunity of a career in IT. This is an eroding national asset as we were once on top as a nation and now, we can't even keep our own jobs. These jobs are not coming back soon. Instead of IT and Engineering, our best and brightest now find themselves in Poetry or Music Classes. With China taking the low end and India taking the high end, where will the American jobs be? Why does this have to be?

What Can I do About Offshoring?

First of all never let your representative off the hook. I am still looking for one of those bills that were sent up that were to reform the process, protect American's jobs or provide a cure for illegal immigration to pass and be implemented. Congress is literally full of baloney. Sometimes I think that the procedures in the House and Senate are there to hide the truth from the constituency and to appear to be doing more than a yeoman's effort when doing nothing. The bills just die. Let's make sure the new House in 2010 (all 435 seats) will get this work done.

By keeping yourself informed along with as many of your friends as you can muster, you will be able to tell the facts from the fiction about these critical issues. It seems that we have all awakened to an unhappy reality that our elected representatives have chosen to ignore.

Offshoring is responsible for losing about 3 million manufacturing jobs and countless others since the Ruling Class decided it was a good thing for America. This issue affects me and my family and my friends in the IT and engineering communities as well as call center personnel and many others who wake up one day and their company is gone.

A Glimmer of Hope

American management does have a history of following the big league consultants. Little league consultants often get on the bandwagon so that there are few management consultants who are not saying the same thing. Whether they are right or not does not matter to them as much as if they are needed to help solve the problems that they identify.

When the consultants were suggesting that good managers should be downsizing in the 1990's, amazingly, these pied pipers had American managers, almost to a one, executing some downsizing or rightsizing option. The same goes for reengineering efforts and restructuring, and onshore outsourcing. Now, the biggie is offshoring. If you are not doing offshoring then you just aren't with it man! Check the management club's recommendations and offshoring is right on the top so what does the good U.S. manager do today-- offshore jobs. And, of course bad managers are not going to be left out in the cold either—so they too follow the leaders and offshoring is now the saving game plan.

Once a management consultant gets it in management's eyes that there is a problem, who gets to solve it? How many times have you heard that where there are problems, consultants are needed more than ever? The truth is that all offshoring does not work for various reasons -- language, real knowledge, core company skills etc. Now that it is time for a new paradigm to be invented by classic management consultants, there may be a break from the constant drumbeat of offshoring. But, the new paradigm is not here yet, although the shift away from offshoring as a management panacea may already have begun.

The outsourcing advisory company TPI released data in early 2008 that showed more evidence that the offshoring bubble was losing some air. TPI ought to know as they work from their Houston offices in helping companies gain major cost benefits through large outsourcing deals. They noted that the total of such contracts in 2007 was down 5% from 2006. This is a glimmer of hope that the problem may solve itself naturally. With some government help it may even be solved sooner. This is the lowest level of outsourcing from a U.S. standpoint in 5 years. It's nice to have good news but 5% is not going to break the bank in either direction. But, if it really signals a trend, it is very good news for America, indeed.

Chapter Summary

America's global corporations are enjoying their unencumbered journey towards labor arbitrage. Using H-1B visas, illegal aliens in the workforce, and offshoring jobs overseas, this trifecta of actions against American workers is saving corporations tons and tons of money and increasing profits dramatically. For American workers, however, things are not so good.

The first types of products to be manufactured overseas were the low-tech items such as toys, shoes and apparel goods.

Eventually, higher value items like high-tech components, computer chips and wafers, and now even high tech jobs and telephone call centers, and Accounts Payable and Payroll operations are easily farmed overseas while the carnage of long-term high-skilled workers on the streets is a new problem for America to solve.

Corporations want this solved by permitting it to be laissez-faire, which today is code word to the government to not invoke any measures to protect workers. Unions seem to have lost their will to engage but this is not a perfect scenario for unions since a strike, a union's best weapon would actually encourage a shift to offshoring to countries where strikes and labor rights are not permitted.

The Apparel industry in the U.S. has just about given up and everything is done overseas other than just a few U.S. apparel companies that still make things here. The textile industry in America wants to stay in America as do its workers, but in order to do so, they want the government to level the playing field so that the Chinese and others no longer have a government sponsored advantage.

A big part of the disadvantages faced by U.S. firms and in fact workers is that our trade negotiators get beat every time out. The NAFTA and GATT agreements crippled U.S. industries and caused a flow of work to Mexico that helped the Ruling Class but hurt American workers. Additionally, the negotiators threw in various visa caps to assure that people from developing countries could come to the U.S. and to assure that when a developing country fights the U.S. in trade, the other guy will win. In many ways, we would be better off not sending anybody to the trade table and taking what we get since it could not be much worse.

Colleges and Universities need to step up to the plate and begin to create students who know how to win in the International arena so that the best worker in high tech and other tech areas is American. There are a number of ways academia can help including more faculty continuity, less emphasis on student opinions, standardized requirements in major disciplines, and integrated courses that span semesters to mention a few.

Corporations do not get a pass here either. It doesn't help to declare American education as bad and then send jobs overseas or bring in foreign educated foreign nationals. Corporations have a role as "citizens" to send top management to actively participate in advisory councils for Academia and tell them what they need to do and give some grant money to help move the ideas along.

The Largest companies in America have joined together in the ITAA to lobby Congress for favorable business legislation that precludes protecting workers. This is unacceptable. Congress needs to enact legislation and create a Workers Body or Council completely funded by the government that is elected by the people and serves as a countervailing force against the combined forces of unions and management and government.

Sources

http://lieberman.senate.gov/documents/whitepapers/Offshoring.pdf
"Offshore Outsourcing and America's competitive edge: Losing out in the high technology R & D and services sector," May 11, 2004, Senator Joseph Lieberman

http://www.freetrade.org/node/38

Chapter 17   Throw the Bums Out!

Big Problems Bring Big Solutions

I began this book by noting the big issues which Americans are facing in this first decade of the 21st Century. There are many. Besides war and peace, the citizens face huge tax bills, an unresponsive democracy, corporate excess, loss of jobs from visas, offshoring, and illegal aliens, and an election system that needs to be repaired. These issues affect every American in a big way. Worse than the problems themselves may be the fact that no help is on the horizon. The white hat guys are not around the corner. Our representatives are AWOL, the President is playing on the other team, and the judiciary think we don't exist.

The citizen taxpayers of the U.S. are angry about a lot of things. The list starts with corporations pushing down the average wage to subsistence levels, jobs being taken at home and abroad by foreigners, labor unions standing idly by, illegal aliens crowding the cities and taking jobs, elections that appear to be rigged, and representatives that do everything but represent the people.

The Citizen Taxpayers of this country are fed up. Yes, they are angry but they have yet chosen to go on the warpath. Some think the time is coming close when there is going to be a spontaneous combustion. You may remember as a little kid, one day you weren't going to take it any more from the school bully and in exasperation, you finally gave the bully a big push and said, "Come on... you want a piece of me." One thing is for sure. It's got to change, and every politician in this election season has caught on to the theme: They are all preaching "Change."

The areas in which we presented problems and general solutions in this book, along with a few others that are prevalent are as follows:

- Representation Democracy & Honorable Congressman
- Taxes, Taxes, Taxes
- Fight for Liberty & Representation
- Forming of American Government
- Corporate Power, Greed, & Corruption
- Robber Barons - Old & New
- Countervailing Power - Labor Unions
- Labor Arbitrage --- H-1 B Visas and Other Visas
- Labor Arbitrage --- Offshoring
- Illegal Immigrants

Let's examine most of these points again over the next several chapters and see what we can come up with as some solutions to help make America, great again. There are certainly enough points above that if we were to be able to effect a solution to them, we would be well on our way to solving many other ills of our country. In no way does the focus on the above points minimize the other issues that need solutions. There are enough topics to be examined in total to create a number of other thick books, to help us be aware and find solutions to the important things we all need to fight to keep America free.

Representation, Democracy & Honorable Congressman

We always have the choice to take action or do nothing. From ancient times to modern times, good advice suggests that we not sit idly by and let things crush around us. The

words of Plato, President James Garfield, the infamous and
the insidious Joseph Goebbels, J. Edgar Hoover, and
Thomas Jefferson give appropriate caution to sitting idly by
or believing that all is OK when it is not:

"The penalty good men and women pay for indifference
to public affairs is to be ruled by evil men." Plato

"Now more than ever before, the people are responsible
for the character of their Congress. If that body be
ignorant, reckless, and corrupt, it is because the people
tolerate ignorance, recklessness, and corruption. If it be
intelligent, brave, and pure, it is because the people
demand these high qualities to represent them in the
national legislature."   James Garfield

"The great masses of people will more easily fall victims
to a 'Big Lie' than a small one, if it is repeated often
enough." Joseph Goebbels

"No matter how paranoid or conspiracy-minded you
are, what the government is actually doing is worse
than you imagine."   J. Edgar Hoover

"To consider the judges as the ultimate arbiters of all
constitutional questions is a very dangerous doctrine
indeed, and on which would place us under the
despotism of an oligarchy. Our judges are as honest as
other men, and not more so. They have, with others,
the same passions for party, for power, and the privilege
of their corps.

... The constitution has erected no such single tribunal,
knowing that to whatever hands confided, with the
corruption of time and party, its members would
become despots." - 1820   Thomas Jefferson

Is Anybody Listening?

Sometimes it seems that nobody in government is listening to the people. Of all the topics of the day, especially those that we discuss in this book, our representatives operate their own agendas and do their own will and don't even seem to hear the people. Is our voice being heard but it is being ignored? The Obamacare debacle of 2009 is the most recent example of this phenomenon.

Has the two-party system merged into the Republicrats or Demicans? Do Congressmen merely put on a small show for the people and pretend to disagree on a few things so that the system of checks and balances still appears not to be broken? Or, was Mitt Romney right in his 2008 campaign speeches, "Washington is completely broken."

Certainly on the issues raised in this book, all very important to the American people, the Senate, the House, and the "new" President -- all members from both parties -- Democrat and Republican alike have taken their stance and somehow it is the same stance. How is that? Thomas Sowell, the great writer was recently quoted as saying that bipartisanism is when they get together and do it doubly wrong. Both parties are mirrors of themselves on the issues. The only one on the other side is "We-the-People." The thinking of the Democrats in Congress and the President's and even the Republicans under the Bush Administration was so unified that it reminds me of one of the great sayings attributed to General George S. Patton:

When everybody is thinking the same thing, somebody is not thinking!

Worse than that fact, consider that if there were another good thought in the chambers of the federal government... it would surely be lonesome. Democrats and Republicans are not supposed to be unified. Congress is not supposed to be unified with the President or the Supreme Court. We have separation of powers. A Democratic Congress is supposed to counter the Republican or Democratic President on matters of public importance such as the problem list above, rather than make political statements in the hallowed chambers. So also for a Republican Congress.

Where are the laws to protect the people? Where are the border fences and increased patrols? Where are the congressional voices screaming bloody murder that their constituent's jobs are going overseas? Where are the Unions? Thank God the Supreme Court is still grumpy and disagreeable or there would be no countervailing power. It is like Gary Cooper as John Doe vs. the United Aristocracy?

The great healthcare and energy tax debate of 2009 did find the donkey and the elephant on different teams. The one thing that Barack Hussein Obama has done is that he has succeeded in making the Democrats and Republicans in Congress hate each other again. I keep thinking that as soon as it sinks in that the President and his pack of czars appear to be on a team of Socialists, Communists, and Marxists, both the GOP and the Dems may find another reason to be on the same team -- the survival team along with the rest of us. .

General Solutions to the Country's Issues

Each of the ills that we identified in all of the prior chapters needs its own specific solution and I offer a number of these in the next several chapters. Along the way to fixing the specific problems, there are few general / generic solutions that if applied to the identified problems would help make the specific solutions that much easier to accomplish. You may actually laugh at some of the solutions because you may think they are far away from ever being possible. You may be right. But, let's look at these solutions in the same light and in the spirit that we would possess after watching one of these Frank Capra films:

Both **Meet John Doe** (1941) and **It's A Wonderful Life**
(1946) are both directed by Frank Capra who had a gift to
make people feel as good as they possibly could feel just by
watching his films. One of seven children, Frank Capra was
an immigrant from Sicily. Though at six years old, he did not
have to deal with coyotes and bribery to make his trip in 1903
to America, he recalled the hell of the voyage on the Ship
Germania quite vividly:

> "There's no ventilation, and it stinks like hell. They're
> all miserable. It's the most degrading place you could
> ever be. Oh, it was awful, awful. It seems to always be
> storming, raining like hell and very windy, with these
> big long rolling Atlantic waves. Everybody was sick,
> vomiting. God, they were sick. And the poor kids were
> always crying."

Meet John Doe

Meet John Doe is Capra's wonderful, message-laden
populist melodramatic tale about the common man. This
sentimental, hard-hitting film is often grouped into a populist
trilogy of Capra films about American individualism -
associated with **Mr. Deeds Goes to Town** (1936) and **Mr.
Smith Goes to Washington** (1939), although it is generally
considered the weakest of the three.

The socially-conscious film was derived from a 1939 film
treatment, titled **The Life and Death of John Doe**. With all-
time persuasive performances by both Barbara Stanwyck and
Gary Cooper, this sobering film remains an important social
commentary.

Contrasted to today, a Capra film about individualism may
not fit so well for the hard left residents of the White House
and their government minions. Individualism is counter to

the group-think that has permeated our government. Yet, if we are to be saved from ourselves, it will be individualism, and not group-think or statism that does it for us.

Back in Capra's day, the media worked with the government for the good of the country, and it challenged the government on behalf of the people when necessary. That's what a free press is to do. Wouldn't that be something if it could happen again today?

Ironically, this film was intended to combat pro-Nazi Fascist forces present in America with its story of a young female newspaper reporter (Barbara Stanwyck) who writes a fraudulent column after threatened with being fired. In the spoof, she invents a fictitious reader as the author of a letter - a suicide-martyr who protests against an unjust political and social system. And then because of public interest and demand (and soaring newspaper sales), she convinces a hobo to take on the role of John Doe as if he were real.

This American ex-minor-league baseball player/hobo becomes John Doe - an Everyman character, and he sells his services as an imposter and he impersonates the non-existent character. John Doe (Gary Cooper) becomes a national figure, and causes the spread of 'John Doe Clubs' across the country.

The public gets excited over all of the goodness represented by the notion of John Doe. But, this spirit was not seen as a good thing by the power brokers who felt their control slipping away. Eventually, the reformed Doe, who is taken up fully by his own cause and who actually becomes the embodiment of the John Doe he represented, is discovered by corrupting, unscrupulous political forces, and a shamed Doe is forced to publicly admit the charade.

The film hits on the dangers of a complacent nation (with hunger amidst a land of plenty) being manipulated and taken over by neo-Fascist forces and Hitler's Third Reich (a reality in the early 1940s). This notion is countered in the film by the actions of the ordinary 'little man,' the John Does of this world (people like you and I) in a very moving way. Fully humiliated upon discovery of what was intended to be an innocent perpetration, John Doe decides to prove his sincerity to the people by fulfilling the suicide promise and leaping from the top of City Hall. But the rest of the world, all the real John Does of the world, convinces him otherwise and without killing himself, his sincerity is recognized on Christmas Eve and like all good films, "all is well."

It's a Wonderful Life

Many more have seen Capra's **It's a Wonderful Life** than **Meet John Doe**. This magically wonderful film portrays a good young man named George Bailey, who marries his sweetheart Mary, has four wonderful children, sacrifices for his father and his brother and his family and then has a tough time one particular Christmas Eve. This puts George on the verge of suicide, thinking he is worth more dead than alive.

The movie starts on Christmas Eve, as all of the citizens of the small town of Bedford Falls, pray to the heavens to help George Bailey. It's then decided in the heavens that Clarence, an angel who hasn't earned his wings, is assigned to help George. The film is emotional and it is uplifting and it again shows the power of the little guy and the power of good over evil and that's why it is suggested viewing before reading / viewing the general solutions outlined below.

Keep both films handy because in this fight against evil and corporate greed, rampant political corruption, and the threat of statism and government takeover of healthcare and other industries. None of us want to become like Potter or the bad guys in this movie. When you and I win as John Does ourselves, you want it to be for the good of the country, and not just to get even. In this spirit, the spirit of real hope and individual goodness, I present a number of general solutions to America's current malaise. They are not meant to be humorous but you may smile because they are unusual.

Throw the Bums Out

This is the overriding theme of *Taxation without Representation* If they do not represent us, then we must throw them out. Since the first and second editions of this book, I have had a few more years to think through the possibility that there may be some other real solutions out there. for these problems. Let me be very frank.

As I give the logic test to all solutions, they all seem to have a common prerequisite. The sitting Congress must have the objectives of the people as its paramount objective. Since its paramount objective, especially as we have seen in the 2009 healthcare debacle, and on to 2016, clearly is to serve themselves by serving special interests. In the sunlight of the day, therefore, the existing Congress--yes, both houses must go.

This simple solution is aptly labeled, "Throw the Bums Out!." Any logical examination of the recent politician (our representatives) and media attacks on the courage of dissenting people dictates that this crew has outlived its usefulness. Consider their fine work in the billion dollar gifts to banks and corporations, the takeover of General Motors, Cap and trade legislation -- which is also called the energy tax, and of course the healthcare debacle. Though it is not funny at all it is actually funny that a Congress of the people would be attacking the people.

The Congress showed its pomposity and disdain towards the concerned citizens at many public forums in the summer of 2009. One major theme emerged from this and from the many calls people made to their legislators -- they know lots more than we do. Congress was not dissuaded from selling out America by the voice of the people -- even though it was delivered clearly and distinctly. The just and proper solution

to such insolence is that we simply and quietly use the 2010
election process to throw all these bums out on the street.
Nobody asked for a change that would destroy America as
we know it. They have served us all very poorly. This will be
the beginning of our chance to regain the future.

Who Replaces the Bums?

We can't just elect anybody, however. When we throw the
bums out, we need to define our requirements so that
whether a Democrat or a Republican is elected, they will
solve the problems identified in this book and swear to
strengthen our representative constitutional democracy.
Since Liberals often have a hard left tendency, the Democrat
or Republican selected would need to be conservative. Why
bring in more of the same?

While we are making a better government for ourselves, it
would also serve us very well to suggest that the candidates
promise to work for an amendment enabling Initiative,
Referendum, and Recall at the national level. This will give
the people the tools to help keep our great country from ever
becoming Communist, Socialist, or Marxist in practice or in
policy.

None of the general solutions can possibly work, nor can the
specific solutions work with the current bums in their seats
right now, for the first time in the history of the U.S. We the
People have little to no power as we have little to no
representation. Members of Congress do not return phone
calls and when they respond to emails and hand written
letters, they send boilerplate, canned responses. If they hear
our messages, they ignore them or they deride them as they
did with the Tea Party participants and the Town Hall
citizens. They no longer care, and we should no longer care
about reelecting any of them. Throw them out! Don't be
afraid!

When you see these pompous "honorables" on display defending the indefensible, they look like fools as their one message in common is that we are fools for electing them. We have no rights. We are beholden to our elected officials for all we have. They must go.

Congress Sold Out Americans

The US Government system as we have discussed in this book is that of representation and built on the theme of "no taxation without representation." So, in 2009 when the taxpayers were paying attention, we noticed that every one of these congressmen and women who voted against the majority of their constituent's wishes sold out our US system of representation and sold out We the People.

So, I reluctantly choose the word traitor to describe their acts. What they did in the last two years was nothing less than traitorous. They were tyrants and traitors to America for how they represented themselves and not the people. The "traded" our rights to representation so they could please the special interests and gain favor with the powerful.

Is traitor too strong a term? It seems to me that when you are elected to represent your constituents and instead you decide to betray their trust and the responsibility they have delegated to you - you are a traitor and you should not hold office. There are a number of definitions of traitor in a number of different dictionaries. They all have similar items as these in the definition.

- A person who betrays another, a cause, or any trust.
- One who betrays another's trust or is false to an obligation or duty
- One who commits treason

I am not suggesting that our representatives have committed treason per se, though surely some may have crossed the line,. This huge majority who voted in socialism for Americanism do fit one of the other two definitions for sure.

As noted in prior chapters, a number of congressmen who voted for many of the socialism bills did not read even read them. Yet, they were advised by their constituencies that the effect of the bills would do great harm to the economy and, in turn, national security. What weak country can be strong in defense? So, perhaps our representatives really are traitors indeed in the truest sense of the word.

They are traitors to the ideals upon which this country was founded and even without a lawyer's opinion, a quick read of the Constitution will quickly show that these bills are all unconstitutional. Thus, our representatives have betrayed their oath of office and the country.

As we noted in Chapter 14, they voted to restrict the manufacturing capability of the United States in what is supposed to solve a farce global warming issue (CAP-AND-TRADE) thus leaving other countries un-affected by the same burdens. The bill cost Americans thousands of dollars each and gives other countries the gift of a competitive advantage at the expense of the taxpayers.

Many of the voices clamoring for the "virtual heads" of our dishonorable "honorables," are frustrated that the wheels of democracy seem to be in a cog, and perhaps they are in fact no longer moving. I have noted many who believe it is past the time when reasoned expressions, position explanations, or scientific reasoning can be used to convince the "honorables," to see the light. It is time to escort them from their positions of trust and throw the bums out.

The science of global warming for example is not complete, and the notion that the land, and the air, and the sea and the animal kingdom below Homo Sapiens should have higher priority than mankind (green / socialism) is just plain bull. Al Gore is an almost billionaire because he misused whatever information he had to create a frenzy about a notion that is not hard science. Many fine scientists have proven that global warming at best is junk science, but it has made Gore a soon-to-be billionaire.

The notion of "green" is part of the hard left's socialist agenda, and Al Gore, well, he is the luckiest man in the world. Right place, right time, the all green Gore knows how to make a buck on the American people. Known as a big polluter himself with his big private jet and huge homes, Gore figured out how to get some stimulus money for himself. You may not believe this but a tiny car company backed by the former Vice President Al Gore in September 2009 with zillions of Americans out of work, got himself a $529 million U.S. government loan to help build a hybrid sports car in Finland that will sell for about $89,000.

The Finland made Goremobile competes with the US handmade Dodge Viper, built at Chrysler's Connor Ave custom facility. Last time I checked Michigan was having some worker employment issues. What a kind government to help out ole Alfi compete against Americans.

Americans have a motley combinations of emotions regarding what they see as a hard left takeover of the country, with much of the damage financed by Progressive Insurance's George Soros. Rush Limbaugh found out how much the hard left can influence life in America as he was denied the right to be an owner of the St. Louis Rams, supposedly because of high level hard left interference. Could it have been the president himself as Obama has called out Limbaugh in the past?

Limbaugh, who like most Americans is dead set against the notion of Obamacare and health rationing, found a way to inject some serious humor into the post mortem about his losing the Rams opportunity. He said, "Everybody ought to be afraid of it [Obamacare]. If they're willing to politicize something as innocuous as the NFL, who's to say they won't politicize kidney transplant or any other kind of medical procedure?"

Having the White House interfere in American's personal lives is at best unforgivable and at worst, unconstitutional. Americans are seeing more dirty play than ever before in recent American history. Their perspective is that junk science and tax increases will just make them broke with few pleasures in life.

Democrats and Republicans alike as well as those who practice any religion, even those who are self-avowed atheists and agnostics find that mankind should have dominion over the land the sea, the birds in the air, the air itself, as well as all the creatures of the land. They know this either because their religions tell them this or they know it because it is common sense. Situations such as the two inch California minnow shutting down the water supply and forcing farmers to stand in food lines for the poor are becoming more commonplace. Yet, our "trusted" honorables are praying to a different power and firing them all is the only way to get a good answer to our prayers.

We may not get the chance again and we may not be so charged up again as we are today's with these big time issues. Don't waste your breath sending the Congress a message. They won't pay attention and they would not comply anyway. As I said earlier in this chapter, all other solutions depend on us acting in a unified voice in 2010. Vote them all out and by then it might be good to launch impeachment proceedings against the master of the Congressional Obamabots. Make sure you go to the polls in 2010 and start the process. Get rid of them all. They are not good for our country.

Here are some solutions that might be employed at a general level to make the situation better. But the primary action is to beat them all at the ballot box

Chapter 18   General Solutions for the Future of the USA

General Solution 1: **Renew Oath of Office**

The gentle and polite way to solve this is to start by simply bringing the Supreme Court Justices into an extended joint session of Congress, with the President in attendance. The Justices would have a big job. Their role would be to swear-in each Senator and each Representative and the President, one more time. The symbolism would be hard not to catch.

This would be a vow renewal just like those who hit a 25th anniversary and they renew their vows, or perhaps a couple who have not been true to each other find a preacher and they decide to recant their old ways and renew the vows they have broken.

Let's bring the Congress and the president into chambers and with C-Span cameras rolling have them humbly and individually renew their oath of office. Let their vow renewal make up for the clear trail of broken oaths leading back to their collective swearing-in.

The President should renew his oath first. Followed by each and every Congressman. Let each hear the other be sworn in individually, not as a group. Let their voices be recorded forever for posterity. And let's bring them in a few times as a matter of course during their terms - at least every six months so they cannot forget their oaths. For the second and third and fourth swearing-in during the same term, there shall be no Inaugural Balls required. The tape of each individual oath, all 536 of them, including the VEEP, can be uploaded to YouTube for all the citizens to enjoy.

My dad always had this little phrase to pipe back with when asked for something he was not willing to give up. It might be the simple request of a dime for the candy store or it could be one of his friends trying to borrow money. He'd say, "Try and Get it." I don't think in a thousand Sundays we could get the Congress, the President, or the Supreme Court to retake their oaths. But, it would have an impact if we could. So, General Solution # 1, admittedly will never work. If the solution itself won't work, the follow-up to the solution will not work either but let's talk about it as it too has merit in an honest world.

How about a second Joint Session, again with the President present. Starting with the president, each one would be asked to take just five minutes to describe how they broke or did not break their oath (no criminal charges for anything confessed.) In this five minutes they should also discuss what they will change if they think change is needed regarding their behavior in order to better perform the people's will. The President can take fifteen minutes if needed for all his confessions. Confession is good for the soul and this public confession would be good for America.

Tell me the truth now, wouldn't that be a good restart if only? Take a look at these oaths of office and ask yourself if this has happened.

President's Oath of Office

> "I do solemnly swear (or affirm) that I will faithfully execute the office of President of the United States, and will to the best of my ability, preserve, protect and defend the Constitution of the United States."

Congress - Oath of Office:

> "I do solemnly swear (or affirm) that I will support and defend the Constitution of the United States against all

enemies, foreign and domestic; that I will bear true faith
and allegiance to the same; that I take this obligation
freely, without any mental reservation or purpose of
evasion; and that I will well and faithfully discharge the
duties of the office on which I am about to enter: So
help me God."

The Constitution is quite a document so what we need in the
oath is well covered in the Constitution. It certainly would
not be bad to have a well-respected religious cleric such as
Anne Graham Lotz or Franklin Graham, children of the
renowned Dr. Billy Graham add a few points of humility into
the oath. Either could make it clear in the swarming inn
speech that our representatives represent the people and not
themselves or other interests.

In his book, Civil Disobedience, Henry David Thoreau, the
great American author and tax resister made his own
recommendations to improve his government of the 19th
century. He called for improving rather than abolishing
government:

> "I ask for, not at once no government, but at once a
> better government..."

Can't we ask for it? Will they submit to the oath renewals? I
surely do not think so. It certainly would be symbolic of a
nation trying to heal itself by having the very perpetrators of
the problem, the elected politicians, promise they won't be
bad anymore. I think it would be a good start. Since we do
not live in Utopia, I do not expect it, but I think it would be
good if we were to collectively and singularly ask our
representatives to retake their oaths.

Unless they are ready to lie right away, it might give us at
least a few good years in which to operate to make the laws
catch up with the times so that we do not have to depend on
the good will of hizzoner. And, by the way, while they are at

it, during the swearing in, the Chief Justice should announce that herewith the Congress and President are not to be referred to in etiquette as "Your Honor." And, not to be left out, the Chief Justices should renew their oaths at the same time"

Supreme Court Justice Oath of Office

"I, [NAME], do solemnly swear (or affirm) that I will administer justice without respect to persons, and do equal right to the poor and to the rich, and that I will faithfully and impartially discharge and perform all the duties incumbent upon me as [TITLE] under the Constitution and laws of the United States. So help me God."

And for good measure it wouldn't be a bad idea to bring the names of the Supreme Court Justice's to the people once every five years during election time. If the people approve, the justice's get five more years before they need re-approval. If the people disapprove, the justices who are not approved are placed on the ballot. If approved, they serve. If not, they are gone.

General Solution 2: Throw the Bums Out

I keep coming back to this because it is the only option we fully control. Simply throw the bums out. Though this will take more time, the people should take an oath if the leaders will not that every current office holder at any level of government that chooses not to renew their oath of office, shall hereby be voted against and thus thrown out of office. No second chances. And we encourage some people from the non-political side of life to take their places. Once they are gone, we get a fresh start.

General Solution 3: Initiative, Referendum, and Recall

The people need to add an amendment to the Constitution to provide the rights of initiative, referendum, and recall. Initiative as it exists in the states is the ability of citizens to suggest legislation for consideration by a state legislature. Referendum is the passage or rejection of a proposed law by the citizens of a state in a statewide vote. Recall is the ability to recall a candidate once he or she has been elected if he/she is not fulfilling the promised duties of office. The most important of these at this time is the right of initiative, though the others are also necessary. There is no such thing provided for in our Constitution for federal leaders. Here's why.

You may recall the civics lesson in Chapter 1 in which we discussed the U.S. as a constitutional democracy. In such a democracy we have a Constitution and representative government. Initiative is a structure of a direct democracy in which the people make the laws without representatives. In order to offer countervailing power to the people against the powerful coalition of the President, Congress, unions, corporations, and to an extent, even the Supreme Court, the people need the power to submit legislation for consideration. The other good part of this is that it would help more people to be more active their government. Therefore, it would be tough for the scoundrels to continually snooker We the people as they have been doing for too long.

An amendment to the Constitution (Citizens' Initiatives Constitutional Amendment) is already in process at http://www.cusdi.org/. This can be the first step of the process and then would come the formation of the committees funded under the power of the Amendment by the government. This in process amendment is good to hop-on and support. I beg you, if you have read this far in this book, to please go to http://www.cusdi.org/ and read their proposal on Initiative.

The folks at the web site address shown above have put together a Citizens "Athenian" Initiatives Amendment which focuses on the Initiative part of this recommendation. It is excellent. This is the first of the process. Encourage your congressman either before or after the great replacement of 2010 to get the amendment passed to start Americans on a path to better assure that we are protected from electing doofusses and buffoons in the future. Additionally, get your state representatives and state senators involved to begin the amendment process in your state.

This is the closest thing I have seen since I first saw the classic movie, <u>Meet John Doe</u> starring Gary Cooper with Barbara Stanwyck, Edward Arnold, Walter Brennan, Spring Byington. This movie was introduced in Chapter 15. The unscrupulous politician is portrayed by Edward Arnold in this movie but in your districts and my district they have different names. But they are actors nonetheless. Picture Gary Cooper as John Doe rallying all of us other John Doe's to work on the Citizens' Initiatives' Constitutional Amendment campaign. And then they all lived happily ever after. It would be nice.

By the way, the framers of the Constitutional Democracy of the United States were smart very men. They were not, however aware of the Athenian democracy notions as archaeology had yet to discover the materials. In fact it was not for over 100 years after the founding fathers put together our government that this other information became available. This would have been a great-add-on to the Constitution, had the founding fathers known about it. Through the amendment process, we can make it part of the Constitution.

A reading of the U.S. Constitution is always a refreshing wake-up experience. The Constitution was not written for slithering rogues or despicable thieves. It was written for good God-fearing people. This amendment and the Initiatives and other amendments that may follow are needed because our politicians have lost their fear of God and their fear of shame and worse than that, their fear of the people.

The corporate god of greed and the self-god of pomposity and self-importance, and the lure of the comfortable life of an elite have mis-directed many of our representatives to be substantially less than they can be. So, the people have no choice but to take back the government using both the same constitutional instrument that has guided us so far, as well as the notions discussed in this section. Let us hope and pray that our representatives are merely good men and women gone bad, rather than bad men and women. The words of our Second President, John Adams, are haunting as they appear to be written for our times:

- "We have no government armed with power capable of contending with human passions unbridled by morality and religion... Our constitution was made only for a moral and religious people. It is wholly inadequate to the government of any other."

- "The church is the moral compass of society."

- "We have no constitution which functions in the absence of a moral people."

- "A standing army, however necessary it may be at some times, is always dangerous to the Liberties of the People."

The words of John Quincy Adams, our sixth president give what one would think might be reason for his election. Though he had big issues before and during his presidency, and he never was popular, he had a message well worth hearing: Perhaps these words are even more haunting than those of his Father, John Adams, the second President.

- "Men, in a word, must necessarily be controlled either by a power within them or by a power without them; either by the word of God or by the strong arm of man: either by the Bible or by the bayonet."

- "The highest glory of the American Revolution was this: It connected in one indissoluble bond the principles of civil government with the principles of Christianity.

- "The experience of all former ages had shown that of all human governments, democracy was the most unstable, fluctuating and short-lived."

Ironically for a man with such insights, Quincy Adams was chosen for the presidency in 1821, not by the people but by the House of Representatives. He and the other two candidates had lost both the popular vote and the electoral vote. Andrew Jackson was the high vote getter but even he did not have the majority. Quincy Adams won the election since the 12th amendment of the constitution prescribes that when no candidate has a majority of electoral votes, the election will be decided among the top three by the House of Representatives. Quincy Adams was an unpopular president and failed to win a second term... but these quotes live on.

One more point: Under the original provisions of the Constitution, the only direct election of any Federal representative was to the House of Representatives. The Presidential system was indirect via the Electoral College and Senators were selected by a state's legislature. Under the provisions of the 17th amendment to the Constitution, Senate elections became direct elections within each individual state.

This change had to have been done via an amendment because it was directly changing what was originally stated in the Constitution. The current version of the Citizens'

Initiatives Constitutional Amendment is already well framed but requires several more edits to be in final form. Then, just as the 12th (President) and 17th (Senate) amendments changed how the voice of the people is expressed, so also will the 28th (People) amendment. Let us work so that we can celebrate.

General Solution 4: Use the Courts.

Find a good trial lawyer. Give them half and take action against the corporations and those who tacitly break our laws. Trial Lawyers may have a moral compass that always points to their wallets but they cannot win without being very adept at the law. There are many abuses of the people's rights today and when Congress chooses to take no action, We the People, collectively or individually can find ourselves a good lawyer and use our right to redress.

Until all the judges are owned by corporations and hopefully that will never happen, this may prove to be a very effective way to curb abuse of all kinds. We do need to learn how to sue our legislators for lack of representations. Find a good lawyer and let's take that one on. If your employer fires you and hires someone with an H-1B visa or an illegal, for example, sue them. The courts are a last resort for the American way. Let's use the courts. Let's find some lawyers who are willing to do this work pro bono, and let's make them famous. The courts can help us gain justice by Civil Law to overcome the criminals, often our legislators, in our midst.

General Solution 5: Pay Attention

I have a great and wonderful friend who like me is Catholic. We don't evaluate the extent of each other's' Catholicism but we respect each other's word as being the truth. Francis X. Kurilla was an IBM Administrative Executive in the New Jersey Area. While he was approaching retirement age, he unexpectedly passed on to the Lord. He was a great friend.

Frank told me a long time ago about a real situation that occurred in his church.

The Church was Catholic but there were a lot of European customs exercised during the mass. At Easter Midnight Mass, for example, the priest would go off on a multi-hour sermon or so it was relayed by Frank.. During the sermon, the priest would look around and see a few "nodding" parishioners. While in the midst of a very serious sermon or readings, both being chanted, the priest, without missing a note, would chant, "Be attentive!" These admonitions were so well blended that if you were not paying attention, you would be startled and if you were paying attention, you would almost not notice. The moral of the story of course is, "Pay Attention!"

Please note that solutions 1 to 4 have some prospects for success only if we want them to be successful. Remember "nothing in life, worth having, is easy." That goes for the right to life, liberty, and the pursuit of happiness. While you work on the real solutions, *pay attention* to your government. Get to know your representatives at all levels. Remember who works for whom.

Send them emails and faxes and real mail and occasionally a registered letter just to get on their true fan list. Prod your local radio and TV personalities. Hound legislators about the major issues of the constituency and ask them to have a program in English each week that talks about the legislation they are working on, what passed last week, and who voted for what and what does it mean. Include yourself in their lives.

This is the ultimate reality show in an age of no writers. Talking about a reality show. How much better can you get? If you can coax the Ozzie family and the Hulk and his family to show up at a legislative session, you can actually see the same stuff on three different TV shows. That's Reality TV.

Our legislators have failed us so miserably that they deserve nothing less than public shame. Unfortunately, since Hollywood threw shame out the window thirty years go, there is no longer such a thing. But, if there were, our legislators would suffer from it. Maybe we can bring some back when we let our legislators go. That way the new guys would have to be concerned about it.

At Marywood University, I have the pleasure of teaching Operational Management. That's the part of the business in which more than 95% of the people work. When I teach my students about quality, I tell them the first message of quality is to pay attention. That's the message in General Solution 5. Pay attention.

Among all the other things that workers are thinking about when they come to work, they are thinking about making the product better or doing a better job or being more pleasant if they have a service mission. But, they are also thinking of the Super-bowl, the Yankees, their girlfriends, etc. in other words, if they can be paying attention to the mission at hand, that will bring its own set of quality rewards to the matter at hand. So, "pay attention" to what your government is doing and you can help bring about a higher quality government. It can happen. Yes it can!

Chapter Summary

The General Solutions are just the start but, they are a very good start to getting this country on the right track

Chapter 19 Help US Solve Taxes, Taxes, & More Taxes

Taxation by Confession

"The United States has a system of taxation by confession." U.S. v. Kahriger Hugo Black, Supreme Court Justice

'A hand from Washington will be stretched out and placed upon every man's business; the eye of the federal inspector will be in every man's counting house.... The law will of necessity have inquisical features, it will provide penalties, it will create complicated machinery. Under it, men will be hauled into courts distant from their homes. Heavy fines imposed by distant and unfamiliar tribunals will constantly menace the taxpayer. An army of federal inspectors, spies, arid detectives will descend upon the state.'

... predicting what would happen if the federal Congress were to enact a federal Income tax. Richard E. Byrd, Virginia House Speaker 1910"

There is a decorative license plate that some cars in Pennsylvania have on the front bumper (no official front plate required) that has a picture of the Keystone State and the words, "Pennsylvania, Land of Taxes," emblazoned on it. We sure pay our fair share of taxes at many levels in Pennsylvania as do the many people of the other states.

Add that to the federal burden and you are talking real money for sure. There are many pork projects, earmarks, and money that is just given to rich people who don't really need it because their work represents whimsical projects, goofy reasons, or simply corporate welfare. There are also some important people who actually "own" a few lawmakers as these honorables must be representing somebody. Surely, we learn every day that there is not proper respect given by lawmakers for what the people give up in taxes to help our government operate efficiently. Why is that?

Perhaps we need something about taxes added to the oaths so our representatives remember whose money they are spending. The poster of government waste is the infamous "bridge to nowhere" standing as part of the legacy of an apparently sincere congressional budgetary proposal. Yet we know that such costly gifts to the special class should not be given to or by various lawmakers just because the special interests are in the good-guys club to help them buy votes with our money.

It is apparent that our government does not respect the value of the dollars we provide. They obviously did not get the lessons we did as kids by our mothers and fathers. They cannot even balance the federal budget and they do not guard its checkbook. Maybe we need to have our finest business academicians create a four week class that our representatives can take before assuming office.

The class should teach, among other things, the value of taxpayer dollars, and how the Congress is to conduct itself (individually of course) as honest representatives of the people. It is actually hard to believe that there would not already be such a class.

The IRS Administers the Problem

The general solutions defined in the last chapter may help our legislators pay more attention to our money but fundamentally, today's income tax system that provides for a pay as you can afford notion is fraught with so many loopholes unavailable to the common person that it is time to throw it all out. Despite perhaps good intentions, all of the deductions in the tax code are written of the rich, by the rich, and for the rich. The Ruling Class certainly has had its input into to the IRS code over the years since, after all, that is the documentation that tells them how much they can keep.

Before the Bush tax cuts which gave the rich people in the country an opportunity to keep more of their income, in 2000, the nation's richest taxpayers, who made an average $173 million each, paid an effective tax rate more than 5 percentage points lower than those making $1.5 million to $5 million. This was documented by economist Martin Sullivan in Tax Notes magazine. How can that be in a "progressive" tax system? Look no further than to the IRS tax code. It is a sham. It is actually a joke if you think you can find anybody who has read the whole code. The really rich have figured how not to pay, and the legislators have legislated them many favors. And, ladies and gentlemen, you know that is true, and that is that.

Besides the code, along comes this agency called the IRS, which, as an agency is about as popular in the U.S. as Osama (not Obama) himself. There is lots of IRS abuse and congressional abuse that can be found in the existing tax code. One might suggest that the folks who work for the IRS are good people just trying to do their job, but how can that be possible when not a one of them can know every clause of every section of a code that is virtually unreadable in its magnitude. They have to first admit they can't do their jobs to be truly honest since nobody can.

At just about 17,000 pages in over 20 printed volumes (That you can buy for just about $1,000), more than 13 times the length of the Bible, it is impossible for the average taxpayer (even the experienced IRS agent) to know, understand, and accurately apply its provisions. It can't work! It is a joke. But, nobody is laughing.

Just think about all the tax lawyers, accountants, auditors, and CFOs who are burdened by all of this prose and challenged to do their job. Because of this code, these positions are essential to commerce though quite burdensome. The IRS code causes so many people who produce no goods and provide only an IRS-assistance-type service to have to be paid. The IRS code itself is a major burden on the economy.

How about the billions that could be saved there. But, a lot of people would be out of work. So, when we really want change enacted like getting rid of the tax code, we need to slowly remove its need so that the CPAs and the accountants and the bookkeepers can be given a more productive role.

From H & R Block for the little guy to the big accounting firms to the biggest law firms to the bookkeepers and in-house accountants who don't see the sun until April 15th every year, there is somebody always ready to profit by the misery built into the U.S. tax code.

Why not just get rid of it? Give the IRS agents their full salary for two years after we shut down the code so they can get other jobs. A part of the IRS would still exist but they would be working on collections, not on income and expense audits, and they would not be in a position to threaten anyone with the code. Did I hear a cheer?

The Flat and the Fair Tax

There were some nice proposals this past election season for an abolishment of the tax code and the institution of a Flat and / or Fair Tax. The proponents did not make it past the primaries but it sure seems that it would be a great deal for America if some of these fine notions were enacted.

What Is the Fair Tax Plan?

The following is from the horses mouth - FairTax.org:

http://www.fairtax.org/site/PageServer?pagename=about_main
The Fair Tax plan is a comprehensive proposal that replaces all federal income and payroll based taxes with an integrated approach including a progressive national retail sales tax, a prebate to ensure no American pays federal taxes on spending up to the poverty level, dollar-for-dollar federal revenue neutrality, and, through companion legislation, the repeal of the 16th Amendment.

The Fair Tax Act (HR 25, S 1025) is nonpartisan legislation. It abolishes all federal personal and corporate income taxes, gift, estate, capital gains, alternative minimum, Social Security, Medicare, and self-employment taxes and replaces them with one simple, visible, federal retail sales tax administered primarily by existing state sales tax authorities.

The Fair Tax taxes us only on what we choose to spend on new goods or services, not on what we earn. The FairTax is a fair, efficient, transparent, and intelligent solution to the frustration and inequity of our current tax system.

The Fair Tax:

- Enables workers to keep their entire paycheck
- Enables retirees to keep their entire pension
- Refunds in advance the tax on purchases of basic necessities
- Allows American products to compete fairly
- Brings transparency and accountability to tax policy

- Ensures Social Security and Medicare funding
- Closes all loopholes and brings fairness to taxation
- Abolishes the IRS

What Is the Flat Tax Plan?

The Flat Tax is an income tax vs. a value add / sales tax. Almost ten years ago in 1998, the Armey-Shelby Flat Tax and H.R. 2001 was proposed and was defeated. All Flat taxes have similar ingredients so repeating the provisions of H.R. 2001 helps put the Flat tax in perspective.

How the Flat Tax Would Work

The flat tax rule simply says this: Everyone -- you, me, even Warren Buffet -- would pay 17% (or the proposed percentage) of what's left of their total annual income from all wages, salaries, and pensions after subtracting a personal allowance. The word allowance does take people back but under this bill at least there were few (Four) and they were simple to understand:

- $23,200 for married filling jointly
- $14,850 for single head of household
- $11,600 for single
- $5,300 for each dependent child

There would be no more, tax credits to figure, deductions to keep up with, or loopholes to look for. In fact, the entire tax return form would be printed -- on a postcard as shown in Figure 13-1 below. Of course so the postal worker doesn't know how much you make, you can put the card in an envelope.

The more you earn (no matter how you earn it), the more you pay. Rep. Armey when he proposed this bill cited these examples: Given the exemptions shown above, a family of four earning $25,000 would owe no tax. A family of four earning $50,000 would owe 6%, and a family of four earning $200,000 would owe 14% in tax.

The flat tax proposal would eliminate the marriage penalty, almost double the deduction for dependent children, and end multiple taxation of savings. Social Security and Medicare payroll taxes would not be affected under this flat tax proposal. Social Security benefits would not be taxed.

Rather than show you the form in place in 1998, it has been given a breath of life recently so let me show you the form used in 2005 as shown in Figure 21-1 below:

Figure 18-1 The Flat Tax Postcard Form

Form 1	Individual Wage Tax		2005
Your first name and initial (if joint return, also give spouse's name and initial)	Last name		Your social security number
Home address (number and street including apartment number or rural route)			Spouse's social security number
City, town, or post office, state and ZIP code	Your occupation		
	Spouse's occupation		
1 Wages, Salary and Pensions		1	
2 Personal allowance			
(a) $20,000 for married filing jointly		2(a)	
(b) $10,000 for single		2(b)	
(c) $13,000 for single head of household		2(c)	
3 Number of dependents, not including spouse		3	_ _ _ _ _ _
4 Personal allowances for dependents (line 3 multiplied by $6,000)		4	_ _ _ _ _ _
5 Total personal allowances (line 2 plus line 4)		5	
6 Taxable wages (line 1 less line 5, if positive: otherwise zero)		6	
7 Tax (17% of line 6)		7	_ _ _ _ _ _
8 Tax already paid		8	
9 Tax due (line 7 less line 8, if positive)		9	
10 Refund due (line 8 less line 7, if positive)		10	

Notice some changes:

- $23,200 for married filling jointly changed to $20,000
- $14,850 for single head of household $13,000
- $11,600 for single $10,000
- $5,300 for each dependent child $6,000

Hey, I'll sign up for it right now. The Fair or Flat tax both accomplish the major goal of tax reform and put the rich on equal footing with the poor instead of paying a smaller percentage after loopholes and lopsided deductions.

Democrats in the 2008 election were not saying this as I heard it as they are poised to raise taxes overall - once the Obama legislative agenda is accomplished. Why get the people upset before you have what you want. That is clearly the new administrations agenda and it is OK, apparently, for them to throw some chicanery into the mix.

Raising taxes is what Democrats do. It is what they have always done. As a Democrat myself, I think they are full of it because those of importance have a million shelters so that only you and I have to pay, Democrat, or Republican. If you pay taxes, you won't be happy.

By eliminating the Bush tax cuts and whacking those at the very top, paying the energy tax, the healthcare tax, the bailout tax, the "porkulus" tax and perhaps the "Pay the Chinese back - thank you tax," only the thieves will have a buck left. Democrats think that they reach the common person. The common person hides their wallet whenever they see a Democrat.

Knowing that the "owned" legislature, Democrat and Republican, has preserved the "necessary" loopholes that the "special people" need to keep their "hard earned money" always makes me feel better. Of course, the real power brokers, who are also rich, like to offer that the rich should be taxed and taxed well.

While they have hidden all of their taxable income, I fear that my professor salary at Marywood will put me in a "rich bracket" by the Democrats, meaning I will have to hand them over more and more and more. Of course because I do work for Academia, most of whom are hard-core, hard left liberals, perhaps I too would benefit from a tax exclusion.

Mitt Romney, after the low-ratings media had crushed George Bush's reputation, had as much life left in the political game as a garden slug placed on the endangered species list. Yet, he endured, but failed nonetheless. He said that he would lower the corporate income-tax rate. His objective was to make US firms more competitive in the world economy. I am not so sure corporations need to be rewarded by America for their poor behavior against American workers. I think Romney had a lot of good points but making life more comfortable for American corporations would not be one I would endorse.

I admit I have not examined the requirements of corporate returns since I cashed out my last corporation about 15 years ago. For me, it just wasn't working. Romney said he would also eliminate all taxes on interest, dividends, and capital gains for those with incomes below $200,000. That does includes me. From my eyes, America cannot punish the successful for the benefit of the unsuccessful. Otherwise, it will not take much time for America itself to be quite unsuccessful, and along with America, would go all of its citizens, both the "haves," and the "have-nots."

Chapter Summary

Taxes, Taxes, Taxes. Make sure they know we care and don't let them take our money to buy votes. I would like to see vote Buying defined by statute and have this federal legislature reluctantly create a felony charge for any congressman in either house who introduces legislation which clearly has violated his oath to the people and has rewarded a single entity among his or her constituency or of the people's other states with more munificence than meets the smell or sniff test. In other words, if they buy votes, they pay.

Chapter 20   Build It or Not; Illegal Aliens Will Come!

What Is Wrong With the Home Country that We Cannot Fix?

"If this were a dictatorship, it'd be a heck of a lot easier, just so long as I'm the dictator." December 18, 2000,   President George W. Bush

We all have experienced to some extent the trauma caused by illegal aliens to America's citizens. Foreign nationals have affected many aspects of life in the United States of America. Though the people of the United States are not necessarily in unison 100% on the matter, upwards of 90% think that the problem should be solved without a Reagan style amnesty program.

The illegal invaders clearly must be stopped at the borders and there is much support for shutting down the employers in the U.S. to solve the drain on taxpayers. This would create a natural attrition back to Mexico without the need for mass deportation.

The right-wing radio talk show hosts have made a big deal about the illegality of illegal migration to the U.S. It is not a good situation for U.S. citizens nor is it a good thing for illegal aliens. U.S. Senators and Congressmen are impervious to the drain on the lives of individuals who are in proximity to the cramped housing and poor living conditions that have become part of their neighborhoods.

For those of us not living in gated communities, we see that somehow the dwellings of illegal foreign nationals are not subject to the same building maximums for fire and health that apply to the rest of the citizenry. There are a number of laws that if you are illegal somehow do not apply to you but if you are a citizen, you may go to jail if you do not comply. This double standard exacerbates an already tenuous situation.

With more children in school from people who do not contribute to the system and more people using social services, and of course healthcare services, the citizens are getting whacked with an ever increasing local tax burden so much so that many cannot endure the expense themselves. If you live in gated communities as most, if not all Senators and House members, you don't ever see it. You can be as munificent and benevolent as you like doling out taxpayer money for a "good cause."

But, if you live in the open neighborhoods of America, it does matter and it matters an awful lot. Additionally, if you are a laborer or a tradesperson - construction, plastering, roofing, it matters also because as the supply of illegal labor increases, you either cannot get work or you no longer can get a decent wage rate for your labor. If you are a meatpacker, you have seen your wages decrease and decrease as your coworkers retire or are displaced by illegal foreign nationals. It is a big problem for Americans that our representatives in their closed neighborhoods do not face every day, and they choose not to address.

When somebody crosses the U.S. border without invitation or prior approval, it's the same as if they came to your house for supper and you have no clue who they are or why they are there? Should they be able to demand dinner? Though you can refer to Illegal aliens as foreign nationals, illegal alien is a proper term for them. When they enter our country uninvited, they have violated our immigration laws and our space and thus they are definitely illegal. They are also definitely aliens.

The Yahoo thesaurus defines alien as "a person coming from another country or into a new community." So, regardless of whether the politically correct do not like the term, it accurately describes the new type of individuals who we see on our streets and in our neighborhoods, and who help keep our wages down..

They are also foreign nationals since they are citizens of a foreign country and not U.S. citizens. Are they immigrants? Now, the answer to this is maybe so and maybe not. The Dictionary defines an immigrant as a person who leaves one country to settle permanently in another. That word "permanently" is a staple of that definition. Some may come permanently while others may come to work or to drop off some drugs, see some relatives, pull a few heists, and eventually go back.

Most may very well be good people but they committed a crime when they entered our country. All illegal immigrants are illegal aliens but not all illegal aliens are illegal immigrants. Nothing about their personhood is illegal. The illegal tag comes because they have broken the law of America by their mere presence in our country just like somebody breaks the law when they come into your house uninvited and they demand dinner.

Pennsylvania Is Not a Border State

The City of Hazleton Pennsylvania saw its population soar from 21,000 to 28,000 in ten years. The new arrivals were not from an unexpected baby boom. They are illegal and they are aliens. They are not citizens of the community but they now live in and take from the community. In Hazleton, the crime rate is up and aliens have committed murders in daylight on

Main Street and they have otherwise caused devastation to what was once a quiet and peaceful place to live.

There are hundreds and thousands of Hazleton's across the U.S. who now have multiples of large families living in single family dwellings, bursting at the seams, ready to erupt. Is it fair to American citizens who do not live in gated communities as do the elite who have foisted this trauma on the population?.

Is it fair that in school districts in Pennsylvania that the rules for potential illegal aliens are more permissive? For as long as I remember students had to present social security numbers before they could enter school? If your kids did not have a social security number, they were not permitted to register for school. I did not make the rule but I had to get my kids SSNs in order for them to go to school. Now, only my kids and the kids of other citizens need to comply with this requirement. Why is that? Who OK'd that?

Call it racial profiling. I don't know what else it could be. Our school district has modified its rules that if somebody "looks" like they may be of an illegal alien family, such that they might not have a social security card, and since this might be a way of identifying a child of an illegal person, the administrators are not permitted even to ask for the number. No, it is not fair and it is not right.

Moreover, is it fair that my kids and the kids of all citizens in Pennsylvania must bring proof that they have received all of their immunizations (shot record) to school before they are permitted to attend even one day? The idea is that a non-immunized child may come down with a major illness and in fact may affect a child who was either not immunized or whose immunization has weakened over the years.

This program is to protect the children from diseases that have been mostly eradicated in the U.S. but have not been eradicated in Mexico or South America or elsewhere. So, now, in addition to not asking the child for a SSN, the administrators are not permitted to ask about immunizations.

Why is this? Because not being immunized may be a sign that the individual is of illegal status and the administrators are not permitted to identify students who are illegal aliens under any circumstances.

Why is it like this when my city has not registered as a sanctuary city? So, instead of Mexico and Mexicans getting healthier because of their relationship with the U.S., now both countries can be more susceptible to disease. Our politicians are so afraid of their shadows and there are so many alternative agendas at play that Americans are being hurt and Americans are demanding real action, not just election rhetoric.

So, let's ask ourselves, Is it wrong to let illegal actions go unpunished and if so, is it wrong to let illegal foreign nationals from many different countries stay in the United States in an illegal status, despite that their mere presence in this country is an illegal act? They are not invisible in regards to their social needs (for which, in most cases, they do not pay). The political right sees border security and deportation as the only viable answer, whereas the political left is not as excited about a border fence and massive patrols and they view deportation as cruel and unusual punishment. They would prefer amnesty. Yet, as both sides look at what is happening to their communities, all have concerns.

The Mexican Government Likes What Is Happening

The preponderance of illegal aliens come from Mexico and are citizens of Mexico. Others come through Mexico to get to the U.S. from the Southern Americas. The Mexican Government assists its citizens on their trips to the U.S. In fact, they create and print pamphlets for their citizens which encourage Mexican nationals to make the run for the border.

The pamphlet makes sure that the soon-to-be illegal alien knows their rights in America. The "Guide for the Mexican Migrant," (Figure 19-1) shows illegal aliens crossing the Rio Grande, traipsing through Arizona, avoiding border patrol agents and it instructs them on how to hide in American society so they aren't caught. Mexico surely does not have a neutral position in this issue. And the U.S. takes no action against Mexico for this obvious abuse of our borders. The cover of this pamphlet is shown in Figure 23-1, and the whole pamphlet is available for downloading at diggersrealm at the following URL:
http://www.diggersrealm.com/mt/illegal_alien_comic_book/GuiaDelM igranteMexicano.pdf

On the Diggersrealm site, the pamphlet's intentions are clear and the paper could be printed from a link gained through a link to the Mexican Government site. The little book helps the illegal alien once in the U.S. in that it covers the rights they have if caught including the right to not disclose their immigration status.

Is that our law? What goof said they do not have to tell us their immigration status? It's really outrageous that rather than actually trying to discourage illegal aliens from making the trip and therefore reducing the death toll, the Mexican government would rather create this colorful cartoon-like manual that encourages and gives a sense of hope to those that may be contemplating the border hopping.

Figure 20-1 Guide for the Mexican Migrant

In case you were wondering, the U.S. has no such pamphlet for Americans. The U.S. has the same instructions for all Americans who wish to travel abroad at http://travel.state.gov/passport/passport_1738.html. This site instructs U.S. Citizens. It says that they must get a passport to visit a foreign country - even Canada and Mexico. The U.S. government does not tell its citizens, "Bon Voyage," go wherever you want; break whatever border laws you want; and don't worry, we'll help you get around the host country's laws with this pamphlet.

What are the rights of U.S. Citizens who travel down into the southern hemisphere without documentation? How many ways can you say, "None?" If we were to evaluate the guidance in the pamphlets to Mexican migrants as an indicator of how nice we would be treated in Mexico, we could logically conclude that Mexico is a sweet, benign democratic country that is very interested in the desires of its citizens. But, their pamphlets don't govern their behavior towards us. They put the pamphlets together to document our laws and ways of behaving here - so that their citizens know their rights! The fact is that the Mexican Government and Mexico in general does not treat illegal foreigners as well as they expect their citizens to be treated in the US. So, you would be at your own peril traveling to Mexico and there would be no welfare net or medical net to catch you if you happened to take a fall.

The Bush Border Legacy

Before El Presidente Jorge Arbusto (Spanish for George Bush) was interested in being the supreme ruler of Canada, the U.S., and Mexico, Vicente Fox was the President of Mexico. There is now a new President of Mexico, Felipe Calderon. Now that Mr. Bush is no longer President of the U.S., the bad news for many Americans, Canadians, and Mexicans is that he can become President of North America. I do think he would have a bit of a problem with getting Mr. Obama's concurrence because that is not the kind of change I think Obama would believe in.

When Bush was the top US guy, he was not received well in Mexico. Funny how that goes. Looks like he would have to rely on the Canadians to help him in his desire to be President of North America.

This is ironic because regarding illegal aliens, George Bush has been a major league friend to Mexico and Mexicans. In fact, he has been their friend much more than he has been a friend to U.S. citizens in their border fight. More than any other President in U.S. history, of which I am aware, George W. Bush bent over backwards and forward and backwards again to please the government of Mexico and the illegal aliens in this country.

For no apparent reason he defended, justified and facilitated an influx of illegal aliens into America and he steadfastly opted not to uphold the Constitution of the United States as executive officer of the country. His team was instructed not to enforce the laws, not to shut down the businesses that hire these people, and not to mess with these people living illegally in America. Yet, the Mexican citizens in Mexico did not like him.

They actually hated him and showed it. They protested his visit to Mexico quite vehemently burning U.S. flags and telling the President to "Go to Hell!" There were a few Americans saying the same thing about the same thing so it did not gain much press coverage.

This was ironic in so many ways since Mr. Bush had done absolutely nothing to stop the Mexican Invasion of the United States. The Mexicans must have been reading the New York Times. It is also ironic that when Bush visited Mexico, the Mexicans could all come together to protest a visiting George Bush and they can hold protests in the United States every May. However these same people refuse to come together to protest their own corrupt government.

George Bush could have made it real tough on these folks and that is what Americans actually expected their President to do. Bush simply chose not to enforce the law. Thanks to George Bush, in fact, Mexicans already had most of what they were protesting for. He never took any real action to control our border. He certainly had the authority for eight years to clean up the mess.

Nobody can say the President failed in his attempts to clean up the border in those eight years. He did not fail at it. He just did not do it. In fact, during the Bush years, the number of raids on businesses hiring illegal foreign nationals and deportations went down substantially compared with even the Clinton years.

If George Bush had taken a stance, his overall legacy could have been more positive and perhaps the Republicans would have been assured a President in 2008. Maybe not! But, by deploying a pro-Mexican strategy on the border, Bush won no American points and no American hearts.

And those Republican politicians that did not criticize his perverse stance on Mexicans having more rights than U.S. Citizens will be remembered for a long time to come in the history books and in the elections In fact, in 2006, the Democrats took care of most of the latter. Even with a pro-Mexican strategy, the irony is that Mr. Bush still was not loved south of the border, and it does not look like that will change now that he's back in Crawford.

Was Obama Worse than Bush?

Some Congressmen care more about America than others. For example, conservative Representative Trey Gowdy (R-SC) is sick and tired of being sick and tired of the illegal alien crisis that President Barack Obama has created on the Southern border. As bad as Bush was Obama is the worst ever in enforcing US immigration law. Gowdy has spent a lot of time exposing Obama in a big way!

Obama's Justice Department for example, according to Gowdy, has refused to enforce current immigration laws and defend the rights of American citizens. That's because the Obama White House is stopping the efforts of the U.S. Border Patrol and immigration enforcement agencies, while simultaneously granting amnesty to millions of illegal aliens by unconstitutional executive orders.

Here are Gowdy's words as he explained at a recent hearing:

"Today there are over 350,000 known criminal aliens in the United States who are not detained by ICE, 350,000," Gowdy, the chairman of the Immigration and Border

Security Subcommittee, said opening a hearing examining the victims of illegal immigrant crime.

"That number may not get your attention — statistics rarely do — so I want you to think about it this way. The number of criminal aliens living in the United States, not in custody, not separated from society, it larger than the city of Pittsburgh, Pennsylvania. Larger than the city of Lexington, Kentucky, larger than the city of Anaheim, California," he asked. "Can you imagine a city the size of Pittsburgh, comprised sole of people who are here unlawfully who have also committed another crime?"

Gowdy offered those at the hearing even more information. He said that according to ICE, between October 2011 and December 2014, ICE released criminal aliens over 100,000 times, though the President has sworn that criminals are not being released.

And so, Gowdy's perception and that of many Americans is that while America continues to struggle with the problems created by illegal aliens, Obama's executive actions are being challenged before the Supreme Court right now. Gowdy is furious at Obama's attorney's deceptive arguments:

"Just yesterday the lawyer for the president was at it again, this time at the United States Supreme Court, arguing for the non-enforcement of the law, arguing for the wholesale failure to enforce the law," Gowdy said. "

Here's what the attorney said – all lies: 'The damage that would be reeked by tearing apart families.' If you want to see that damage, Mr. Solicitor General, if you want to see what tearing apart looks like, I hope you're watching this morning."

The hearing also gave an opportunity to many victims who have been hurt by violent criminals who were in this country illegally. There were two mothers of children killed by illegal aliens who offered their testimony. Many of us owe a great amount of thank you's to Rep. Gowdy, for bolding exposing Obama's radical amnesty agenda! For the good of America, it is time to secure the border now, before it's too late!

Treat Them Like They Treat You

We can learn something by examining how the Mexican government would treat Americans if we crossed illegally into Mexico. Like my father-in-law, Smokey Piotroski always said, "Treat people the way they treat you." So, let's take a peek at how the Mexicans treat immigrants from the poorer countries to their southern areas when they sneak into Mexico. How does Mexico handle its own "illegal aliens?"

Visitors from Central and South America

Statistics tell us that every year a large number, as many as 250,000 people from Central and South America cross the Mexican border. This is nowhere close to the 1.5 million who cross the Ro-Grande illegally each year. There are no reporters following this contingent from way south. There is no enraged Mexican citizenry. The official Mexican reports suggest that these illegal aliens to Mexico are treated with respect, and are offered a better place to stay and new opportunities. What a great deal? Then why do they work their way up through the country, unless caught, so they can have the opportunity to cross the U.S. border?

Maybe Mexico is not such a nice place to be for an illegal from another country and maybe the official reports are just propaganda. There are also lots of other reports from areas of South and Central America and even from Mexican migrants that in Mexico, illegal aliens are subject to abuse at the hands of police and military personnel. These hapless and defenseless immigrants are often robbed by police and detained in municipal prisons.

Can it be as some suggest that the Mexican government mistreats indocumentados (undocumented people) who cross its territory? Do they keep them in jails, and in overcrowded conditions, many times without food, without medical attention and overall, violating their human rights? Who do we ask for these answers? The ones who agree to talk are few and far between. They are lucky to survive. These poor souls are incarcerated in crowded municipal jails for days and weeks, with dozens often detained in small rooms in which men and women are not separated.

When these survivors, who often have been brutally treated on their journey north arrive in America, where nobody denies their innate right to exist, in short order they join those who demand that they be treated to all the benefits of a U.S. citizen. Mexico detained just under 1/4 million illegal aliens in its territory in 2005. Of that total, as the sterile statistics indicate 42% were from Guatemala, 33% from Honduras and most of the others were from El Salvador.

The Price Illegal Aliens Pay in Mexico

All of this irony comes about because on May 1, 2006, a nationwide protest, dubbed "A Day Without Immigrants," was organized and held to show the U.S. a thing or two about who has the real economic power in our country. The idea was that those opposing tighter restrictions on immigration -- the illegal aliens themselves -- flexed their economic muscle by boycotting everything they could - no shopping, no working, and no going to school. Those depending on their cheap labor surely were inconvenienced, and they should have been.

The irony comes about since if in Mexico, for example, illegal immigrants took to the streets in such a demonstration of protest, they would be breaking the laws of Mexico. There, the constitution blocks all non-citizens from participating in public political demonstrations. Mexican law is really tough on illegal aliens and it is enforced even more harshly than it is written. It is hypocrisy that the illegal aliens make such demands of U.S. citizens.

The words of Michael Waller, vice president of the Center for Security Policy cut to the chase on this perspective:

> "By making increasing demands that the U.S. not to enforce its immigration laws and, indeed, that it liberalize them, Mexico is throwing stones within its own glass house."

Though there are some major similarities between the constitutions of our two countries, Mexico has its own set of standards regarding immigration and those heading north would not have such a sweet experience if they were heading south of the Rio Grande. For example, in Mexico, under Article 123, illegal aliens receive two years in prison and a fine of up to 5,000 pesos, or about $500.

Additionally, the perpetrator is then considered a convicted felon. Article 118 makes it even worse if once you were deported and you choose to come back without invitation, you can get as much as 10 years in prison. With Article 73, the local police who are not permitted in the mix under our laws, must cooperate with Mexican federal immigration authorities to enforce their nation's immigration laws.

More than likely because of the rush to get to the U.S., Mexico has recently witnessed a rapid rise in the number of people entering its borders illegally, primarily from Central America. As noted previously, those who get caught wish they only had to endure the penalties that are on the books but, unfortunately, they face a far worse plight in practice. Rape, robbery and assault by and for corrupt police and soldiers is commonplace. Overall, Mexico has a deplorable record of human-rights violations on its southern border that is well documented.

Tough Mexican Citizenship Requirements

Mexico is also very selective as to whom it ultimately grants citizenship or even admittance. To be in Mexico legally, you must have the potential to "contribute to the national progress" and you must have the income needed to support yourself. In other words, there is no welfare for new legal admittances. Since illegals are deported, they never become a welfare issue.

Mexico did not want its sovereignty compromised since at the time these laws were made, foreigners had been coming in and not only settling but they were buying up huge masses of land. They were in effect taking over the country by owning huge areas of the country. The "taking over the country" notion seems pretty familiar to those Americans who see the same thing here and now.

Think of the last time you planned a trip out of the U.S. Americans who travel to Mexico or Ireland, or France or any other country, have to enter that country according to the laws of that country. Passports are the minimum requirement granted for tourists, not immigrants. Mexico does not advise its citizens to treat the laws of other countries with respect and it permits its citizens to go wherever they please with no documentation.

Independent observers from other countries looking at the laws and the policies of Mexico and the U.S. would note that a U.S. citizen could not get away in Mexico with what a Mexican gets away with in the U.S. So, they do see the hypocrisy in Mexico's treatment of the poor from Central America but they also see hypocrisy in how the U.S. operates.

U.S. Hypocrisy re: Illegal Aliens

Those without a horse in the race see the U.S. discouraging illegal immigration while simultaneously attracting cheap labor by providing a safe place to work. This becomes an implied promise that the worker will not get turned over to the police. Some go so far as to compare the treatment of illegal aliens in the U.S. to the treatment of blacks and the notion of slavery.

Those of us who are not part of the Ruling Class of elites know that this is not discrimination in any form because the Ruling Class and their corporate fictitious citizens would be pleased to have all Americans, legal and illegal, black and white, working for sub subsistence wages. The fact is that any mixed signals that are given to the potential migrant from Mexico, are not coming from U.S. citizens. Citizens in the U.S. want this charade ended and they want corporations and government agencies, who violate American law, and who violate illegal aliens along the way, to be punished big time. No hypocrisy - just end it.

Solving the Illegal Alien Problem: Some Other Solutions

So, with all of this rhetoric, how do we really solve the problem? In this next section, we look at six totally different solutions for you to examine but before that... There is just one more vexing issue that I would like to sprinkle in the mix with regard to an equitable end to this perplexing problem. Who is at fault here?

The fault for this problem is the "it's OK signal" that our President and Congress send to the would-be border crosser. "We will do nothing... even though we have sworn to uphold the law" is the Bush administration's unwritten policy for the last eight years and perhaps longer. Obama has granted de-facto amnesty as the new residents may be the only chance for a Democrat to win the next election. We are about 60 million more illegal aliens on the wrong side of the ledger because of these poor policies.

"Smoke 'Em Out" Is O-U-T!

I can't see a better way of punishing those representatives who permitted this to happen than by assuring that they never get elected to anything ever again. You know who they are. What about punishing the President? Bush is gone and can't run again and mostly everybody thinks that is good. Additionally, Mexico and the U.S. seem ready to vote against ole "Smoke 'Em Out" from Crawford as the President of North America, Canada probably won't be able to save the day for his eminence either. And, that is also good! Obama is so crafty, there may already be lines in the healthcare bill or something else that nobody has read that have already given illegal aliens citizenship. Obama is someone to fear in the illegal alien battle. He is not a friend of America in this regard. He is a friend of Obama.

Follow the Money

Though it certainly helped, illegal aliens did not come to America just because of the welcome packets provided personally by the President and Congress, though clearly they were welcomed if not encouraged to come. In criminology they always suggest that investigators follow the money. That's what needs to be done here. Who benefited from this perpetration? Did border guards benefit? I can't really see how. Did federal U.S. lawmakers gain from illegal immigration? Hopefully not and it is safe to say "no" to that one.

Did George Bush benefit? Not really though we might not convince him of that. Did state or local U. S. lawmakers gain from illegal immigration? No again. Did the illegal alien get any gain from their own illegal immigration? Definitely yes. They gained jobs and they gained in many cases high cost social services from American taxpayers. Did the Mexican government gain and / or get money from illegal immigration? The answer is yes. They saved the expense of providing for the care of their most poor and their economy benefits from the $30 Billion sent back to Mexico each year by the illegal aliens in America.

Did the U. S. Corporations gain revenue or save costs from illegal immigration? The answer here is absolutely yes. They gained a supply of semi "slave" laborers that they could pay under the table or knowingly pay via false identification and it increased their profits immensely. This permitted the agricultural industry to participate in the rewards of globalization and "offshoring." In this case, the politicians brought and delivered "the mountain to Mohammad." Agriculture could not offshore its production so the borders were opened originally just for agriculture. Corporations saw this as such a good idea for all corporations that all types of industries began to derive the major benefit of cheap labor. And all the President and his minions had to do was misplace the border keys.

Make no mistake about it, the biggest gainer in all of this is the American corporation. In fact, in all of the ills identified in this book that are facing the country today, the corporation is the major perpetrator. All of the bad things in this book are caused mostly by huge corporations. In fact, in this book, none times out of ten, "the corporation" is the answer to the question, "Who did it?"

In just about every issue we brought forth, it is the dirty-trick playing, greedy, straw-hearted American corporation playing the part of the perpetrator. it is clearly a problem that these fictitious behemoths have brought on America by reaching out for slave labor. Therefore, no matter how the problem is solved, corporations should pick up the part of the tab that America cannot extract from the Mexican Government.

Amnesty for Illegals - Yes!

The amnesty that I think does belong to the illegal aliens is the knowledge that up to a certain point of time, say a year or two from now, they will not be prosecuted for being in this country illegally. So, they have a year or whatever the right number is to return to Mexico. During this period, If they need any emergency services or payouts of any kind from taxpayers, then, upon receiving those services, they get deported immediately. That is an amnesty I can believe in. It is the same amnesty that draft evaders from Vietnam got when they came home from Canada or elsewhere. It's been done before.

In 1977, President Jimmy Carter issued an amnesty in the form of a pardon. Some estimates are that there were as many as 50,000 draft evaders in Canada and those that had not come back home by 1977 were pardoned by Carter's amnesty. Getting amnesty for a past crime, however, does not mean that you get a license to commit the same crime continually in the future and in this plan, you don't get to collect money for having crossed GO! You don't get a comeback ticket.

Lifetime Guest Plan

The best approach to solve this problem permanently is a plan I cobbled together called the Lifetime Guest Plan. I wrote a book about it in 2015. You can access the book at bookhawkers.com -- http://bookhawkers.com/products/the-lifetime-guest-plan-a-long-term-immigration-fix-that-puts-americans-first

Mexico Needs to Pay for Its Own Poor

There are many opinions brought forth on this issue by liberals in the American mainstream press, who always seem to have a better way to spend your money than you would choose yourself. Many opine that full and immediate legalization is the only fair, just and humane thing for the U.S. to do. After all, since our economy is dependent on the hard work of Mexicans and others who come north to make a better life for their families, undocumented workers must be allowed to come out of the shadows, etc. etc.

Reagan proved this would not work and the government of Mexico has proven this cannot work as they choose to continually export their poor northward. How about sending a few billionaires? Mexico plays the U.S. for a sucker and we are. W. C. Fields used to say, "never give a sucker an even break and never smarten up a chump!" Mexico does neither and they have us right where they want us. Let's figure out how to legally collect some payback from Mexico.

Meanwhile read The Lifetime Guest Plan

Chapter Summary

The bottom line folks is that American corporations have to figure out a legal way to do business and they need to pay back those profits they made while disrupting our country. Mexico also needs to pay back the U.S. for its caretaking of Mexican citizens.

Non-Americans need to go back to their home countries but fairly and humanely. They need to be stopped from coming in illegally by building a big fence and putting whatever we need on the border to assure that illegal traffic is kept to absolute zero.

If illegal aliens send $20 to $30 Billion back to Mexico and elsewhere, each year from what they make here, they probably should be alerted to keep some for the trip home. Give warning but slowly and surely shut down the companies who choose to operate in the dark with illegal aliens despite the crackdown. Other companies will take their places.

The exodus of Mexican and other illegal foreign nationals must soon begin. Our representatives and the new President must make this happen. The time is now. We have to recognize that all aliens will not be able to get home immediately. We have been patient and we don't expect the government to begin to charter a zillion trains and busses to Mexico (paid by corporations and Mexico) and elsewhere. But it probably would be good if they chartered some.

Of course the Lifetime Guest Plan is an even better idea: http://bookhawkers.com/products/the-lifetime-guest-plan-a-long-term-immigration-fix-that-puts-americans-first

Book Summary

Well, that's just about all folks. Just one last caveat. When you feel that you are not represented and your taxes are higher than appropriate, please remember that this is your country and politicians serve at the pleasure of the citizens. When you go into the voting booth, please remember that your vote counts.

Throw the Bums Out! They'd throw you out first if they had the chance. Don't give it to them!

God bless you and God bless all Americans!

LETS GO PUBLISH! Books by Brian W. Kelly
www.letsgopublish.com; Sold at

www.bookhawkers.com
Email info@ letsgopublish.com for specific ordering info. Our titles include the following:

Great Moments in Penn State Football The story about the beginning of US football and Penn State football in the US as well as the great moments and great PSU coaches and players over the years.

I Had a Dream IBM Could Be #1 Again The story of how IBM can again hist the top as the #1 IT company in the world

Whatever Happened to the IBM AS/400? The story of the AS/400 and how and why it disappeared.

Great Moments in Notre Dame Football The story about the beginning of US football and ND football in the US as well as the great moments and great ND coaches and players over the years.

Thank You IBM The story of how IBM helped today's technology millionaires and billionaires gain their vast fortunes

WineDiets.Com PresentsThe Wine Diet Learn how to lose weight while having fun. Four specific diets and some great anecdotes fill this book with fun.

Wilkes-Barre, PA; Return to Glory Wilkes-Barre City's return to glory begins with dreams and ideas. Along with plans and actions, this equals leadership.

The Lifetime Guest Plan. This is a plan which if deployed today would immediately solve the problem of 60 million illegal aliens in the United States.

Geoffrey Parsons' Epoch... The Land of Fair Play Better than the original. The greatest re-mastering of the greatest book ever written on American Civics. It was built for all Americans as the best govt. design in the history of the world.

The Bill of Rights 4 Dummmies This is the best book to learn about your rights. Be the first, to have a "Rights Fest" on your block. You will win for sure!

Sol Bloom's Epoch ...Story of the Constitution This work by Sol Bloom was written to commemorate the Sesquicentennial celebration of the Constitution. It has been remastered by Lets Go Publish! – an excellent read!

The Constitution 4 Dummmies This is the best book to learn about the Constitution. Learn all about the fundamental laws of America.

America for Dummmies!
All Americans should read to learn about this great country.

Just Say No to Chris Christie for President!
Discusses the reasons why Chris Christie is a poor choice for US President

The Federalist Papers by Hamilton, Jay, Madison w/ intro by Brian Kelly
Complete unabridged, easier to read version of the original Federalist Papers

Bring On the American Party!

Demonstrates how Americans can be free from Parties of wimps by starting our own national party called the American Party.

Saving America
This how-to book is about saving our country using strong mercantilist principles. These are the same principles that helped the country from its founding.

RRR:
A unique plan for economic recovery and job creation

Kill the EPA
The EPA seems to hate mankind and love nature. They are also making it tough for asthmatics to breathe and for those with malaria to live. It's time they go.

Taxation Without Representation Second Edition
At the time of the Boston Tea Party, there was no representation. Now, there is no representation again but there are "representatives."

Healthcare Accountability
Who should pay for your healthcare? Whose healthcare should you pay for? Is it a lifetime free ride on others or should those once in need of help have to pay it back when their lives improve?

Jobs! Jobs! Jobs!
Where have all the American Jobs gone and how can we get them back?

IBM I Technical Books

The All Everything Operating System:
The story about IBM's finest operating system, its facilities, and how it came to be.

The All-Everything Machine
The story about IBM's finest computer server.

Chip Wars
The story of the ongoing war between Intel and AMD and the upcoming was between Intel and IBM. This book may cause you to buy or sell somebody's stock.

Can the AS/400 Survive IBM?
Exciting book about the AS/400 in an System i5 World.

The IBM i Pocket SQL Guide.
Complete Pocket Guide to SQL as implemented on System i5. A must have for SQL developers new to System i5. It is very compact yet very comprehensive and it is example driven. Written in a part tutorial and part reference style, this book has tons of SQL coding samples, from the simple to the sublime.

The IBM i Pocket Query Guide.
If you have been spending money for years educating your Query users, and you find you are still spending, or you've given up, this book is right for you. This one QuikCourse covers all Query options.

The IBM I Pocket RPG & RPG IV Guide.
Comprehensive RPG & RPGIV Textbook -- Over 900 pages. This is the one RPG book to have if you are not having more than one. All areas of the language covered smartly in a convenient sized book Annotated PowerPoint's available for self-study (extra fee for self-study package

www.ingramcontent.com/pod-product-compliance
Lightning Source LLC
Chambersburg PA
CBHW070341090426
42733CB00009B/1246